T0266415

48 PEAKS

HIKING AND HEALING
IN THE WHITE MOUNTAINS

CHERYL SUCHORS

SHE WRITES PRESS

Published September 11, 2018
Printed in the United States of America
Print ISBN: 978-1-63152-473-8
E-ISBN: 978-1-63152-474-5
Library of Congress Control Number: 2018939600

For information, address:
She Writes Press
1563 Solano Ave #546
Berkeley, CA 94707

She Writes Press is a division of SparkPoint Studio, LLC.

Interior design: Tabitha Lahr
Map credit: Mike Morgenfeld
Line drawings: Windy Waite

Names and identifying characteristics have been changed to
protect the privacy of certain individuals.

For Larry, this book's and my *sine qua non*

48 PEAKS
Over 4,000 feet
White Mountain National Forest

VERMONT

NEW HAMPSHIRE

N

0　　　　5　　　　10
Miles

0　　　　5　　　　10
Kilometers

Mount Cabot
4,170 ft

Mount Waumbek
4,006 Ft

North Twin
Mountain
4,761 ft

Mount Hale
4,054 ft

Mount Tom
4,051 ft

Mount Garfield
4,500 ft

Galehead
Mountain
4,024 ft

South Twin
Mountain
4,902 ft

Mount Field
4,340 ft

Mount Lafayette
5,260 ft

Mount Zealand
4,260 ft

Mount Willey
4,285 ft

Cannon Mountain
4,100 ft

West Bond
4,540 ft

Kinsman Mountain
North Peak
4,293 ft

Mount Bond
4,698 ft

Mount Lincoln
5,089 ft

Owl's
Head
4,025

Bondcliff
4,265 ft

Kinsman Mountain
South Peak
4,358 ft

Mount Liberty
4,459 ft

Mount Flume
4,328 ft

Mount Carrigain
4,700 ft

Mount Hancock
4,420 ft

Mount Hancock,
South Peak
4,319 ft

KANCAMAGUS

HWY

Mount Moosilauke
4,802 ft

East Osceola
4,156 ft

Mount Osceola
4,340 ft

Mount Tripyramid,
North Peak
4,180 ft

Mount Tecumseh
4,003 ft

Mount Tripyramid,
Middle Peak
4,140 ft

Waterville
Valley

Mount Whiteface
4,020 ft

2

2

3

93

302

302

93

93

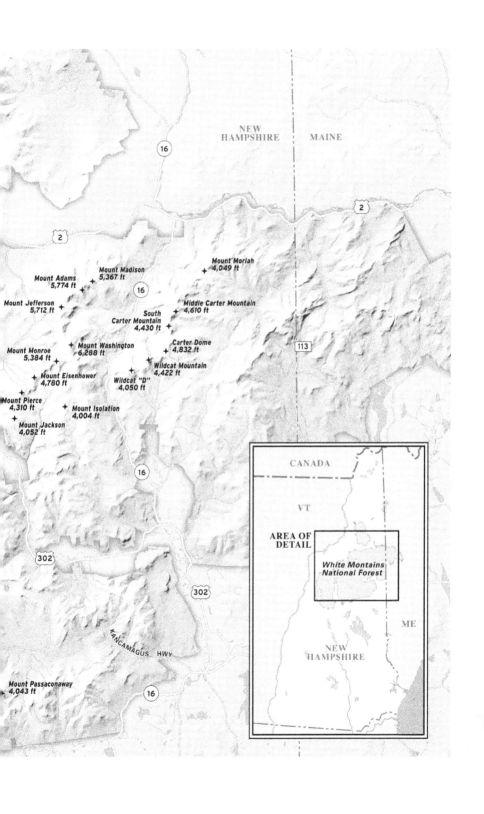

NEW
HAMPSHIRE | MAINE

16

2

Mount Moriah
4,049 ft

Mount Madison
5,367 ft

Mount Adams
5,774 ft

16

Mount Jefferson
5,712 ft

Middle Carter Mountain
4,610 ft

South
Carter Mountain
4,430 ft

Carter Dome
4,832 ft

Mount Monroe
5,384 ft

Mount Washington
6,288 ft

113

Wildcat Mountain
4,422 ft

Mount Eisenhower
4,780 ft

Wildcat "D"
4,050 ft

Mount Pierce
4,310 ft

Mount Isolation
4,004 ft

Mount Jackson
4,052 ft

16

302

CANADA

VT

AREA OF
DETAIL

White Montains
National Forest

302

ME

KANCAMAGUS HWY

Mount Passaconaway
4,043 ft

16

NEW
HAMPSHIRE

AUTHOR'S NOTE

The memories and interpretations of events are mine and mine alone, told as truthfully as I can by relying on journals kept over the years. The only things that have been changed are the names and details of friends and one institution.

PART ONE

"The bitterest tears shed over graves are for words left unsaid and deeds left undone."

—Harriet Beecher Stowe

PROLOGUE

2002

Hours of tunneling through clammy forest up the shoulder of a ravine bring us to the invisible line beyond which trees do not survive. Our boots strike only stone, an endless upward tilt of stone. Emphatically not noticing the steepness of the ledge, I pause, catch my breath and wait, my hand straying protectively to my hip pack. Again I wish I weren't so slow and wonder if, pushing fifty-two, I'll make it to the top. I'm afraid I may not, but I'm afraid of more than that.

Though midsummer, the White Mountain sky hangs low, a cold and mournful gray. Rain threatens but so far hasn't fallen, and I'm grateful. The trail is chancy enough without being slick. I'm already worried about the descent. Climbing up allows me to face into the mountain, but climbing down means swallowing vertigo, relying on muscles stiff with fear and ignoring the shrieking in my head.

Thirty feet below me, Sarah yells that she's scraped her shin on a boulder, one of many that constitute our trail. Though she has joined me on a journey that most would have found any excuse to avoid and I love her for it, I can't summon the energy to reverse course and help her. I simply stand, locking my knees, and rest on my bones.

Sarah drops her pack to search for the first aid kit. So far the slow pace she allows me to set doesn't seem to frustrate her too much. Bless Sarah. We both know I couldn't make this journey without her. Today I can't—I refuse—to worry about my larger quest.

Which brings me to Kate, as most everything these days does. Would my best friend have liked today's hike? Would our first climb in the craggy Presidentials, the mightiest range in the East, have taxed her too greatly? Or would she have soldiered on the way she did, breaking her silent counsel to find things along the way to delight and fortify us?

Though I can't be certain, I think I've chosen wisely with Mt. Monroe, the fourth highest peak in the Presidential Range. This way Kate can join us to test the Presidentials together and she can remain in a place known for its expansive, heart-thumping view. I considered Mt. Washington, the biggest of them all, but I'm not strong enough yet. My second choice was the 360° panorama atop Mt. Eisenhower—until I reconsidered. Kate would never have forgiven me for leaving her on a mountain named for a Republican.

I won't know for sure about Monroe until Sarah and I reach the summit and something inside me says *yes* or, God forbid, *no*. If it's *no*, I don't know what I will do. Leave without performing the ceremony for which Sarah and I have hauled ourselves up these body-busting rocks and slabs? Or will we figure out some way to make this mountain the right mountain?

Maybe it's crazy to think I can manage this seven-mile trail with an elevation gain of 2900 feet, the final third of which the *White Mountain Guide* characterizes as "extremely steep and rough." My will may be sharp as a spike but the body I inhabit is small, flimsy, and middle-aged. One knee hasn't worked properly for decades. My spine twists from a scoliosis that causes everything else to hang off-kilter.

Perhaps my limitations themselves propel me toward mountains that wring from me everything I've got. I want to be sleek and fast and tough. I don't tell anyone, I hardly admit it to myself, but I want to be every bit as good as the men who wrote the *White Mountain Guide*. I want to lope up and rattle down something as big and demanding as these intimidating mountains, confident and unafraid. If the hiking book guys say a hike should take seven hours, I want to do it in six.

Time gnaws at me. At my age, climbing won't likely get any easier.

The small sounds of Sarah's tearing open adhesive strips float up to me. I remember Kate's making those same sounds, our first big hike together. Sarah was with us on the Mt. Tripyramid venture and cut her leg then, too. I applied the antiseptic and Kate applied the Band-Aids. As usual, we worked as a team.

On that same hike four years ago, we learned there was a list of forty-eight mountains over 4,000 feet in New Hampshire and that the titan we women had just climbed was one of them. "Peak baggers" who finished all forty-eight could apply to the venerable Appalachian Mountain Club, caretakers of these and other mountains in the Northeastern and Mid-Atlantic regions since 1876, for membership in the Four Thousand Footer Club.

Novices still, Kate and I vowed that someday we would join that elite society. That is, I took up the quest and Kate didn't say no. For the following year, she planned and trained and learned right beside me. She hadn't yet committed herself to more than one trek at a time, but I believe we'd have wound up doing The 48 together. In one way or another, we had carried each other through a number of things.

I carry her today. She is a weight of ashes that can be measured in pounds and a weight of memory and loss far greater, one that cannot be measured at all. I am on my way as promised, to set her free at 5,372 feet in the raw wild winds atop Monroe. I can only hope that when the moment comes I'll be able to let go my last physical hold on her.

She and I had presumed we had a future together. In that future, she would overcome the six years and extra pounds she had on me and I would conquer my troublesome body and fear of heights. However long it might take, we would meet the 4000-Footers together.

Now I must do them without her. If I can. For both our sakes, although at the moment the precipitous trail weaves knots in my stomach and I'm so drained I dare not sit for fear I won't pull myself up again.

Sarah has finished bandaging her leg and I see a flash of red as she tucks away the nylon aid kit. I hear her small involuntary grunt as, in one motion, she hoists her pack and swings it onto her back. Her hip and chest belts snick shut. If Sarah and I are able to make it up and down Monroe today, if I am able to let Kate go, if after that I can find the heart and the strength and the will, then I have thirty-nine more mountains to climb.

1. CHALLENGE

Kate, my next-door-neighbor, best friend, and now hiking buddy, just explained why heavy leather sandals dangled from her overstuffed backpack. "My boots might be too tight." She confessed this now, at the beginning of a 12.1-mile climb, causing tiny frogs to trampoline from my belly to my throat.

Nothing could be done now, so instead I re-checked the sky. Still full of thick pewter clouds. On a Saturday in 1998 at the height of fall color in New Hampshire, mine was the only car at the trailhead. Did everyone else think it would warm up? On the drive over, the car had registered 34°F. I'd rather not have known that.

I shouldn't worry about Kate. I was just as likely to be the one who had to quit and ruin the day for us all. At least, I assumed if I turned back my friends would too. I glanced at Kate, then Sarah. Would they abandon me to reach the top?

I pushed the pack belt firmly down on my hips. That wasn't going to happen. This wasn't the Himalayas. Though hikers got injured, lost, and even died in the White Mountains, I didn't expect any of that to happen to us. No, what wound my clock was finishing. I had to finish.

In the Sandwich Range Wilderness of the Whites, Mt. Tripyramid would push me to my limits. Twelve miles was more than double the longest hike I'd ever done—two decades ago. No matter. Though I might be a month shy of forty-eight and potentially a fool for giving up a lucrative business career to write a novel, I would complete this "event."

For months, Kate and I had climbed subway steps in Cambridge and tested ourselves on small Massachusetts mountains. Even so, she had delayed committing to today's venture. Maybe she worried about her age, too. She had signed on only after two weeks out west tramping the Cascades with her friend Pauline, a fact that still rankled.

When Kate dithered about Tripyramid, I'd invited my college classmate Sarah as well. I'd get to spend a whole day as well as the nights before and after with Sarah, at my place in New Hampshire. We'd never hiked before, but we had rambled through Spain together on our junior year abroad. Though we went way back, we usually only saw each other if I initiated our getting together, a pattern we'd talked about over the years but one that hadn't much changed. I would have liked her to show she cared as much as I did by reaching out more. She was busy, of course. When I'd asked her to join us, I thought she'd take weeks to consult her patient schedule, her teaching calendar, her husband and kids, ponder for a while, and have to be asked again. Instead, she had agreed instantly. Neither of my friends had responded to the Tripyramid adventure the way I'd expected. How would we fare, driving ourselves up and down a rough mountain today, especially when they had just met?

Older than Sarah and I, Kate was an intellectual who also loved to cook, a feminist who didn't resort to sly jokes about men. With two kids who were already young men, and a marriage far longer than my own, she was a more experienced wife and mother. I looked up to her.

The looking-up-to part began even before we met. Kate and her family had moved onto our street five years ago, a year after my family, and the woman showed moxie. Within weeks she held an open house, something no one else had done, inviting everyone on the street.

When my husband Larry, our three-year-old daughter Casey, and I arrived, Casey began her long love fest with Kate's enormous golden retriever by lying on the floor, her little corn-silk head propped on a red-gold canine belly as Marla thunked her tail against the oak floor. Tom, Kate's husband, welcomed Larry and me, got us drinks, and asked the usual questions people do when they first meet. I excused myself to check out the food. After three astonishing brownies, I noticed Kate. She stood behind a counter separating the kitchen and dining rooms, a tall, pale woman with light gray hair, broad shoulders, and good posture. She was cooking, admirably calm despite the strangers filling her home, but keeping busy at your own party was an introvert's strategy I knew well. I walked over. "What do you do to your brownies? I'm addicted."

Her smile turned her from someone you might overlook to someone you could not. "Dried cherries." She pulled a tray from the oven. "Shrimp puff chaser?"

We got talking about books. We both loved the novel *A Thousand Acres* and had just finished *Getting to Yes*, about negotiating without giving in. I felt so in tune with her I shyly ventured that I'd just picked up *The Tibetan Book of Living and Dying* to help me handle the news about my mother's pancreatic cancer.

"I've found the book comforting," Kate said softly. "I'm so sorry about your mother." She didn't need to be told the diagnosis was a death sentence. Her own mother, when I asked, was a woman full of personality and verve, like mine. Both mothers lived in the South, something else we had in common.

My friend Sarah was a somewhat different story. She, too, was interested in many things and noticeably smart. Unlike Kate or me, though, you couldn't miss her in a crowd. I'd noticed Sarah immediately that first day back in Portuguese 101, and because the hunky professor called on her more, felt jealous. She had long, naturally platinum hair and big aqua eyes. Taking the same Spanish and Portuguese classes, we'd necessarily competed for grades. I thought an occasional frisson of competition still arose between us, but maybe it was only on my side. Sarah, like me, was an achiever. She was now at the top of her profession as a psychiatrist, not only because she was bright and worked hard but also because people fascinated her. She could always find a fresh angle on a situation or person. Her quirky sense of humor had taken some getting used to in college, but in the decades since then she had kept me in stitches.

If I sometimes cast Kate in the role of wise woman, Sarah stood in at times for the smart sister I yearned for, one who didn't have Down Syndrome and against whom it was fair to measure myself. I cared for both friends deeply and differently. I could only hope they'd get along and—I was counting on this—get me through the climb.

Despite the cold, Sarah wore teal-colored shorts, her pale legs mottling red. She must have known what she was doing, she ran in this weather. Kate tended to train only when she was with me. She had on shorts, too, but beneath a pair of dark pants. She had packed away her fleece, but now zipped her navy rain jacket up to her chin. The wind lifted her short gray hair into soft peaks. Sarah's long blonde hair sailed around her head into her eyes and across the shoulders of a neon purple windbreaker.

My spiky (dyed) reddish brown hair stood at attention. Beneath my rain jacket and heavy fleece I wore a green

T-shirt (*Smith College Class of 1972—One Hundred Years of Women On Top.*) Over that a red cotton long underwear shirt fell to the tops of my thighs. I didn't know yet that cotton was a hiker's bane. The fabric that felt so friendly retained up to forty times its weight in water, so my own absorbed sweat could put me at risk for hypothermia. The waistband of a pair of royal blue spandex leggings squeezed my belly, tender still from bouts of anxiety-induced diarrhea in the early hours. I pulled on a puckered pair of leather gloves, antsy to get going. The longer we delayed, the more time I had to question my readiness. Kate wore gloves, too, but after buckling on her pack, Sarah shoved her hands into her shorts' pockets.

Sarah was here, I suspected, mainly for a lark. A few years ago, she and her family had hiked up Washington, the biggest, deadliest mountain in the Whites and, by my lights, that made her an expert. Kate viewed hiking as a great way to lose weight, the only motivation she ever voiced. Maybe she hiked just because friends asked her. I preferred to believe she came today because we were in this together, shoulder-to-shoulder, hiking buddies and all.

And me? I was here because I needed to find a place where I could still succeed. After twenty years in the business world, I left to attempt something I'd aspired to since the age of six. For a couple of years now I'd been a raw beginner, a baby novelist living off of my husband's salary and our savings with no promotions or raises of my own, alone at my desk. Each day taught me how little I knew about writing fiction. Being a voracious reader didn't enable me to create the quality of prose I was used to reading. My business colleagues had considered me a good writer but expository writing and fiction, it had become clear, were as alike as construction projects and gazelles. I'd been taking classes and working on the novel part-time for two years and not only hadn't I finished my book, it was so bad I kept chucking it out and starting over.

I was also the older mother of an eight-year-old, with no benchmarks or comparative analyses to know if I was doing right by or inadvertently scuppering her. I'd been the youngest of three and my own mother, deceased for several years, wasn't available to consult. Apart from the terrible clarity of death, too much of my life felt uncertain at the advanced age of forty-eight. Things were not how I had expected.

∽

Tripyramid rested in the emerald flats and folds of the White Mountain National Forest. From above, the mountain resembled a reclining elephant, the very one that felt like it had lain across my chest all night. Her head pointed north, her trunk unfurled westward and the rest of her body sprawled south. The triangular shape that suggested a pyramid, a word that clothed her in ancient mystery, was North Peak. We had to hike six miles to reach this summit that jutted from the top of her shoulders. From there, the knobby ridge of Tripyramid's spine marched southward a full mile before arriving at the second bulge, Middle Peak. Then her backbone curled for another half mile to reach South Peak, the final summit at her tail.

A lesser mountain called The Fool Killer guarded Tripyramid's back. Another subsidiary, the Scaur, a Scottish word for "sharp precipice," stood watch over her head. These neighbors with the ominous, foreboding names added to my trepidation.

I marked our official starting time—how it had gotten to be 8:00 a.m. none of us could figure—and we took off on Livermore Trail, a sandy, gravelly old logging road wide enough for five hikers to link arms. Though the way was easy, the trail immediately let us feel the silent embrace of wilderness. I craned my neck upward at soaring blue-green trees that topped their shorter, darker sibling firs whose names, besides balsam, I didn't know. Amongst the green and smoky blue gleamed ghostly white birches, their yellow leaves fluttered by a breeze that now, in the shelter of these woods, was too high for me to feel. Maples had gone red and gold, rich and wine dark against the wooly gray light. I breathed in deeply, happy to be moving, to begin our adventure at last. The fragrance of pine and balsam, sharp and Christmassy, tingled.

Within minutes, however, I found myself struggling to keep up with Sarah and Kate. Kate was six inches taller but how could Sarah be faster? We were the same height, same age, same Hispanics Studies major. I remembered she got a Distinction on our senior comprehensive exam when I did not, but I couldn't go any faster. I stomped along three steps behind, rushing when I wanted to be gently warming up. I had planned on a slow, easy start. At this pace, could I hang in till the end? Not-finishing would be outright failure. I felt the weight of the pack with every step, my scoliotic back twitching from strain. I didn't like being last. It reminded me of trying to keep up with my nine-years-older, bigger, smarter brother and, though I should have known better by now, apparently I did not.

An hour later, the real hiking began. We climbed. The Scaur Ridge Trail was ridiculously steep. We hoisted ourselves and our packs over big rocks we had to clamber up onto, sometimes on our knees, and my back felt every twist. We used our hands to haul ourselves up. In my hiking experience, hands went along for the ride. Hikes were for feet. And, I was learning, for shoulders. My shoulders had developed a voice. A rather whiny voice. Trying not to worry about the shoulder with the three-inch surgical scar, I conjured up images of thick foam slabs beneath the straps of my pack. At least my hands had leather gloves to protect them from the granite surfaces that scraped off skin like a cheese grater.

Sweating, we paused to stuff jackets and fleeces into our packs. Of the three of us, only Sarah didn't seem challenged by verticality. When we started up again, she rapidly regained her lead. Looking up, I mostly saw her butt and then her smaller and smaller self, scaling boulders as if she had sticky pads on her hands and feet. She turned and yelled down, "This is gorgeous! Isn't it fun?" Then she took off and disappeared from sight.

I could have smacked her.

After months of preparing for this hike, I still didn't know if I was strong enough, tough enough, brave enough. As it had during the night, worry eroded my confidence. *Would I finish?* Other possible problems—storms, rutting moose, bears—I didn't have the experience to be troubled by. It was me that worried me.

We continued leveraging and hoisting, maintaining the line-up that would continue for much of the day: Sarah in the lead, me in the middle, and Kate slowly and with no apparent angst about it, bringing up the rear. Kate's face was sweaty, but determined. I thought, *She really is stronger than I am.* Not as fast, but stronger. At some core level, she was unfazed by this trail. Sarah was fast and Kate was sure, but what was I? I no longer defined myself as a partner in a national organization or president of my own consulting firm and I could hardly call myself a writer. I needed to be a hiker, a good one. But I relied on a blend of fear and willpower with neither Sarah's agility nor Kate's character. At least, I consoled myself, the hardest part of the hike would be over early and the day wouldn't further test my fear of heights.

❧

"Hey, look at that," Kate called up, gesturing. She unzipped the small pouch belted at her navel and pulled out a camera. Moving to her side, I leaned down to where she crouched on the trail. She pointed out a whole row of icicles hanging from a boulder to our right. They glistened, wetly silver against a backdrop of emerald moss.

"Wow," I whispered as Kate moved in for a close-up. I stood to yell to Sarah, but she was nowhere in sight. I pulled off a glove and reached out to slide my finger down one of the six-inch sparkling daggers. Cold, slick, solid. I yearned to break one off and lick it, but they were too beautiful to ruin. I remembered my mother coming into my childhood room in the early morning dark to murmur, "It's a snow day." The exhilaration. The sense of freedom. A day in the white glare of snow making lopsided snowballs and forts, plucking icicles from tree branches until I grew chilled, then the warmth inside the house that fogged my glasses. My mother pressing her warm cheek to my cold one, saying this was her favorite part of winter. Offering her a bit of icicle that still clung to my mitten. The taste—gritty, with bits of bark and the strange, bloody tang of dirt.

Perhaps Kate was remembering, too. "Aren't they amazing?"

I looked at her and she looked at me, and it settled into my brain that we were here on the spine of one enormous mountain, just as we'd planned, just as we'd trained for, and it was cold and cloudy but we were warm and we were climbing and we'd probably hiked five miles already, as long as I'd ever hiked in my life. We grinned big wolf grins at each other.

As we resumed our upward scramble, I didn't mind how loudly I sucked in air or how my right knee complained. On the lookout now, I saw more mini-forests of icicles and slowed down to share them with Kate, wondering if Sarah had seen them, too. Kate marveled at clumps of red berries that blazed from tangled gray branches. We were slower than Sarah, but slow had become advantageous.

It occurred to me that I wasn't worried about Kate the way I sometimes was when we trained. Sarah and I were younger and more active, but Kate was doing just fine. The quiet aloofness that could exasperate me in the city made her a perfect companion in the mountains. She didn't need a thing from me beyond my staying within shouting distance—a restful rarity for the mother of a young child. I was free to fully engage with my surroundings, a gift of rare value.

An hour before noon I spied a tiny glen to the left of the trail, a circle of rocks with elegant little mosses jutting up like tiny trees in the middle of the ring. Stonehenge Reduced. The place exuded a sense of serenity and comfort and, somehow, beguilement. The sun came out for the first time and drenched the spot with warm golden light.

"I found a fairy circle," I shouted. If there were such things, this surely had to be one.

Sarah bounded back down the path without a moment's hesitation about retracing her steps and regarded my glowing circle.

"Isn't it perfect for lunch?"

In a little-girl voice that made me laugh she chirped, "Oh, Cheryl, you don't think the fairies will mind?" She strode through the circle and plunked herself down, dropping her pack at her feet. Even her purple shorts didn't dispel the magic. In fact, her white-blonde hair looked just right lighting up the glen. I hadn't expected enchantment when I set out to make something of myself today.

"We taking a break?" Kate arrived panting and sunk onto a rock.

I unearthed the disposable camera I'd brought in case I dropped it. The sun bounced off their smiles in a thoroughly magical way.

When Kate announced we'd lingered an hour over lunch, my stomach went queasy. The days were shorter now and light faded quickly in the mountains. Leaving the fairies, we struck a lively pace.

Thirty minutes later, we reached a crest and turned onto Pine Bend Brook Trail. The gently graded ridge was studded with tall pines. Open woods rolled west, more or less endlessly, just like Sherwood Forest. We unconsciously slowed our pace. Something in this old forest patched with sunlight spoke to the soul. For the next quarter of an hour, we fell into a natural silence rich with the fragrance of pine needles and the creaking of boughs in the wind. Now this was hiking, I thought. I could do this.

Too soon, we scrambled up boulders again. I had assumed that from now on we would sally forth to the top. But here we were again, packing away layers of clothing and grunting like sows. I pondered the meaning of 3000 feet, the elevation we had to gain on this hike. Before today, I'd been clueless. Now I pictured it in terms of a house. If a two-story house with an attic was thirty feet tall, we were climbing up one hundred houses.

I looked back at Kate. Had she understood this? I considered asking her, but suddenly we left the evergreens and found ourselves in a small open space that had to be the top of North Peak.

Sarah glanced around. "This is it?"

"Hallelujah," I gasped. I'd managed 5.8 miles and our first of three summits.

We dumped our packs with relief. Sarah sank onto a log to snack while Kate climbed up some boulders to snap pictures. I pulled out the map and joined her, sorting out mountains. After we identified the far off peaks of the Presidentials, I elbowed her. "Someday, we'll tackle those babies."

～

After North Peak's summit, rocks and tree roots clotted the trail. Yuk. We hiked down for a while then up for a while, down for a while then up for a while. Trails between summits of nearly the same height, it seemed to me, should be level.

We checked the map. Before reaching Middle Peak, we had to descend twelve houses then ascend twelve houses in what the *White Mountain Guide* called "a saddle". I slurped water, then dribbled some on my head. Kate mopped her face and neck with a bandana.

"You're in great shape," Kate complimented Sarah. "How do you do it?"

"I swim." Sarah recapped her water bottle. "And run."

Swimming and running. Two pastimes injuries had forced me to give up.

I remembered when I had flown from Boston to Albuquerque where Sarah was doing her psychiatric residency years ago. Her husband Nolan and I had gone for a jog. After a couple of days, Sarah joined us. Finding she liked it, she asked me how often I jogged. I replied that I was a fair weather runner. A few months later I got a postcard:

> *Dear Cheryl, I tried to be a fair weather runner, but it's fair weather here all the time! Just finished my first marathon. Love, Sarah.*

If you ever want to show yourself up on a hike, be sure to bring along somebody who considers marathons the natural consequence of learning to jog.

I adjusted the shoulder straps of my pack searching for a spot that didn't hurt and told Sarah, "Kate and I did some training hikes on Mt. Wachusett, that little ski mountain west of Boston." I turned around to Kate. "How many Wachusetts did we do?"

"I did three. You did four."

"Yeah, but you hiked two weeks in the Cascades."

"Sounds pretty determined," observed the psychiatrist.

"Cheryl dragged me into it."

"You signed up for the Cascades with somebody else!" It

still smarted how blithely she'd gone off with Pauline for two entire weeks yet hesitated to commit to a one-day climb with me. Maybe with a therapist present, I should work through my feelings.

Kate preempted me by marching off. "I need a pit stop."

I chickened out and dropped the subject. Besides, I needed to hoard my energy to finish.

We were quiet as we slogged on, having been hiking for five-and-a-half hours. Even Sarah didn't start a conversation, just drifted farther ahead. Fifteen minutes later I was calculating, again, how many miles remained when I looked up the trail. And I do mean *up*. We must have finished the low part of the saddle because now a steep, rocky ascent confronted me.

"Again?" I threw up my arms. "I am so sick of this boulder crap. This trail sucks!" I yelled. I shut up and looked around. Sarah was far ahead, but Kate was close enough behind to have heard. She kindly appeared not to notice. I said no more, but I was ready to quit. We were just past the halfway point, I was already spent, and now understood that we'd have to do the whole uphill-over-rocks thing again not just for Middle Peak but probably South Peak too. I had loved the icicles and the Pine Bend Brook ridge and Sherwood Forest, but what if this hike was simply more than I could do?

I waited for Kate. Her cheeks drooped with exhaustion. For the first time I wondered if she had lain awake last night, too. "It can't be far," she said in a monotone.

I saw how hard she was working and how drained she was and how she wasn't complaining but gamely enduring and suddenly I wanted to kick something. After our hard, painful, tedious training, we *couldn't* be tired. We'd drunk our water and eaten our food and taken our breaks and done everything we were supposed to do, yet success seemed unattainable. I stood there with my teeth shut hard on the words boiling in my throat. In a kind of psychological alchemy, the swampy folds of my brain transformed fear of failure into high-minded fury. I stomped off to tackle the unending procession of boulders ahead. Once I got far enough ahead of Kate, I allowed myself to swear continuously, which seemed to help.

I clomped and cursed my way upward one lunge at a time, breathing harshly. I didn't feel my back or knees or shoulders or feet. I didn't find nature beautiful. I wanted to get my hands on the sadists who had cut this trail.

Every now and then, I heard Kate's water bottle clink against a rock. I kept going until I had to stop to catch my breath. Looking ahead, I was surprised to see Sarah sitting down wiping the front of her leg with a tissue, a tissue with red splotches.

I clambered up to her. She'd scraped a four-inch patch from her shin and little runnels of blood trickled down her leg. I groaned in sympathy. "It's just a scratch," the doctor said.

Kate arrived and ferreted out the first aid kit. I moved out of the way while she used her water bottle to wash the cut, then her shirt to pat it dry. I followed with ointment and Band-Aids.

When we hiked on, we marched in a close threesome. My worry about finishing the hike or my novel dropped away. I simply moved.

At some point, voices broke our reverie, making me realize that we hadn't seen anyone else all day. At the wooded summit of Middle Tripyramid stood three men in a clearing so small they pretty much filled it. Two of them had shaken out a map and were pointing out mountains. The other guy looked like a human oriole. He had black hair, white skin, and a black beard atop an orange shirt, orange down vest, and orange backpack. He bounced up and down on the balls of his feet. In one hand he held a camera mounted with a most impressive lens. "Hello!" he hailed us. "Which way'd you come up?"

He had parked off the Kancamagus Highway on the north side of the mountain and had ascended on a different trail. He was so friendly I asked him to take a picture of Sarah, Kate, and me. "You bet!" He took my disposable without a trace of scorn and positioned us against the sliver of vista. The sun peeked out, but we zipped up against a biting wind. As we posed, we learned he shot photos for a living, he was single, and we were the first women he'd seen on Tripyramid. "This is my fifteenth 4000-Footer." He handed back my camera. "You ladies peak bagging?"

"Sure," Sarah quipped, raising her eyebrows. "Is that legal?"

He looked uncertain she was kidding. After a pause, he explained about the forty-eight 4000-Footers and the Four Thousand Footer Club. He spoke with enough relish that Kate asked, "What happens when you join?"

"You get a patch."

"That's it?"

"Well, yeah," he said in a tone that suggested maybe there was a reason he hadn't seen many women here. But his enthusiasm reappeared. "Tripyramid is great because it counts for two peaks!"

"Why not three?" Kate asked. "It only seems fair." Kate was an extremely fair-minded person.

"Rules. There's got to be two hundred feet of elevation gain or loss between peaks for them to count separately. South Peak doesn't cut it."

Tramping on to the peak that didn't cut it, the three of us soon dropped into our second saddle of the day. Sarah queried Kate about the African American newsletter she edited and what it was like to be the only white person on staff. I pondered the Four Thousand Footer Club. Who'd do such a crazy thing? Probably only elite hikers got in—few of them women, I bet.

As if traveling similar thoughts, Kate suddenly piped up. "What kind of people do you think are in that Four Thousand Footer Club?"

"Tall people," Sarah answered.

⌒

Twenty minutes later as we trudged up South Peak, a gap in the trees offered a view backward. As the past so often did, North and Middle Peaks seemed both distant and near, both familiar and strange. Seeing their size and knowing I had traversed them made me feel every minute of my age. Yet here in the crystal air, using my body as I had in my twenties, I was in touch with a younger me that lingered inside middle-aged me.

We moved on. The sun stayed with us. The sky, scrubbed clean by the clouds, burned a deep lapis lazuli. When we arrived at South Peak's summit, a wooded area with no views, we guzzled water and peeled off clothing. It was two o'clock in the afternoon, maybe 60°F in the sun.

"So how long is this hike?" For the first time, Sarah sounded weary.

"A bit over five miles left," Kate answered. "We've done seven. No turning back now."

Soon we inched down large slabs of granite. This was different. So was the fact that we had stumbled onto other hikers. Occasionally a rocky slab stuck out perpendicular to the mountain and on these warm surfaces lay guys with their shirts off. Young show-offs. It wasn't *that* warm.

"It looks like Boston University on the first day of spring," Sarah said.

Kate smiled. "Except for the slope of the trail."

"I wouldn't call this a trail," I muttered, crisscrossing a tilted table of granite so I didn't have to walk—or look—straight down. I appreciated, in retrospect, our prior ups and downs. Where there were trees and boulders around me. Where there were handholds. Where I could ignore vertical drops because I was going uphill. Sweat bloomed on my forehead and in my armpits. Nausea roiled my gut. I began to feel pulled by a giant magnet to the ground far below. Somehow in all the planning for this hike, my terror of precipices had never come up.

Soon we arrived at a point where the slabs were littered with loose gravel and scattered stones and sheered off like a plumb line, taking my courage with them. The South Slide looked as if a giant bulldozer had sunk teeth into the top of the mountain and scraped downward, slicing off Tripyramid's skin of trees and soil, digging through to granite muscle. The scar that was our trail plunged, at a pitch that dizzied me, down the mountainside for nearly a thousand feet—the height of the Eiffel Tower.

I couldn't draw a full breath. I had to sip air. I thought about turning back, but that way was longer. Below me Sarah started down the Slide, more cautious than she'd been all day. *Follow Sarah*, I commanded myself. As I cringed after her, she soon put thirty feet between us. I couldn't spare a thought for how Kate fared. I placed one boot and then the other, testing each step of the treacherous footing. I couldn't speak. I was too scared to tell anyone how scared I was.

I went so slowly I moved in tree time.

The scrape of boots on rock higher up suggested Kate had begun her way down. Behind her floated new voices. I focused on the scree and shifting stones as the voices grew nearer. Then I heard sounds I couldn't believe. Someone behind me was *running*. A shower of stones and pebbles exploded down the cliff face and a sharp rock struck the back of my calf. "Christ!" I blurted, just as a black Labrador wearing a red kerchief hurtled past. Rubbing my calf, I turned uphill, furious.

A young man called out an apology. Then he yelled, "Pinkus! Stop!" But Pinkus was booking it. Everyone stopped to watch, caught up in the drama of his flight. When his back legs slid on the scree and splayed out from under him, hindquarters hitting rock, he whined but saved himself with his forelegs and vice-versa as he seesawed down the mountain.

Sarah looked up as Pinkus slid toward her, preceded and followed by a dusty cloud of flying scree. She ducked, covering her head with her arms. After the dog careened past, she straightened up to stare downhill like the rest. Eventually, all I could make out of Pinkus was a distant patch of black and in that moment, when I knew he had made it safely down, I hated his lucky guts.

"You all right?" I yelled to Sarah.

She made an OK sign, but stayed put. She must have decided to wait for me.

There was only one problem. I had stopped to watch Pinkus and now my engine was stalled. A knee-high boulder stood before me and though I knew I had to go around it, somehow the decision of right or left eluded me. I wasn't proceeding. I was debating, and debating was not a good thing. My feet awaited marching orders, but my brain was in meltdown. Little muscles around my knees, weary from seven miles and three peaks, quivered. Now that I couldn't move, fear flooded my system. I stood there panting while images of myself flying through the sun-washed air to crash into treetops below scrolled through my mind.

I was paralyzed—frozen—halfway down the Slide.

2. OVERNIGHT SUCCESS

I hadn't set out to be a hiker. The road to hiking began three years before Tripyramid, in a kitchen. It's also fair to say that what led me to that kitchen was my mother's death. The last nine years of her life, when she wasn't drinking, had been precious.

Christmas, birthdays, and Mother's Days, I had always known what my mother wanted. I knew that she preferred gold jewelry to silver, that she could only wear tomato red because other reds clashed with her auburn hair. I knew her favorite bite of a roast chicken, one of the two small buds on the underside of the bird nestled close to the bone, the tenderest morsel of dark meat.

By the time I was eight, I could mix her go-to summer drink, gin and tonic, with an extra chunk of lime squeezed in. In the winter, I fixed her scotch on the rocks with just a splash of water. She gossiped with me about her friends whose husbands cheated. When she and my father fought, she recounted his harsh words while I hugged her tight. My mother and I were closer than moth and flame. She made sure to tell me whenever she thought she would kill herself.

Then she stopped drinking for those nine years in my thirties and early forties and, though things weren't perfect between us, it wasn't always about her when she called. After Casey was born, she was the best grandmother a little girl could have and a mother I could turn to with questions about my child. Since her death, I missed her right down to my teeth.

When my father had died a decade earlier, it had changed my life and made me cry, but I wasn't sure I could survive losing my mother. Even though I'd known for a year that she was dying, I wasn't ready when she left me. Nevertheless, I was a grown up orphan at forty-four.

Her death had catapulted me into the older generation, the ones who were supposed to know what to do. With me in that generation were my sister Cindy, who had Downs, and our big brother Bill. Cindy resided at Piney Ponds, a community for mentally challenged adults not far from Bill, his wife Mardy, and their two adult children. All of them lived in another country—Texas—far from Massachusetts, my adopted home. Though I was married to a man who loved me and knew I was stricken, Larry's litigation cases and political activism consumed him. Casey had just entered kindergarten, an absorbing journey of her own. Kate and I had met but weren't yet close. Other friends had busy lives and little time to spare. I sought professional help, but talking about the bleakness wasn't enough. I was never really alone in the weeks after my mother died, it just felt that way.

I had a job, though I had trouble doing it. After graduating from business school late in the 1970s, I'd worked as a general management consultant, a marketing officer for a bank, and a partner in a national accounting and consulting firm. When Casey was two, I'd started a consulting practice that I ran from my home office but now, as I mourned my mother, I wanted no part of my work.

While the phone went unanswered and my business drifted, I sat in the small wing chair in my office on the top floor of our old house and read science fiction and mystery novels, wrapping myself up in worlds in which desperate problems were solved by wise, strong, indefatigable women— the kind I wanted to be. Or I simply sat and stared at the framed picture of my mother and father.

I had to do something about myself.

A friend had told me she'd hired this trainer she saw once a week to plan her running schedule and review her workouts. "I have a new goal," my friend had bubbled. "I've entered my first race!"

I looked at her. She glowed. Her skin looked clear and fresh. She had cut her hair and the feathery new look flattered her.

I put my hand up to see if I had remembered to brush my hair that day. From the sour taste in my mouth, I figured I probably hadn't brushed my teeth either.

Eight weeks after my mother died I walked, numb and bereft, into a kitchen in Chestnut Hill, Massachusetts, the home of trainer and world-class runner Cathy Utzschneider.

"Why do you want a coach?" she asked.

"My mother just died," I said. "You can be my new mother."

Cathy blinked.

In the ensuing silence, we sat across from one another at her kitchen table. A blue, late-autumn sky poured sunlight through the window, highlighting her short blonde hair. Though she had to be near forty, she looked younger. "Okay," she said and picked up a pen. "Let's start with what you want to accomplish. What's your long-term goal?"

I appreciated her professionalism, but I hadn't had a goal, long term or otherwise, since my mother died. I had supposed a trainer would, like a teacher handing out homework, give me one.

Cathy waited. "Toning up?" I suggested. Surely toning up would beget all sorts of goals—maybe even a new hairstyle.

Cathy tapped her pen on the blank form. She was lean

and fit, her blue eyes warm. She wore what I assumed was a training outfit, a close-fitting top and shiny black leggings with blue and green racing stripes that outlined her muscles. She smiled sympathetically. "I know this is about grieving your mom, but it's important to have a goal that's related to a sport, something you enjoy. The more fun you have, the more likely you are to stick with your training."

Fun? I hadn't come here for fun. I needed to get back to work, to stop weeping, to quit inhaling novels like a chain smoker.

Cathy patiently asked me to list any sports I'd ever played, her pen ready. I wanted to comply, but tennis and badminton had been my sports until my right elbow wouldn't allow me to pick up a briefcase much less swing a racket. After elbow surgery and months of physical therapy, I was reluctant to take up racquet sports again. I needed to protect my right elbow until I didn't need to lift Casey anymore. Like when she went off to college.

"How about running?" Cathy prompted. "Have you ever tried that?"

"Sure." Half the country had tried running. "I did a couple of 10K races. But my feet gave out six, eight years ago." It had taken two years of wearing orthotics to be able to walk comfortably again. I'd also had to give up wearing heels, not easily done in the business world when you're a short woman.

By process of elimination, Cathy and I settled on swimming as the sport that would provide a way back into my life. I left her kitchen that day clutching a piece of paper that told me I had to buy a training calendar and get to a pool three times before I saw her again. Even if I sat on the edge of the pool all suited up and couldn't make myself get in, it counted. "The hardest part is getting there," Cathy had said. "The rest will come." She told me about a guy who came out of nowhere one year to win the Boston Marathon. "Yeah," he'd quipped to a reporter, "I've become an overnight success in ten years."

Cathy warned that it took ten years or 10,000 hours to succeed in sports or pretty much anything. Patient, steady, small steps over a long period of time forged champions. As someone who tended to dive into everything headlong, this was not my usual approach, but I needed her.

꧁

Cathy held the long view for me all that year while I mourned my mother. She and I grew closer as I leaned on her knowledge and her generous heart. She pestered me to create small, frequent goals. Four laps. Ten. I felt good when I accomplished them, discovering again the simple pleasure of using my body in a sport that didn't cause pain.

I swam. I learned that a person could, if she swam slowly enough, cry at the same time. I added stretches to my routine and graduated to the intermediate lane, even daring the fast lane from time to time. Though there were days I could not make myself get to the pool, times when I reverted to sci-fi and hot fudge sundaes to get through waves of grief, each month I got a little faster and swam a little longer.

After my family and I survived the first Thanksgiving and the first Christmas without my mother, when I had waited on each of our birthdays for the calls that never came, when I had cradled the phone in my hands on Mother's Day, and after I had mailed twice my usual number of presents to my sister Cindy on her birthday, Cathy told me I needed an event. "Something that really challenges you, something that gives meaning to all this training. You know, like a race."

My heart thumped. I shook my head. When I competed, I wanted to win. Though my parents had found competitiveness unbecoming in girls and women they liked it when, in grade school, I had beaten Gail Sabatini and Patrick O'Shea for the little St. Christopher medal the nuns awarded the kid with the highest grades. Somehow competing in academics slipped right past the sugar-and-spice clause. They even liked it when, fifteen years later, I got an MBA, though they didn't care so much for my actually using it, the way a son would. But I had learned that competition—in the business world, playing tennis, driving in Boston—could be sweet. Sweet, that is, if I won.

I wasn't a good enough swimmer to win so much as a wet towel. Now Cathy wanted to turn swimming-as-therapy into swimming-for-real. "Part of training," she insisted.

Because I'd come to trust her, I entered a breast cancer fundraiser called Swim Against The Tide. In honor of my mother. Four months hence, in late April when it sometimes still snowed, women would swim a mile across Thoreau's Walden Pond in Concord, Massachusetts. I had never swum competitively and certainly not in water that had, mere weeks earlier, been ice. Though I didn't have to race, I could be one of those who entered just to raise money, I felt compelled to swim my fastest.

During childhood I'd absorbed my parents' command to always do my best, but this was a special case. Late one morning when I was twenty-eight, my office phone had rung. My father, who mostly left the calling to my mother and never called me at work, greeted me with, "Your mother's been in the hospital. They found breast cancer. She's already had a mastectomy and she's doing fine. We just got the results from the bone scan and the cancer hasn't spread. She'll be over the staph infection soon. So it's good news."

"What?" I stammered. "She what?"

I found it hard to breathe, to talk, to think. My throat closed like a fist. After a silence during which I understood my father did not want my help, that he was desperate to end this awful conversation and hang up, I blurted, "Can I talk to Mom?"

His voice turned away. "Nance, you want to talk?" Then I heard frictiony fuzz as he handed over the phone.

"Cher?" Her rich contralto was scratched and thin.

"Mom! Are you okay?"

She said she was fine.

"Do you want me to fly out there?"

"No, honey, you don't have to do that. I'll be fine. You have your work."

"I'll grab the first plane."

"Please," she had whispered.

~

My mother's death encouraged me to change careers. I rationalized that I'd proven myself enough in business, but the truth was it had struck home that I wouldn't be around forever. Without my parents' reactions to worry about, I could finally become the writer I yearned to be, knowing instinctively that all good writing was about telling the truth.

I persuaded Larry that I needed a year off to write my Great American Novel. Twelve months focused on nothing but a book should do.

~

As my workouts in the pool grew more demanding, I went to writing class at the Radcliffe Institute and invented characters. I clung to my husband and daughter. I missed my mother and I swam, enjoying the idea that an athletic event was something I could plan for and control. My arms and shoulders ached, but I no longer woke up at four a.m., the anxiety hour. I worked out with hand weights to develop strength and definition in my arms and shoulders. I swam a mile three times a week. My mother would have chided me I was doing too much. "Be careful," she always said. "You're such a Little Bit."

I tended to ignore advice like that. I yearned to be a big, bold warrior, a Viking disguised as a street urchin. Somersaulting and shooting away from the wall at the end of each lap made me feel like a real swimmer, doubly important now that I was no longer a real anything career-wise. Feeling like a real swimmer also gave me something to feel besides loss. Swimming connected me back to my body and from there into life. Some days, as the water slid smoothly over my skin, joy bubbled up right alongside the streaming bubbles of air.

After fifteen months of swimming, I began to feel a hitch, a pull in my left shoulder. I assumed it would go away, but the twinge intensified. I continued training. I was used to ignoring pain. Denial was a skill so proficiently honed that, though I'd recognized my mother's drinking problem in my twenties, I hadn't acknowledged my father's alcoholism until after he died and my brother confirmed my suspicion. We didn't usually mention drinking in the family I thought of as my lottery family, into which I'd landed by chance. In my lottery family, we kept our secrets.

My brother's confirmation left me standing alone in the family, the lucky one un-afflicted by Downs or alcoholism. I wanted to doubt him, but I couldn't. He had gotten sober a few years before, going cold turkey after decades of hard drinking. No AA meetings, no therapy or support of any kind, he just quit overnight. If Bill said our father had a drinking problem—despite his ability to give up booze for Lent and to keep getting jobs—then, no matter how I hated Bill's answer, I had to accept it.

My father had a powerful will on him. He had converted to Catholicism, my mother's and our religion, when I was in sixth grade. I'd asked him why, expecting to hear something about heavenly salvation or the Blessed Virgin or my mother's example, but he had said none of that. Now I understood the truth in his reply.

"For the discipline."

~

Three weeks before the Swim Against The Tide, I couldn't swim at all. On land, I couldn't lift my left arm higher than my waist. I lost my forward motion and felt like a failure. Desperation led me to healing methods I knew nothing about, like acupuncture and Reiki energy work. Though they eliminated the pain, only surgery could repair the rotator cuff muscles and acromion process bone. The body I had counted on to restore color to a world without my mother and that I needed to help me honor her struggle could not, after all, swim against the tide.

3. ENGAGING

With my feet glued to bedrock on the South Slide of Tripyramid and my legs shaking, my mind screamed at me. *You idiot! Daylight's short, you've got five miles. Get ahold of yourself!*

But nothing I told myself turned the key of my ignition. I was utterly, horrifyingly, shamefully stuck and unable to appeal for help. It took all my concentration to control the raging panic.

After what could have been minutes or hours, a tapping sound came closer, grew louder.

A hiking pole appeared at my side and stopped. "My knees are talking," Kate's voice said calmly. She sounded tired, but not afraid. I heard the whip of air as she yanked a bandana from her pocket. I imagined she mopped her face, but didn't dare lift my head to see. "You okay? How come you stopped?"

I couldn't answer.

She touched my arm, held it. "Cheryl?"

Her hand felt warm. Her voice, unlike my internal voice, was concerned and caring and safe. I had a fleeting impulse to fling myself into her arms and burst into tears. Instead, I managed a cautious nod. That tiny movement somehow unlocked my brain, maybe because Kate stood next to me blocking the steepness on that side, her body solid and known. My rickety knees took me to the right of the boulder in front of me, closer to Kate, the decision that had thwarted me finally made. I listed toward her in a kind of animal tropism and, as she took a few cautious steps, I did too. I breathed. I focused on the backs of her long legs and stayed close, inhaling the sharp stink of my fear. For the first time, I followed instead of led her.

Kate and I picked our way down to Sarah. She fell in behind me without speaking, reversing our usual order as the three of us scrabbled slowly downhill. A kinship had come alive. Regardless of other hikers or the separate steps we took or our many differences, an almost physical webbing secured us to one another. I felt this so strongly I wanted to make a joke about it before I cried. I blinked and blinked, creeping down the South Slide bracketed by my friends.

In the days after successfully finishing the hike, my event, I floated on a cloud of euphoria. Though it took a week before my quadriceps unclenched enough for me to descend stairs without wincing, on flat ground I was invincible. I didn't know if Sarah's post-hike joy continued once she disappeared back into her life, but Kate shared the rapture. During our daily walks, we strutted around the neighborhood wanting to pick up cars and save babies.

Within two weeks we climbed a New Hampshire icon, Mt. Monadnock, using only the steepest trails. It wasn't a 4000-Footer, but it was a challenge. Despite spending half an hour on lunch, we finished in *book* time—the exact amount of time the *White Mountain Guide* guys said it should take. If I could do that and Tripyramid, I reasoned, I had a shot at mastering hiking. And if I could master hiking I could get into that Four Thousand Footer Club with its air of exclusivity. Joining the Club couldn't be too dissimilar from getting into grad school or joining the three percent of partners who were women in my old firm. A long list of mountains offered tons of goals and opportunities to flourish. Hiking could occupy the Type-A personality that not only didn't suit but actually hindered my career as a writer. And wasn't it propitious, karmic even, that the number of peaks matched the upcoming birthday I'd been dreading? I could prove there was plenty of achievement left in my forty-eight-year-old self.

I realized the White Mountains were no cakewalk. They were old, far older than, say, the Rocky Mountains. Those Western youngsters routinely poked 6,000 to 16,000 feet into the sky, but many of their trails were less difficult. Out West you could climb thousands of feet on paths with long, gradual switchbacks and excellent footing that took advantage of the larger mountains' width and height. New Hampshire's tallest mountains had been scrubbed and pummeled by glaciers and erosion for so long that much of what remained was the kind of cone you might reach in the West at 12,000 feet. Through-hikers on the Appalachian Trail typically found the Whites, even after months of continuous hiking, the toughest section of their 2,100-mile journey. But the more demanding my goal, the more successful and in charge I'd feel.

Reading the *White Mountain Guide* one night in bed, I thumbed to the index listing trails and mountains. With a highlighter, I underlined all the peaks over 4000 feet, making the index dance with optimistic blazes of yellow. About to close the book, I discovered a history of the Four Thousand Footer Club. Nathaniel Goodrich had founded the Club in 1957, when I was a seven-year-old living on the plains of Skokie, Illinois, with nary a hill in sight. Goodrich also happened to have written *The Waterville Valley*, a book about the very same Waterville Valley nestled in a bowl of the White

Mountains in which my family now owned a small apartment where we spent every weekend we could.

I wasn't the only one whose pulse raced at the thought of forty-eight mountains. By spring of 1997, forty years after the Club's founding, over five thousand people had been recognized as members. An extremely select group of two-hundred-thirteen hikers had climbed all the 4000-Footers in *winter*. Jeez Louise, what a deranged idea that was.

I calculated, on average, 146 people were admitted each year. Surely the number was larger in more recent years, but even if a thousand people had joined last year, that was still only one percent or less of those who hiked in the Whites.

I glanced over at my sleeping husband with a secret smile and turned out the lights. Behind my closed lids, Kate and I marched up and down 4000-Footers, each more fabulous than the last.

Two mornings later as Casey and I walked to school, we paused at the corner mailbox. With a flourish, I deposited my application to the Four Thousand Footer Club.

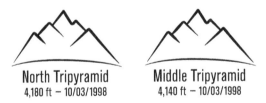

North Tripyramid
4,180 ft – 10/03/1998

Middle Tripyramid
4,140 ft – 10/03/1998

4. PERSPECTIVE

I'd have gushed to Larry in microscopic detail about my victories on Tripyramid and Monadnock, but, crazed with work and with leading volunteers in a gubernatorial campaign, he didn't have the time. When I told him I was taking on The 48, he'd given me a quick kiss and said, "That's great." These days, two weeks before the election, he was gone before I got up each morning and found his way into bed long after I'd fallen asleep. It had been like this frequently for almost two years.

I had no idea how he survived such a grueling schedule, and I knew he hated abandoning Casey and me. But my patience, as I struggled to fill Larry's place in our lives, had evaporated. I wasn't surprised when the doctor confirmed I was anemic, I was pissed. Who had time to be anemic? I had to run our lives, write, and train.

"Have you been able to work?" Kate asked on our morning walk.

My shoulders slumped. "Not really. Are you writing?"

"I just ordered three books on the Jim Crow laws I can't wait to dive into." No matter that she was writing a children's book, Kate would ensure the slightest detail was historically accurate.

We turned a corner. Our immediate neighborhood sat on a broad hill crisscrossed by short streets. I could recognize a Victorian home, but on our walks Kate pointed out brick Georgian Colonials, clapboard Cape Cods, one or two 1960s Moderns tucked behind dense foliage, and even a lone Craftsman style house. Groups of townhouses had sprung up on some of the old properties. We traversed the area admiring the changing colors of tall old trees.

"Even if what I write absolutely sucks," I said, "when I write I'm a better person. If I can't work for days, weeks, or a month like it's been recently, I get cranky. A little nuts. Homemaking just never ends. It's like being eaten alive by an army of ants."

"Oh, I know," Kate said. "Hence *The Feminine Mystique.*"

I nodded. "My mother's generation may have turned to liquor, but hiking is my drug of choice."

We laughed, but even anemic, with the house in shambles and my writing momentum broken, maybe especially then, I couldn't give up hiking. Neither could Kate. The next week we stole half a day to blister up and down Wachusett, our training mountain, chortling over how easy we found it compared to the year before. Nothing like a twelve-mile climb to change one's perspective.

⌒∽

Miraculously, Casey was fed and dressed on time. I either loved or hated our walk to school. On rushed days, I dragged her along as she dawdled to look at everything and we both got testy. But today—sunny, November-brisk, and one day before the election that, win or lose, would return Larry to us—we sauntered happily, petting dogs and picking up giant gold sycamore leaves from the sidewalk.

Until I lurched to a sudden stop. "Jesus H. Christ," I gasped, sounding precisely like my father. My right knee had just been speared. I bent over, fighting nausea, to pull up the leg of my jeans, half expecting to see blood.

"Mommy, what's wrong?" Casey helped me balance on one leg. She glanced at other folks walking around us on the sidewalk and whispered, "You're not supposed to say swears."

"Take your lunch box." With my hands free, I worked to unglue my knee from its bent position. More nausea, more white starbursts. "It's frozen up like the goddamned Tin Woodsman." My father's voice again.

"Lean on me," my girl said.

After a few minutes, I managed to straighten my leg. Gingerly, I put some weight on it, dredging up a wobbly smile. "Dorothy, you've cured me."

We were still riffing on *The Wizard of Oz* a block later when, one month to the day after Tripyramid, my knee failed so suddenly I collapsed to the sidewalk.

The orthopedist who had operated on both my elbow and shoulder wasn't available, but the nurse who worked with him saw me right away. I wasn't fooling around this time waiting for a joint to get better.

"The X-rays don't show any visible fractures. I think you've torn the medial meniscus," she said, probing distressingly all around my knee. "That's the rubbery cartilage that acts like a shock absorber and helps stabilize the knee. A loose piece of cartilage can get stuck in the joint, which is probably what happened on the sidewalk." She pointed. "You can see the area's inflamed."

I stared. When you really looked at it, a kneecap was a weird piece of equipment.

"Have you been doing anything particularly hard on the knees?"

Sitting on the raised patient table, I shrugged. "Hiking, climbing stairs, walking, shoulder exercises, squats."

"Squats!" she shrieked.

I jumped a little. "I use a ball behind my back and—"

"Squats are *guaranteed* to give you knee injuries. It's just a matter of time. I *hate* squats! Everybody in this office hates squats! How many were you doing?"

"Thirty-five. But my trainer said if I used the ball—"

"Trainers!"

Was she saying this was Cathy's fault? "How long will it take to heal?"

It was her turn to shrug. "Three weeks. Six. Depends on how bad the damage is."

She instructed me to stay away from all exercise, ice until the swelling disappeared, and never do another squat of any kind. Along with a blooming case of depression, she handed me a cane. Then she landed her final blow. "If you haven't improved in two weeks, come back to discuss surgery."

5. IN

When the candidate Larry had given so much time to and for whom Casey and I had also volunteered lost the race, my husband didn't cry. I did. Larry's schedule didn't return to normal right away, he had too much litigation work to catch up on. But as we saw more of him over the following months, our family gradually knit itself back together. My beloved strongly supported my refusal to have more surgery or to give up another sport. We decided I should try physical therapy (PT) instead. I was determined to control my body. Hiking was *mine*. I would summit forty-eight mountains and I would join the Four Thousand Footer Club too.

Losing the campaign and getting sidelined by injury left me mopey enough that not even writing consoled me. I'd lost touch with my main characters and new ones popped up without warning. I couldn't tell if they belonged or if it was just easier to mess around with them rather than dig back into the old ones. The only things I seemed to enjoy were Christmas shopping with Kate and the holidays with my family.

As winter dragged on, my hiking gear sulked in the basement, but once crocuses poked from the ground, though I could still only do knee exercises the physical therapist prescribed, Kate and I decided to choose our next 4000 Footer.

I, for one, needed an event in my future. My face-off with the carnivorous blank page was still going poorly and I'd begun to despair.

Sitting at Kate's teak dining table after lunch together, I watched for indications she'd joined my forty-eight-mountain quest. When she slapped a brand new edition of the *White Mountain Guide* onto the table, I smiled.

I'd brought my copy of our mountain bible, too. Within minutes, hardly any teak showed beneath our books and yellow pads. We read each other sections aloud and bent over maps to trace trails, passing possible mountains back and forth like bonbons.

I wanted to net two peaks again, the way we had on Tripyramid. Kate concurred, another good sign. We both wanted something as memorable and challenging as Tripyramid and, we hoped, as beautiful. Since Kate spent chunks of the summer at the second home she and Tom were building in Maine, she wanted to hike in the fall, again like Tripyramid. Fall suited me. When Casey was out of school, I had trouble finding time even to work. And I'd need the summer to train, as would Kate. After some thought, we ruled out mountains that required long drives from Waterville Valley where we'd stay at my place. We needed to start early to finish in daylight.

The 4000-Footers seemed so formidable it never occurred to us to climb more than once a year, especially when we netted two peaks at a time, but I did yearn to finish my second event in better time. I didn't see why, with training, we couldn't hike faster. It bothered me that we had exceeded book time on Tripyramid. Being considered "fast" was part of who I was: fast learner, fast problem-solver, fast to make friends in a new town. Fast to be different from my sister who epitomized "slow." Somehow I'd lost sight of the fact that simply finishing spelled success for me.

Kate and I chose the Franconia Ridge Loop that topped both Mt. Lincoln and Mt. Lafayette. The trail provided dramatic views from the Franconia Ridge between them, the second highest mountain chain in the Whites, bowing only to the Presidentials. The classic trail loomed above tree line on open rock, providing a stunning panorama but also exposing hikers to the elements. Things to worry about included cold, rain, heavy winds, and lightning. The Ridge was the first barrier to storms gusting down from points north, so poor weather blew in quickly. Trickier yet, the hike boasted a *knife-edge*, a section where the trail narrowed and the ground sheared off dizzily on both sides of the rocky spine. Neither Kate nor I had ever seen a knife-edge and it sounded harrowing. She sensibly wondered if this was a wise choice for our second event, but since childhood I'd been forced to suppress fear, instead mixing it up with excitement. The knife-edge only made me crave the hike more, glossing over inconvenient realities like my problem with heights. If Kate wondered about me on open ledges after the South Slide, she didn't say so.

As well as dramatic, Lincoln and Lafayette were big. They soared a thousand feet higher than Tripyramid, with 30 percent more elevation gain. But after twelve punishing miles on Tripyramid, we were delighted that the 8.9-mile Franconia Ridge Loop was shorter. Thinking strictly with our feet, we neglected to perceive that this meant we'd have *less* trail in which to acquire *more* altitude, meaning more sustained steepness than we could imagine.

"How long do you think it'll take?" I sat on the edge of Kate's dining room chair, my good left knee jigging up and down. "We were kind of slow on Tripyramid."

"I've been thinking about that."

She had?

Kate rooted through a manila folder in which she'd apparently filed everything on Tripyramid—just like I did—and pulled out the yellow paper from our hike, wrinkled and stained, on which we'd jotted times for milestones, lunch, and breaks. Stapled behind this page was a crisp new one on which she'd written a column of numbers. She was in, she was definitely in. "I think we can do book time."

"Oh?" I remained polite, not wanting to disturb any progress Kate had made from city buddy to also-hiking-The-48 buddy.

"I read the introduction to the bible."

Who did that? There must have been thirty pages of it.

She gazed at me over her half glasses. "Would you agree it took ten minutes for every pit stop?"

"Sure."

"Multiplying by the number of stops, we spent one entire hour of our ten and a half hours relieving ourselves."

I rocked back in my chair. "No way! We can pee faster than that."

"I agree." Kate moved a finger down her column of figures. "You want to know how much time we spent on breaks?"

I bobbed my head.

"Thirty minutes for lunch. Sixty minutes on the three summits. Another twenty, give or take, for photo-ops. Altogether, one hour and fifty minutes of non-hiking activity." She peered at me to see if I followed. "If you add it together with—"

"Two hours and fifty minutes of those things means we actually *hiked* Tripyramid in—"

"Seven hours and forty minutes. *Book time!*" Kate beamed. Her smile was hard to resist.

We scheduled our event for the end of September. Training for Tripyramid, we'd climbed the staircase of the Porter Square subway station. Now, eight months after it had dropped me to the sidewalk, I figured my right knee was ready to resume Porters. It had been an endless recovery period mitigated only by Cathy's frequent assurance that even top athletes took a long time with injuries. Insisting that I record my PT exercises each week—the color of the stretchy band I used, the number of repetitions and sets—she made me focus on the growing strength that showed up in black-and-white in my sports log. That sense of progress saved me from going in for surgery.

One unseasonably hot morning in early June, at 6:45 a.m. to avoid the commuter rush, Kate and I headed over to the subway station wearing gym shorts, baggy T-shirts, and sneakers. It was already 80°F. The air was so humid it pressed against our lungs with every breath.

"Tom and I counted the subway steps this weekend as we rode up the escalator," Kate informed me. She uncapped her water bottle and drank. "One hundred thirteen steps." One Porter, then, equaled climbing down eight-and-a-half stories and back up. No wonder I hadn't missed them.

We rode the normal-sized escalator down from the street to the large tiled plaza below ground. A long row of gates each with a metal bar across them, the human version of starting stalls for racehorses, prevented us from entering without a pass or metal token. The army of gates was guarded by a glassed-in booth in which sat the subway official who changed money into transportation and ruled this subterranean world. Along one wall, vendors sold sweatshirts, leather goods, and woven items from Latin America. A man wearing a kelly-green apron stood behind a pile of newspapers and boomed out when he saw us, "Bahston Globe! Getcha Globe heah!" In the far corner by the elevator, there was even a coffee and donut stand. The sweet smell of baked sugar immediately made my stomach rumble.

One of the newer stations on the Red Line, Porter Square offered architectural delights. High above us, white seagulls painted against a blue ceiling called to mind open spaces and salty sea air. Daylight brightened the toll plaza through a bank of tilted glass panes like those of a greenhouse. Unfortunately the place was as humid as a greenhouse, too. Kate pulled her T-shirt away from her chest. "You think they still have the heat on?"

We approached the tollbooth. Behind it sat a heavy, grayhaired white man whose glasses had bifocals large enough to notice. He didn't look familiar from last summer. I leaned into the hole cut in his glass cubicle. "Hi. Uh, we're just going to climb the stairs." When he gazed vacantly back at me, I waved my hand up and down. "You know. For exercise."

"In this heat?"

We nodded.

"You ladies got more guts than I do." He smiled, showing the glint of several gold crowns. "Don't faint on me now." He motioned us through the tollgate next to his booth that unlocked with an audible click, calling after us, "And don't fall!"

In front of us gleamed three escalators in perpetual motion, two going down and one coming up. To either side of these beauties lay a beast of a cement staircase.

We stood at the top step of the left-hand staircase looking down what was surely the Mt. Washington of subway steps. Though we were only twenty yards away, I couldn't smell the coffee anymore. The damp air was drenched with the eye-watering pungency of bathroom cleanser beneath which floated the tang of fresh urine. I noticed a few steps had puddles on them.

"You ready?" Kate asked. We agreed we'd switch sides after each Porter to share the puddles.

Our first descent wasn't bad. I felt twinges in my knee, but no real pain. I reminded myself going down was harder on knees. At the bottom when I looked up, I could barely see the top. I'd managed to forget that.

"Let's just go nice and slow," Kate said, and up we started.

To distract us, I told Kate about my phone call to my sister the night before. Cindy had just returned to her home, Piney Ponds Community in Texas, after a five-day visit with Larry, Casey, and me. "She was back to monosyllables, like when she first arrived. I couldn't get her to say anything. Maybe I should find her a place around here instead of Piney Ponds. There has to be something I can do." Though Bill, my sister-in-law Mardy, and I felt our responsibility for her keenly after my mother's death, too often it was unclear what Cindy wanted or needed.

Her visit tormented me. Now fifty-three, she'd become even more rigid and stubborn over the years and so debilitated that for the first time she had trouble controlling her bowels. I spent part of each day cleaning up after her and hours trying to get her dressed and fed each morning, even with Casey running around the house fetching and finding things for her so we could actually get to the outings my sister demanded. Even her birthday had been mixed. When Cindy opened her last present, a silver-sequined vest with butterflies, she'd beamed. "Cool, man!"

"Mom, can I get one for my birthday?" Casey asked.

"Yeah," Cindy said. "You could wear it like this!" She had thrown the vest on top of her head, where it flopped over her face, covering one eye like a pirate. Casey laughed so hard she got the hiccups. "Take another pic!" my sister ordered Larry.

But when the hilarity died down, Cindy had gazed around the room. She cracked her knuckles a few times and turned to me, suddenly quiet. "Where's the rest of them?"

"The rest of who?"

"You know."

I hated when she said that. "I don't know, honey. Tell me."

"You mean Aunt Mardy and Uncle Bill?" Casey asked.

46

CHERYL SUCHORS

"They'll give you presents when they pick you up from the airport tomorrow, in Texas. No doubt they'll have lots," I assured my sister.

She bounced on the sofa in frustration. "They sent a truck. Here. Tonight."

"I'll go look for you, Cinbad." Casey dashed to the front door and out into the dark. Larry went after her.

I didn't know why Cindy had fixed in her mind that her Texas presents would show up in a truck Saturday night in Massachusetts, but all three of us combined could not persuade her otherwise. The only way we'd gotten her to bed was by Larry carrying her piggyback.

"I hung up the phone feeling like a dog," I told Kate. "No matter what I do or say, I seem to fail her."

"Do you think she was angry? I mean, having to go back and all?"

"Could be." I noticed I sounded out of breath. "Honestly? She seemed depressed." I turned to Kate. "You think we should ask her doctor about anti-depressants?"

"I wish I knew. Rather, I wish you knew." Kate paused to breathe. "Maybe these things are unknowable. Even to Cindy."

I grunted. I hated unknowables. I wished our hike were next week. I could have used the hard clarity of a mountain right now. I pulled the bottom of my T-shirt up to swipe my forehead, leaning over so I didn't flash my sports bra. Only three years older than me, Cindy now insisted she was eighty-nine. Maybe she was right.

My legs had gained ten pounds. By the seventieth step both of us audibly sucked air. "Almost there," I wheezed.

Ninety steps, one hundred, one hundred ten and, at last, one hundred thirteen. One Porter, down and up. Seventeen stories.

We limped slowly back and forth across our side of the tiled plaza to catch our breath. My right knee was hot and grouchy. I couldn't believe we used to do this every week. What had happened to those wonderful muscles? My cardio fitness? Scoliosis rotated my ribcage enough to cramp my lungs but still, I had to be in better shape than this.

I turned to Kate. "Let's do another."

We managed three Porters before we waved a shaky good-bye to our friend in the booth. We hobbled home to Kate's backyard where we split an iced tea and a jumbo-sized chocolate bar, sitting with our legs up on her Adirondack chairs, a bag of frozen peas on my knee.

6. SUNK COST

While Casey was away at summer camp in July, I vacationed part of the time at our apartment, walking the woods of Waterville Valley with six-month-old Juniper, the puppy Kate had helped me pick out. That was one thing I loved about my best friend; she helped me out on projects just like family, and she'd do anything for Casey, whom Larry and I had finally agreed could have a dog. His allergies had dictated a dog that didn't shed, so Casey had researched breeds and chosen the Bichon Frisé. Kate had made the hunt for the right little dog fun, and I valued her opinion—she'd been a dog mother for years.

Kate and I chose well and Casey had approved. Though Juniper looked like a little fu-fu dog who should be home protecting her nails, she came from solid New Hampshire stock. The pup knew a trail when she saw one. Despite short forays into the brush and trees, she never ranged too far from Grandma. Which would be me, Casey having immediately declared herself Juniper's mother.

Besides training for Lincoln and Lafayette and getting Juniper used to hiking, I planned to pack in as much recreation as I could before another surgery. Two suspicious areas had to be removed from my breast, my third breast cancer scare. The first time, ten years earlier, I'd found a lump that blessedly turned out benign. The second time, my annual mammogram found a pattern of calcifications in the other breast, worrisome since calcifications tended to form near tumors. Again, the result was benign, but how many times could a woman play cancer roulette and win?

Kate and Sarah would join me for a practice hike to Sandwich Dome, a peak that missed being a 4000-Footer by a scant ten feet. ("Shoot," Kate had said. "If we stood on a rock and jumped, shouldn't it count?") I'd already entertained one visitor, a writer friend with whom I'd founded the April Fools Writers' Group. We'd tramped the pleasant, largely flat Greeley Ponds Trail with Juniper, six miles round trip. My friend had just left and I intended to rest up for Sandwich Dome three days hence, but as I lay on the sofa that afternoon, the ski mountain outside my window beckoned. Mt. Tecumseh was a 4000-Footer right in my back yard. Shouldn't I be able to do a mere five-mile climb tomorrow? I imagined Kate and Sarah's faces when I bragged that I'd done a 4000-Footer on my own.

I had not yet learned that, while some were easier than others, every 4000-Footer in the Whites . . . was a 4000-Footer in the Whites.

Normally I organized my backpack the night before, but instead, I'd watched a movie. Now I flitted around the apartment slinging stuff into my pack, serenading Juniper about hills full of music. I threw in dog biscuits and a water dish along with my lunch, too cocky to worry about our late start, though I did stop off at my downstairs neighbors' to tell Zoe and Lindsey where I was going.

Zoe checked her watch. "Don't you think eleven's kinda late? A storm's due in."

"We'll be back before you know it." With that, Juniper and I sailed off. I was still singing, though it was 87°F and humid. I turned the air conditioning up full blast for our five-minute drive. Tecumseh, named for a Shawnee Chief, meant "Panther Passing Across." That's exactly how I intended to hike, loping up and down the mountain like a big, sure-footed cat.

I parked at the upper end of the ski resort lot, familiar to me from ski season but now strangely foreign with bare macadam showing. There were no other cars or people and it was eerily quiet. No music blared; no chair lift or gondola whirred. All I heard was the tyrannical whine of mosquitoes.

I was prepared to foil not only mosquitoes but also their evil cousin, the black fly. These spawn of Satan plagued the area for several weeks in June or July. You could barely see them, but black flies attacked like silent, heat-seeking missiles. You couldn't avoid them except by staying indoors and their bites swelled to the size of silver dollars and itched like poison ivy. If they went extinct, New Hampshire would declare a state holiday.

Before I got out of the car, I pulled my secret weapon over my head, a contraption something like a net hoodie. From my shoulders up, I was now covered with black netting so dense that not even a black fly could get in. Buttoning the cuffs of my long-sleeved shirt and rolling down the legs on my combo pants, I hit the trail looking like a badly dressed mummy.

I kept Juniper leashed for her first 4000-Footer. We found the trailhead and entered the woods. Having a willful, energetic pup yank me off-trail into the underbrush turned out not to be very enjoyable, so after a few minutes I unclipped her lead and let her go. She behaved much better, investigating smells while staying in sight.

The early part of the Mount Tecumseh Trail followed an eponymous brook. After three-tenths of a mile we crossed the brook, Juniper—after looking a question at me—splashing delightedly across as I stepped sedately from rock to rock.

After the brook, we enjoyed an easy ramble up and down long swells of open forest, having a wonderful time.

Except that my face was melting.

The tiny mesh of my hood protected me not only from blood-sucking vermin but also from air. So much sweat flowed from beneath the hood that I expected my nose to slide into my socks. I stopped in the middle of the trail and yanked off the netted hood. I unzipped the legs of my combo-pants, balancing on one boot at a time. I rolled up the sleeves of my shirt. I sucked in a great lungful of forest air that tasted slightly green and definitely damp.

Soon we arrived at a part of the trail that looked like a drunken, scattered stairway of rocks heading relentlessly up. Clomping on nothing but rock seemed to bruise the bottoms of my feet, even through my boots. Tree roots stretched across the rocks trying to trip me and slippery dead leaves covered everything.

I sweat so much my shorts dripped. Juniper suffered too. She had eagerly lapped up stream water, but now her sides heaved like a little bellows. I sat on a stone and filled her dish with water. While she slurped, I set a handful of puppy chow near the water dish, making myself chew half a limp peanut-butter sandwich that, despite the jelly, stuck to the roof of my dry mouth.

We marched upward again. Somehow it hadn't occurred to me that any trail that gained 2200 feet of elevation in 2.5 miles would have no room to dilly-dally. Rocks continued to rise ahead of me like an escalator. As we ground on, I found myself thinking about breast cancer. Somehow it was easier to probe my fears on a mountain.

Was I doomed because of my mother's history? Her tumor was discovered in her early sixties. Surely, at forty-nine, I was too young. I couldn't have cancer when my baby was only nine.

As a teenager, like most of my friends, I had been desperate for the airbrushed cleavage we saw in magazines, worrying our breasts would never grow. Then at business school a busty classmate had bitterly confided how she was subjected to constant harassment and the assumption that she was stupid. Another friend endured breast reduction surgery to rid herself, she said, of a weight that felt like carrying around a bag of groceries she could never put down, one that made her back ache. Over the years, I'd also heard women say their breasts were too tilted, too hairy, or too differently shaped.

I'd succumbed to the cultural hype and had always wanted bigger breasts—until I got pregnant and had them. After losing my large breasts along with my pregnancy weight I had finally come, in my early forties, to appreciate my breasts. Now that they had been threatened and cut into, they seemed precious and I damned well wanted to keep them.

Sweat stung my eyes. Every few feet I had to mop my face with a bandana. Then I mopped my arms. I'd never seen arms sweat before. By now I'd drunk most of my water and was eyeing Juniper's bottle.

"We're almost there, Big June." After I'd said this a number of times, it proved true. I looked around. There were some views down a side spur but I was too drained to care. I slumped onto the trunk of a fallen tree, fed Junie more kibble and water, and dug out the rest of my sandwich. As I chewed, it dawned on me we'd done it. I'd summited my third 4000-Footer! Alone, except for Juniper.

Thunder boomed so hugely it was as if the mountain shuddered. Where had that come from? I thought I was watching the sky.

"We've gotta boogie," I yelled to Junie, who furiously crunched her last bite of chow. I threw the rest of my sandwich and the water dish in my pack and yanked on a rain jacket. "Come on!" I hurtled off the peak down to the protection of the wooded ridge trail below, Junie right beside me. Between one breath and the next the sunlight was extinguished. Thick black clouds scudded overhead and a wild wind sprang up. Serrated yellow blades of lightning sliced the sky. I started counting: *one one-thousand, two one-thousand* . . . By the time I reached *five one-thousand*—five seconds—thunder crashed again. I remembered to count like this from going on a hike with Larry fifteen years ago. What I couldn't remember was what five seconds meant. Were we safe?

I promised myself when I got home I'd research the subject of lightning. When I did, I learned that five seconds for the sound of thunder to reach my ears after seeing a flash of lightning meant it was probably a mile away. Which was close, way too close. Some experts said six miles was their danger line, lightning being too fickle and unpredictable, even for them, to let it come any closer.

I didn't know this atop Tecumseh, but I felt it. The small hairs on my arms and the back of my neck lifted. Suddenly, cold torrents poured from the sky. Within minutes my shorts were plastered to my thighs and my boots were soaked. I wasn't hot anymore.

The lightning and booming continued, punctuated by a heavy waiting silence between blasts. As more lightning split the sky, my counts suggested the storm was coming closer. As we neared the top of the rocky staircase we'd trudged up, I made a spur-of-the-moment decision.

Snap decisions on a hike could flow one after the other like water, downhill, as many major hiking accidents proved. Hikers made a poor choice initially, like betting the weather would hold or they were strong enough to deal with whatever happened, then felt committed to their choices and stayed the course—the wrong course—toward more and greater danger. Even the most experienced hikers could succumb to their own cockiness.

For my part, I decided my knee and I would never make it safely down the rocks and roots of Tecumseh Trail, slippery enough on the way up and perilous, I reasoned, when wet. I turned instead onto the Sosman Trail that led to the top of one of the ski resort runs, figuring we'd hike down a nice meadow, sure and soft on the feet and knees. I shook out the map to check my memory of the trail, but the downpour obscured now-soggy lines. I moved as fast as I could to get us off the ridge and make myself less of a target. "Don't worry, Short Stuff," I hollered to Junie. "Lightning will go for me first." I didn't know that when lightning struck, it often ran along the ground.

I knew lightning sought the tallest, easiest, objects. But standing near a tree didn't guarantee safety, I would learn. Having struck a tree near you, lightning might notice you, a tall yummy column of salt water, and leap to your highly conductive body. Lightning could also, having struck that tree, scurry along the trail, catch you by the boots and run right up your legs. Better to crouch down and balance on heels or toes or stand on an insulated sleeping pad to lessen your contact with the ground. Or better still, try not to get caught in a thunderstorm with your daughter's puppy in the first place.

Under other circumstances, I would have enjoyed this trail softened by pine needles with their sharp, clean scent. Sosman didn't need the storm to have a sense of wildness about it. Already there were so many blow-downs I had to climb over or crawl under, I began to wonder if we were on a trail at all, the week's thunderstorms having apparently left their mark. At last, I could just make out through the downpour the line of trees that signaled the edge of the ski runs. "Almost home, Junie-June. Come on, Pup!"

But once we cleared the trees, I discovered that what looked like neatly mown lawn from the distance of my living room window was, in fact, a sea of grasses that rose to mid-thigh. My first thought was of deer ticks and Lyme disease. My second thought was that, when I put down a boot, I had no idea whether I was stepping on a rock, in a hole, or on top of something alive. There were rustlings in the grass.

"Shit." I scanned the fields. "Shit, shit, shit!" Having come this far, chilled and shaking, I refused to retrace our steps to the trail we came up. I should have turned around, but I didn't. Instead I waded in, Juniper following faithfully in my wake.

Rain hammered the hood of my jacket. My head began to ache, either from rain or the pounding thunder. My toes throbbed from kicking rocks I couldn't see in the deep, wet grass. I prayed I wouldn't sprain an ankle. That my knee wouldn't fail. All I clearly understood was that I had a visceral compulsion to move. Something louder than my brain was shouting at me: *Get OUT of here!* I was awash not only in rainwater, but adrenaline.

Lightning stabbed the sky. I practically jogged down the mountain while trying to figure my way out of another conundrum. The ski run was a swath of grassy plain fringed by a thin line of firs to either side. When out in the open, I was exposed as the tallest thing in the middle of a field. But if I stayed near the protective height of the trees, wasn't their narrow row the most likely target? Which course was safer? My brain skittered from one option to the other, arriving at exactly no good choice. I wound up crisscrossing the steep field from one side to the other in a downward zigzag, precisely as if I were skiing.

I hoped I was aimed at the parking lot. My map didn't show ski trails, so I tried to imagine the one I was on covered with snow. Did it look familiar? I kept moving, consoling myself that a moving target was harder for lightning to catch and hoping it was true.

I swiped soaking hair from my eyes to check on the dog. Juniper still trooped along at my heels, but her head was down, her little tail between her legs. The rain had plastered her kinky curls to her body and pale freckles showed on the tender pink skin of her back.

"Oh, my sweet little dogga. Look what I've gotten you into." I bent down and picked her up. Unzipping my rain jacket, I stuffed her cold wet self inside. Only her head and dripping ears poked out, scared brown eyes staring into mine. I pressed her chilly head onto my chest offering her whatever body heat I had. Movement. I had to keep us warm. As cold rain needled my bare legs, I crooned to Junie and willed my shivering self to keep going.

With Juniper's added weight, it wasn't long before my right knee throbbed and wobbled. Periodically, the thigh above it spasmed. I was jeopardizing my grand-dog, Casey's baby. My conscience lashed while the rest of me chattered and shook and kept going, one sloshing boot step at a time.

By the time we reached the parking lot, the rain had softened to a drizzle and I was so relieved I wanted to kiss the car. When I unzipped Juniper from my jacket to wrap her in the towel I kept for her in the car, her head and ears dripped onto a doggie body that was nicely warm and nearly dry. She immediately curled up on the back seat, laid her head on her paws, and slept.

I leaned against the car, upending my boots to dump out rainwater and struggling to peel off wet socks. I drove home in bare feet that were slightly blue, remembering a concept I'd learned decades before in business school—*sunk cost dilemma*. It was the main reason smart people threw good money after bad. We'd invested so much already that we continued the same path trying to recoup. We insisted to ourselves that going forward had to be better than changing course or stopping. As I turned onto Valley Road, I wondered if the best way to improve my novel would be to chuck all two hundred pages and start over for the third time. Then I put this application of sunk cost aside to consider the day's adventure.

Some climbers got into trouble because they hadn't hiked much and were simply ignorant, others because they'd hiked a great deal and had grown arrogant. My experience on Tecumseh had ushered me into that unique subset of trampers both ignorant *and* arrogant. Still, I now had three 4000-Footers under my belt. I just hoped it wasn't sunk cost that kept me thirsting for more.

Tecumseh
4,003 ft – 06/24/1999

7. THE PLAN

A few days later Kate, Sarah, and I tackled Sandwich Dome. Though the Dome didn't make it onto the list of 4000-Footers, it was a rugged practice hike. When Kate inexplicably wanted to turn back about two-thirds of the way up, I protested. This was training for Lincoln and Lafayette! She responded, "And I'm well trained. You two go on." I could never have done that. How would I feel victorious if I did that? Sarah and I went on.

Back in Cambridge, my right knee swelled, requiring frequent icing. I even took aspirin, though I hated pills of any kind. Call it hubris or good fortune, but all I swallowed each day was a multi-vitamin. My left shoulder, the post-surgical one, required cold packs too. Apparently, a 4000-Footer and almost-4000-Footer in one week were more than my body could handle. Unacceptable. I'd have to train harder for Lincoln and Lafayette.

Despite the pain, I felt grand. Two big climbs, one by myself! Hiking in the White Mountains, even in a thunderstorm carrying a hypothermic pup, seemed to have filled up some deep inner reservoir I hadn't known was parched, something that went beyond mere accomplishment. I wasn't sure what it was or how it happened, but had I been able to persuade my family, I'd have gone out that very weekend and hiked again.

～

Everything would be different, I told Larry, Kate, and my trainer Cathy. I'd be strong and calm for the upcoming breast surgery.

It would take some doing. After elbow surgery, shoulder surgery, an appendectomy, a Cesarean, and two breast surgeries, I hated hospitals. I hated operations. I came to afterward with the disorienting, frightened sense that a piece of my life was missing, that things had happened to me that I not only didn't control but couldn't even remember. Picturing my mother's anxious eyes so many mornings, I wondered if this was how a blackout felt to an alcoholic. Worse yet, anesthesia didn't agree with me. One time I'd woken up in the recovery room convulsed, legs slamming up and down on the gurney, jaw clenched shut, torso lurching side to side. Most pain medications made me sick. Finding my way back to normal took at least twice the time surgeons predicted. For far too long, recovery ran my life.

Underneath and through my days now, pulsed a river of fear. Would cancer claim me? To reduce my anxiety, Cathy and I treated the surgery as an event. I pulled together what I'd learned from prior operations to develop a plan for making the whole experience better. I read Peggy Huddleston's valuable book, *Prepare for Surgery, Heal Faster*. She advised treating physicians and nurses as part of your team, people there not to take control of your body, but to help you.

I trained for my surgical mountain by playing the tape that came with Huddleston's book. Over and over, I visualized myself well and strong after surgery, my body healing quickly. I pictured myself walking the neighborhood, pounding through Porters, speeding like a centipede up the side of a

4000-Footer. The visualizations lessened my anxiety and that, in turn, was meant to reduce the amount of anesthetic I'd need. Moreover, Huddleston's advice provided a sense of control as I hitched my mind to the task of helping myself heal.

In the weeks leading up to breast surgery, my knee grew less painful. My shoulder stopped hurting. Whenever I felt afraid, I played my tape. I was doing everything right. Surely they wouldn't find cancer.

8. CLASSICS

Wind and rain had torn most of the crimson and gold from the trees. On the drive north neither Kate nor I voiced any doubt, but Lincoln and Lafayette were over a thousand feet—nearly an Empire State Building—taller than Tripyramid. I stared out at the dreary wet day, almost as cold as when we'd climbed Tripyramid a year ago and a far cry from the oppressive June heat when Juniper and I'd scaled Tecumseh, my last 4000-Footer.

I shouldn't worry, I told myself, I should be happy. I was happy. I'd recovered from breast surgery faster than usual, though the surgeon had needed to perform a lumpectomy, cutting out much more of my breast than expected. The surgery had gone smoothly and all my preparations had paid off. The surgeon promised my breast would recover and look almost normal.

And I didn't have cancer. They had discovered atypical ductal hyperplasia (ADH), a condition in which cells lining the milk ducts grow numerously and differently from normal. Most surgeons and researchers viewed ADH as pre-cancerous.

But because of the operation and recovery period, I hadn't trained the way I had for Tripyramid, which meant neither had Kate. On the loop up and down Lincoln and Lafayette we faced an elevation gain of 3900 feet, thirty houses more than Tripyramid, numbers at which my mind poked like a sore tooth. I didn't know what Kate was thinking. We'd fallen into a potent silence.

Out of the blue she asked, "Are you hungry?"

We'd finished breakfast roughly an hour ago. "Sure," I said.

There wasn't even time to put on her blinker before veering off into a fast food joint beside Route 93. She careened into the parking lot and slammed on the brakes. Switching off the engine, she said, "We should load up on carbs."

What other reason could we have for stopping?

⌒

By 7:55 a.m., we were boots to trail. My heart drumming, I reminded myself this was just an experiment, a strategy that came from Cathy. She told the Olympians who worked with her to think of their first Olympic competition as an experiment, a scouting mission for the next Olympics. Most athletes, she said, didn't medal their first time out because there was so much to learn. She advised everyday clients like me that an experiment was never a failure because an experiment always taught you something.

I tried to persuade myself that if I had to quit this trail and try again another day, I wouldn't be a complete loser. As Kate and I began our 8.9-mile trek in a freezing drizzle, I whispered to myself, *It's just an experiment.*

We chose to ascend Falling Waters Trail, the southern branch of the loop, because it was steeper and Kate thought it would be easier on her knees. The bible agreed, describing the trail as "steep and rough in parts and better for ascent than descent, but not normally dangerous unless there is ice on the ledgey sections near the brook."

We started off slowly, bellies bulging, stiff from the car and the cold. The pleasant grade gave us a chance to warm up and work off some fast food. I snapped a photo of Kate crossing Dry Brook. She posed with one foot on a peeling birch log, the other about six inches higher on another log, these two damp trunks forming a slippery, uneven bridge across. She raised her arms in a "Look, Ma, no hands" kind of way. Our quest for two more 4000-Footers, our second big climb together, had begun.

Rain engorged the waterfalls beside the aptly named Falling Waters Trail and we stopped to admire each one, mesmerized as water tumbled and swirled—white, powerful, kinetic. Our exuberance grew as if we soaked up energy along with the spray. Everything else in life fell away. I didn't think about my mother-in-law battling oral cancer, the chapter of my novel I didn't know how to finish, the boy who'd bullied Casey, or whether I'd made the right decision about not taking Tamoxifen. A senior oncologist had recommended I take the drug usually given to women with breast cancer, despite the fact I didn't have breast cancer. Larry and I'd done research and gotten second opinions. In the end, I didn't want to take a powerful medication for five years and risk side effects if I didn't have to. I prayed I'd chosen wisely.

Kate and I navigated slick roots and chunks of rock, inhaled the mossy smell of wet earth, and inspected shy colonies of toadstools. I liked today's experiment.

Just as I settled into happiness, the trail did an abrupt personality change. What we faced now was demandingly, diabolically steep. For the next two miles, we'd average 100 feet of elevation gain for every tenth of a mile. The final half-mile of trail would punish our legs and pulsing hearts with an average slope of 31 percent. Roads with inclines of only 10 percent carried warning signs.

The verticality quickly translated into panting and body heat. Kate and I stripped down to T-shirts, wishing we could peel off more. Our breath forming tiny clouds, we felt grateful for the spitting rain. From time to time, the rain quit and wisps of fog blew in, making it hard to see the trail above us. We had to stop for a breather every ten or fifteen minutes, the degree of difficulty battering my equanimity. Who knew Tripyramid had been a waltz?

Kate climbed slower than I, significantly slower. I didn't think our age difference mattered much—until I hit fifty-six myself, Kate's age that day. As I kept her company, another worry ping-ponged inside me. I feared at this pace I'd never make it to the top. Plodding bled both my energy and my nerve. I couldn't explain what I felt to Kate, I just jittered, sure that our slowness and constant stopping foretold my failure.

I hadn't understood yet that, like any sport, hiking required a rhythm, a rhythm that differed for each person. Hikers developed a beat, a pace that kept them going. Every stop and start exhausted more fuel and, worse, broke one's concentration. A regular rhythm helped a hiker overlook aching lungs and quadriceps to sink into a fugue state in which the body moved automatically, unquestioned. This meditative zone was where a hiker instinctively yearned to be. I only grasped, as I struggled along, that I needed to go at my own pace. When Kate generously didn't mind my going ahead, I left her to find my rhythm.

We didn't expect this to be our last 4000-Footer together. Were I able to go back in time, I'd stay beside her every step.

⟶

I hauled myself upward accompanied only by trees and ferns and bits of fog, my mind a blank, all perception absorbed by the footing and the sound of my labored breath. My lungs were working and my legs pumping and I was sweating in forty-degree weather and, though my calves screamed and I huffed like a steam engine, the whole thing made me feel extraordinarily good. Strong. Right where I needed to be. My body was an instrument the mountain played, and I found, amazingly, that I was happy to cede control.

⌒

Rapid-fire French broke into my mountain harmony as two forty-something couples crowded up on my heels. I stepped off trail and mustered a breathless, "*Bonjour!*"

"*Bonjour*," they returned gaily as they whizzed past. I watched them for a few breaths while I slurped water and wished I spoke more French. I turned my face up to the cold, welcome drops of intermittent rain.

Before I could step back on the trail, another group of French speakers passed. We exchanged greetings and smiles. Just as I started up again, more hikers appeared at my shoulder. Also speaking French. Had we been invaded?

I questioned the next person who showed up, a young man. "We are from Montreal," he informed me. "The hiking club."

I blinked. "You drove here from Montreal this morning?"

He smiled happily. "Oh yes. We come the bus. Sleep." He mimed putting his head on a pillow.

For the next half hour I became the clunker that pulled over to let sports cars zip by, making me feel like I didn't belong on such a challenging mountain. When I wanted to trip the next Montrealer who passed me, I made myself sit on a rock and wait for Kate. How big was that bus?

Kate finally arrived. "Two buses," she puffed.

While she rested, I calculated our time between milestones, hoping to soothe my ego. "Hey, guess what? For the first 1.6 miles, we were only ten minutes off book time."

"And all those waterfall photos took time." Kate uncapped her water bottle. "Pretty good, I'd say."

"Yup. But call me crazy, I think we've slowed down."

We manufactured smiles for a woman bounding past.

"She looks like she's on a pogo stick," Kate murmured. We snickered behind our hands like kindergarteners.

While Kate enjoyed trail mix and chocolate, I dug out a piece of apricot cake I'd intended as a summit treat, rationalizing that I needed the sugar now. I unwrapped the cake and took tiny bites to make it last. When Kate hoisted on her pack, I still had half the cake left. Determined to savor it, I buckled on my backpack and climbed, cake in hand. I asked Kate how far she thought we were from Shining Rock, a feature of the trail I was eager to see. I was listening to Kate say she guessed we were a mile away and licking up every crumb of cake when a root snagged my boot. I pitched forward, throwing out my hands to protect my face. Hands, knees, elbows and then belly slammed into granite, my hands bearing the brunt of my backpacked weight.

Cursing loudly, I rolled over onto my pack to relieve my right hand. My knees and elbows hurt, but my hand had my attention. Something was very wrong. I lay there trying not to faint and clutching my hand to my chest. Kate helped haul me to standing. I stood in the trail doing a little pain dance while waves of nausea surged. I held out my shaky right hand to examine it. The whole palm had turned a violet so deep it was nearly black. The thumb, also violet-black, had already doubled in size.

∼

How often I wished I could talk to my mother about the fact that, despite prior successes, I always feared failure. The best way I knew to keep the fear at bay was to master the new thing, and quickly. I remembered the visit home to my parents' when I was twenty-three. I'd asked them to come into the den, a room wallpapered in warm tan grass cloth and filled with shelves of my father's history books and biographies of military men and politicians. Once they had settled, my dad in a persimmon plaid armchair and my mom on a golden-hued floral sofa, I took the other end of the sofa and told them I wanted to apply to Harvard Business School. What did they think? Could they help with tuition?

My father broke into one of his rare, delighted smiles where one corner of his mouth tipped up more than the other. My mother looked stunned. Maybe she remembered the job offer I had turned down after college, the one that would have paid for me to get an MBA, opting instead, to use the vernacular of the 1970s, to "drop out" for a year, sailing, working odd jobs, and living with a boyfriend. Perhaps she was amazed that the countless novenas she prayed on my behalf had finally paid off.

My father, an engineer who had gotten a master's degree from MIT before advanced degrees were common, said he'd be delighted to pay for further schooling. If I couldn't find a husband, he explained, at least with an MBA I'd be able to support myself. He added he could now die in peace, then went off to the dry bar in the living room to fix drinks all around.

My mother beamed at me. The happier she and my father got, the more I worried.

"What if I don't get in?" I asked her, keeping my voice low so that my father, rattling bottles and glasses, wouldn't hear.

"Don't be silly. You always say things like that."

"Alright, what if I get in and flunk out?"

"Why should you flunk out? You've got your father's brains."

"This is *Harvard*, Mom. *The B School.* Future captains of industry. Sheiks. Princes. What do I know about business anyway?"

"Isn't that why you go to school? To learn?" She looked away from me, swinging the leg crossed over her knee. When she turned back, she said brusquely, "So you fall on your face. So what?"

"*So what?*" I cried. If I flunked out of graduate school, I assumed my life would effectively be over.

"So what," she had repeated and leaned forward, closer to me, her eyes sparking. "So then you pick yourself up just like everybody else and you say, 'Well at least I had the guts to try,' and you move on to the next thing. Just like we all do."

On the Falling Waters Trail, I slumped on a boulder, cradling my right elbow to keep anything from touching my hand. Kate pawed through my pack for the first aid kit, keeping up a running commentary on what she found—menstrual pads, snake bite tourniquet, eye dropper—talking so much I knew she was trying to distract me. I sat there breathing slowly through my mouth to keep from vomiting.

I was livid. I hated that fucking cake. I hated this miserable trail. I hated the jaunty Montrealers.

Kate muttered, "We seem to have everything but the two things you need: a cold pack and an ace bandage. We do have this." She held up a thick packet of gauze. "I could wrap it around your hand then hospital-tape it."

"I'll do it myself," I hissed. I didn't want to have to be nice when she hurt me. By now my head ached and I was shivering from shock.

Kate handed me two ibuprofen tablets and uncapped my water bottle.

I held out my left hand for two more. After downing them, I tried to rip open the gauze packet with my teeth until Kate reached over and pried it away from me. Wrapping myself up left-handed was an arduous process that had me inhaling fiercely whenever my right thumb or fingers were shifted by the gauze. I let Kate do the taping. Twice—she couldn't help it—I grunted in pain. We sipped water while I waited for my pulse to approach normal.

"So what are we doing?" Kate asked.

"For chrissake, give me a minute!"

"No, I mean should we head back and get that taken care of?" She nodded toward my hand, large and white with wrappings.

"No way," I snapped. What was the matter with her? "I'll be fine."

I learned the hard way not to use my dominant hand. The first time I forgot and instinctively reached out to climb a boulder, my pain sensors whited out. After that I imagined my brain was a closet. I stuffed the pain into a small box, hid it on the back shelf and locked the closet door.

Having an injured hand changed my gait. I felt awkward and unstable, desperately keen to avoid another fall. To stay alert, I noted the feel of damp air on my skin, the sound of breath wheezing through my nose. I debated ways to describe the pewter light that forced its way through the clouds. I refused to give up on this hike, this experiment.

Kate and I struggled down the rough spur to Shining Rock until the path dead-ended in a clearing that left us beside an incredibly steep, enormous, upright slab. It rose, my best guess, at a 100° angle. The "slab" was a side of mountain over two hundred feet high and eight hundred feet wide. Water sluiced down Shining Rock to create an eight-hundred-foot wide waterfall that was just half an inch deep. Because of its flat watery face, the slab reflected every hint of light, blazing like a giant mirror.

The bible cautioned hikers not to climb Shining Rock without technical gear. Serious injuries had occurred. It was fortunate that I remembered this warning because, despite my injury, I could feel Shining Rock's magnetic pull.

A bit of level trail crossed in front of the slab. Kate wouldn't join me, but I shucked my pack and eased out to the middle of the rock face on the trail that wasn't much wider than a hiking boot. The slab tilted so strongly that it was hard to stay upright against its slanted message to the brain. I stretched out my left hand and touched through the waterfall to the slab beneath. Water cold as icicles streamed to either side of the small obstacles of my fingertips. Kate and I smiled in wonder.

Back on Falling Waters Trail (which now had a whole other resonance for me) we toiled upward. I slowly pulled ahead of Kate as still more folks from Montreal pulled ahead of me. A pair of men in their twenties wearing jeans and sneakers seemed to have strayed onto the bus without realizing what they were getting into. They rushed past me but ten minutes later I passed them collapsed on a rock, sides heaving. We did this so often we now waved at each other like old pals. I wondered who in our game of human checkers would reach the summit first to get crowned. Me, I hoped.

Periodically I put on my fleece and sat to wait for Kate, snacking and asking passersby, "Do you speak English?" If not, I waited for the next person. "Have you seen a woman with gray hair, friendly, about so tall"—I measured above my head. "Very red in the face?"

When they assured me she was still climbing, I swallowed more ibuprofen. As the minutes stretched, I thought about Kate's being so much slower today than on Tripyramid. She couldn't be giving up on the 4000-Footers, I assured myself; she was just having a bad day. I wasn't having my best day myself. Sitting still made it hard to get past the drumbeat in my hand, but my conscience wouldn't let me give in to the desire to get moving. When Kate at last arrived, relief lit up my smile. As soon as she dropped her pack to sit beside me, I plied her with food. Food was fuel.

71

Soon we faced the last wicked half-mile to the summit of Little Haystack, 620 feet higher than Tripyramid and our first peak of the Franconia Ridge Trail. Like South Peak on Tripyramid, Little Haystack didn't count as a 4000-Footer because of the rules requiring independent summits.

"You still okay with my going ahead?" I asked Kate.

"Of course." Kate was good at allowing people plenty of space. I was pretty sure that, in her position, I wouldn't be. I'd be too afraid of never catching up.

I lurched ahead as the chunky rock trail pushed straight up, tamping down guilt and curling my right arm into my chest to prevent using it. I passed the young men in jeans for the last time. Despite the cold and spatters of rain and my bare arms, sweat stung my eyes. More boulders appeared. I looked behind me. I thought I could pick out Kate among the hikers below. Reassured, I pushed myself harder. Though I couldn't see the summit, it pulled at me.

When I finally dragged myself over the last rock to the plateau atop Little Haystack, I had to hunch over to catch my breath. Despite that, I felt like waving a victory flag in the thick fog. If Kate were here I'd make her do something silly, like dance with me. Others on the summit wandered around or crouched on the ground using boulders for a windbreak while they ate lunch. Lunch? I pulled a watch out of my pocket. Noon. It had taken me four hours and five minutes to make the trek whose book time was three hours, ten minutes. Damn.

As I strolled the summit hoping for a view through the fog, I noticed my body shivering. I didn't *feel* cold but my skin, when I touched it, was icy. I looked around. Hikers who'd just arrived were, like me, half naked and sweating. Everyone else wore jackets and mittens and hats. I followed their example, even added a scarf. Somebody with a gadget on his jacket read the temperature aloud. "32°F. Without the wind chill."

The wind that had felt refreshing when I first arrived now numbed my cheeks.

I recorded Kate's arrival twelve minutes later. I hugged her sweaty self then suggested she layer up. Even pacing with all my outerwear on, I couldn't get warm. It was if my bones had been refrigerated.

Kate ignored my advice to turn in a circle. "This is our great view?"

"If you go over to the edge, you can see a bit of hillside. When the wind blows the mist away."

"This is absolutely not mist," she replied in disgust. "This is *fog*. I can't believe I climbed all morning to the *classic* views and I can't see a damned thing! If I actually want to *see* the fabulous views, I'm going to have to haul myself up here *again*."

Complaining was not like her. I had never seen Kate so put out. She stomped away from me to a bunch of rocks, dropped her pack and sat. She didn't layer up. She just sat. Nor did she appear to want company.

I sank down out of the wind to wait.

After a while, Kate put on extra clothes. Hauled out food. I gathered she intended to eat lunch. I was not hungry and I was too cold to linger here. My hand throbbed hard enough to burst the skin but it wasn't time for more ibuprofen. I just needed to get moving.

I went over and joined Kate.

She greeted me with, "This is certainly a snake-bitten venture." Food was not improving her mood. Should I say something positive? Point out how much worse it could be? No. I hated it when people played Pollyanna with me.

"I suppose the whole knife trail will be like this. Pea damn soup." Kate threw lunch remains into her pack. "We would pick the day the whole city of Montreal emptied out to hike our trail."

I glanced around.

"Oh, for heaven's sake," she snapped. "Nobody can hear anything in this godforsaken wind."

Ridiculously, I insisted on someone's taking our picture by the lichen-spattered boulders where we sat. Kate pushed her farmer's cap emblazoned with "John Deere" so far down on her face that, in the photograph, you can't see her eyes. Though I had my fleeced and jacketed arm around her, neither one of us smiled.

Kate led off on the famous Ridge Trail, the knife-edge. Perhaps the change-up would cheer her. Gingerly, I tucked my bulky hand into the pocket of my rain jacket as if in a sling, while the fog thickened to pudding. I made myself catalog the good stuff. It wasn't raining anymore nor was there thunder or lightning. My legs lifted my feet and my lungs pumped air. Stones bleached to silver. And how would I describe the lichen in my journal? *Shades of ivy, cucumber, and citrine.*

Sometimes Kate was hidden by the fog. I wondered if she'd remain disenchanted for the rest of the day and, if so, what that meant for the future if my hiking partner decided she hated 4000-Footers.

❧

Though it was our second summit and the first one that counted as a 4000-Footer, I found it hard to work up enthusiasm for the top of Lincoln, a small cairn of rocks in a sea of fog. No doubt on a clear day it offered life-enhancing views. Would our final peak, Lafayette, be the same? Kate groaned. "If it weren't so damned cold, I'd lie down and take a nap."

I hid my dismay behind my uplifted water bottle. Would she make it? Would she turn around here like she had on Sandwich Dome? No, she wouldn't. By now it was no shorter to go back. But I so wanted Kate to enjoy the hike more, for both our sakes. With the fog pressing down and my hand aching, I couldn't figure out how to help her. I was carefully watching my footing going down the rocks from Lincoln's summit when Kate suddenly reached out to a white-haired woman in the line of hikers marching past, up Lincoln toward Little Haystack. "Frances?"

"Kate?" said a woman who seemed to be wearing a trench coat. Was that possible? In the drippy fog, I was flabbergasted at her lack not only of layers but of gear in general. She carried a daypack just big enough for a sandwich and a water bottle. Where was the rest of her stuff? Apparently, Frances had just climbed up massive Lafayette and trekked a mile along Franconia Ridge looking as if she were strolling through a park. And Frances had to be in her seventies.

She and Kate hugged and reminisced about the hiking trip in the Cascades where they had met last year. Kate was the most animated she'd been all day. Ebullient. Laughing. I stood around lifting and lowering my feet to keep the blood flowing, trying not to notice how happy Frances made my best friend when I hadn't been able to pry a sunny word out of her since Shining Rock. Kate turned to me. "Frances is the one who loaned me her hiking poles that time my knees gave out. I could never have gotten off the mountain without her."

Clearly Frances was made of sterner stuff than us. She was a walking, talking role model. A classic. Since she had last seen Kate, she'd hiked in South America and Colorado and all sorts of places. She and her hiking buddies, women and men her age, hiked all over the world together. I developed a serious case of hero worship.

Eventually, even Frances succumbed to the cold. She regretted she had to get moving. She and Kate parted with another big hug, promising to stay in touch.

"Wow," I said as we watched Frances goat-foot-it up the rocks we had just picked our way down.

Kate threw an arm across my shoulders. "One day we'll be like that."

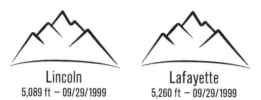

Lincoln
5,089 ft — 09/29/1999

Lafayette
5,260 ft — 09/29/1999

9. DIGGING IN

An MRI revealed that my mishap on Lincoln and Lafayette had broken two small bones in my right wrist. The doctor predicted an eight-week recovery. No one expected it would take six months to recover full use of the fingers and thumb of my dominant hand or that it would be a year before the hand could bear any significant weight.

The doctor forbade hiking, and it would have been risky and awkward in a cast. Normally, I'd have poured my frustration into writing, journaling myself into a better place and then working on my novel. But keyboarding one-handed made me want to slam my good hand into a wall. Not hiking *and* not writing left me homicidal.

My rational, reasonable husband asked, "Suchs,"—a nickname, derived from my last name, that rhymed with *cukes*—"don't you think you should re-evaluate the forty-eight mountain mission?"

"What?"

"Your first climb hurt your knee and sent you to PT for eight months. On the second one, lightning could have killed you and Junie. The third one just broke your wrist."

When you put it like that, it wasn't an encouraging picture.

Then one afternoon while Casey did homework at the kitchen table and I prepared dinner one-handed, she looked up. "Mama, I did the math." Pointing to some calculations with her pencil, she explained, "If you and Auntie Kate do two 4000-Footers every year, when you finish you'll be seventy. She'll be seventy-six."

I had never done the math. I didn't think Kate had either. Planning and executing one expedition a year had seemed like plenty to us. Now a clock ticked. Loudly. Not only did we have to hike faster to match book time, we needed to hike more mountains per year. I had no time to loll around with a broken wrist. We needed to get stronger, more knowledgeable, and faster. Each hike had given me enormous satisfaction and fueled my writing for weeks, but that didn't add up to *mastery*. Joining the Four Thousand Footer Club and becoming a venerable mountain goat like Frances, however, qualified.

"My God, you're pig-headed," my father used to say.

I'd inherited a double dose of stubborn, Austrian/Lemko/Polish on his side and Irish/Welsh on my mother's. Everybody in my lottery family had a mulish tenacity that led to an unshakeable conviction that we were always right.

After Cathy and I completed our post-event analysis of Lincoln and Lafayette—what had happened, what I thought about it, how well training had prepared me, and what I'd do differently—she grew thoughtful. "Every serious athlete has somebody in their sport they strive to be like. Meeting Frances is a real milestone for you."

Another beacon came from Larry. Despite his concerns, for my birthday he presented me with a four-foot National Survey Map of New Hampshire mounted on poster board. On each 4000-Footer he'd placed a pin topped with a round blue bead. Enchanted, I ran off to a map store and bought some red-topped pins emblazoned with black numbers from one to forty-eight. I removed the five blue pins of the mountains I'd climbed on my treks with Kate and the solo with Junie and managed to replace them, left handed, with red pins one through five. Then I stood before the map for a long time, gazing at the potent red pins marking my progress through the throng of blues, one dream in the making.

⁓

Cathy was doing Porters with me as I tried to shave a second off my Porter time. I complained that my right hand was taking forever to heal.

"Cheryl, you're on your way to becoming an expert hiker," she responded.

I stumbled on the stairs, grabbing the handrail with my left hand to prevent another fall. "Expert hiker" made heat crawl up my cheeks. I knew she was trying to encourage me, but this was over the top. I was too slow, I gasped out to her as we climbed steps, too injured, and still too worried I couldn't finish whatever hike I was on, much less the next forty-three.

As we reached the top of the staircase and started down again, she thought for a bit. "Maybe since you can't go hiking, it's a good time to deepen your understanding of the sport itself."

Kate found us a course organized by the Appalachian Mountain Club. "The Winter Hiking Program" met one evening a week for eight weeks. I couldn't imagine hiking in snow and ice, but Kate could and she took the lead. "We could bag peaks year-round," she observed.

That meant more success sooner. Maybe I'd write year-round too, and become a real writer.

Which is why one evening in November 1999, I walked into a huge room at the Appalachian Mountain Club's Boston headquarters. The place vibrated. Over a hundred people sat in ranks of folding chairs chatting, most of them male, most of them young. I searched the rows for Kate's gray head. She had arrived early to get us seats and to sign us up for the January weekend at Cardigan Lodge in New Hampshire. The weekend would be the culmination of the course, a workshop where our instructors helped us turn instruction into skill.

Kate sat in the front row next to the only other gray-hairs, a man and woman. I introduced myself. Kate informed me the pair intended to ring in the new millennium from the top of a White mountain. Let the millennium bug "Y2K" (short for Year 2000) wreak havoc with computers that numbered years using only two digits, making it impossible to distinguish 2000 from 1900; let the banks fail and the utility companies stop producing electricity or heat. This couple would be counting the stars overhead before nestling snugly in their tent. As Kate recounted the couple's plan, her eyes danced. She and they kept interrupting each other, their excitement palpable. Could I possibly do that? Did Kate want to?

She handed me a spiral bound manual an inch thick. I thumbed through it. There were appendices. Diagrams. Chapters called: Heat Management; Energy Management; Equipment and Technique Above Tree Line; Bushwhacking; Health and Safety; Hazards; Emergencies. We would be taught by no fewer than eighteen people. I turned, wide-eyed, to Kate.

"I know," she grinned. "Heavy duty."

That night we learned that most of Kate's and my hiking gear was either worthless or perilous in winter. That air was a terrific insulator. That we not only had to dress to capture the heat our bodies radiated, we had to be just as careful to release it. Sweating was very bad, a shortcut to hypothermia. Consequently, we had to wear a *wicking* layer next to our skin, a middle layer with plenty of *loft* and an outer layer with *baffling*, taped zippers, and *pit zips* under the arms. The outer layer had to be treated for wind, rain, and snow. The middle and outer layers might involve more than one layer each. In fact, we could put on and take off eight or more layers on a single climb.

I glanced down at my right hand in its second cast. Would it be ready to get in and out of all that stuff by our training weekend on Cardigan? Speaking of hands, if we were unfortunate enough to spill gasoline on our hands in 0° weather—"What would we be doing with gasoline in the first place?" I whispered to Kate—our hands would instantly become frostbitten.

Then our instructors covered food. Good news here. Staying warm required consuming high caloric, high fat foods like chocolate, peanut butter, and cheese. Constantly. Hikers should start eating within the first ten minutes and graze from then on. "I like the sound of that," Kate whispered.

Food needed to be pre-cut into small bites and kept close to the body to avoid freezing, all extraneous wrappers removed and containers opened *before* the hike because these actions were hard to perform wearing mittens. Bare skin should never be exposed, so whenever you removed the mammoth snow-proof mittens they showed us, you kept on the light wicking gloves worn beneath them.

I raised my hand. "If exposing skin risks frostbite, how do you go to the bathroom?"

Everyone laughed. The three lecturers, two middle-aged men and a young woman, looked at each other. "I don't know how it works," one of the men finally said. "But it's never a problem."

The woman chimed in. "Obviously you want to minimize the time you're exposed." She advised bringing anti-diarrhea pills as well as urinating into funnels and pee bottles at night to prevent having to leave our tents.

Throughout the class I seesawed between the thrill of learning something new, challenging, and dangerous— and panic that I was in way over my head. As our shoulders bumped each other on the subway home, Kate said, "There's a lot more to it than I imagined."

~

Each week, Kate and I piled up knowledge. We plotted to store pointy objects like ice axes and crampons outside the tent at night. In the vestibule—the tent we had yet to purchase would require a vestibule—we would stack our snowy boots and lumbering packs.

We would need to share our sleeping bags' warmth with any damp (but not soaking) clothes we wished to dry, our boot liners, head lamps or anything else with batteries along with our water bottles and any food we didn't want to freeze. We'd carry two sleeping pads to place under our bags to prevent our body heat from melting the snow beneath us. We'd do jumping jacks in the howling wind to build up body heat before crawling into those sleeping bags. We, after all, were our tent's sole generators of heat and our gear depended on us. "I thought it was the other way around," Kate murmured.

It unnerved me to see instructors demonstrating how they wore three pairs of gloves or socks to stay warm. I had enough trouble staying warm inside my house.

We moved on to stoves. A "stove" was a small piece of metal that looked like it had been wrenched from a lunar landing module. We should avoid touching the fuel. Kate poked me. "No gasoline on the hands."

We were exhorted never to light the stove in the tent with all that plastic waiting to go up like a torch. We had to cook outside on the snow. Our teachers reminded us, as if we had always known, to put some plywood between snow and stove to keep melting snow from tipping over the stove and burning us. Kate and I glanced at each other. "Of course," she whispered. "Who would ever go hiking without a piece of plywood?"

We learned how to handle emergencies. Kate grimaced during the brief lesson on splinting our own broken legs using a hiking pole, but I found the subject, in a weird way, calming, even hopeful. Besides, nothing could be worse than the slides showing frostbite—a stream of blackened feet and missing fingers, toes, and noses. In the margin of that section in my course manual remains the cryptic advice I scrawled left-handed that night: "Better not to become a stretcher patient."

In spite of the dangers of winter hiking, despite the massive amount of funds required to equip ourselves, Kate and I loved the course and all the shopping for new gear. I couldn't wait to tackle Cardigan in the teeth of winter, not letting myself add up the pounds of equipment I'd be carrying. Somehow, I would manage. Climbing a mountain when bears took cover in caves frightened me so much I knew I had to try it. Standing up to fear, controlling it by doing what scared me most, was not only thrilling but deeply gratifying.

I'd been a fearful child. We moved a lot in my family of corporate gypsies. I always seemed to be facing new homes, neighborhoods, and classes of kids—four grade schools, four different high schools. After a drink or two, my parents had a hard time seeing past themselves to their children's troubles, to any desires not consonant with their own, to the fact that we were actually not extensions of them. Whatever town we lived in felt like Pompeii. I was never sure when scalding lava, my parents' fury, would burst through the thin crust of their self-restraint.

I was always startled to discover we were pulling up stakes again, kids' preferences never being taken into consideration. Moving from place to place for different or better jobs for my father helped maintain our cover. Both my parents had enough control to function well despite their drinking. We always lived in a nice home, went to Catholic or special education or private schools, kept a neatly mown lawn. My mother made sure we dressed well. My father made sure we had table manners. We duped casual observers, at least I thought we did.

My role as the good kid who didn't have Downs or a drinking problem was to obey without question, to cause no trouble, and to never make a mistake. I remembered one Thanksgiving when I was nine or ten. My mother and I were making Cindy's bed, something she was supposed to do but never did when she came home from the special boarding school we called her "college" so she could feel like Bill, who was a college student. Soon Cindy's friend Carol would arrive and I'd babysit while my mother ran errands.

My mother talked as we tucked in sheets. "Cindy should be well-mannered and easy like Carol. Carol does what she's told. She's smarter than Carol, but your sister is plain . . . damned . . . hard to deal with. She's funny, yes—funnier than Carol—but my God she's stubborn. And ungrateful." My mother yanked up the bedspread. "It's my own fault. I should make Cindy toe the line like Carol's parents do. Instead, she acts like a spoiled brat."

Though I loved having her home, Cindy was spoiled. Everybody in the family knew it. "I guess when I have kids, Cindy shouldn't be around them too much."

My mother turned on me quick as a snake. "Cheryl Suchors! How could you say such a thing!"

"But you said— . . ."

"God gave us Cindy to love and protect! How can you be so cruel, after all the gifts God's given you, after all your father and I've done for you?"

What did I know about having kids? "I'm sorry! I didn't mean it. I love Cindy. You know I do." I rushed over to hug my mother, but she pushed me away and stalked to the door, where she stood staring back at me cold as ice.

I went hollow inside. My mother had always told me that I was her favorite.

To win her back I cried, "It wasn't me who said that! It was Lizzie Tish." Lizzie Tish was a girl, like my twin, that my mother invented and blamed whenever I did something she didn't like. After yelling at and spanking me, once her anger dwindled, she would say in a voice like silk, "It wasn't my good girl Cheryl who did that. My Cheryl would never be so selfish and bad. It must have been that Lizzie Tish." My mother would wait until I agreed. The whole idea of Lizzie Tish confused and unsettled me, but I did understand I was never to do anything wrong, so maybe Lizzie Tish could rescue me now.

My mother looked down at me like I was someone else's problem and shook her head. "It wasn't Lizzie Tish. That nasty, selfish, ugly person was you." She walked away.

"Mom," I had cried, running after her into the hallway. "Will you ever love me again?"

"I don't know."

It was easy to be scared most of the time. Scared to reveal myself, to make a mistake, to need anything. Scared of loud noises or sudden movements. Scared to be present at the wrong moment. Scared to be found wanting. Scared of the hand grenade that could come hurtling over my wall at any moment.

Acting despite fear—controlling the fear somehow—was necessary if I weren't to lose myself entirely.

⌒

Various news commentators believed Y2K would turn the country upside down. On the first day of the new century, they warned, the ensuing chaos could bankrupt everyone with savings, including Larry and me and our relatives. Other commentators were more optimistic, expecting at worst a few days' economic shutdown. A few experts predicted nothing at all would happen. To be safe, Larry and I stocked extra provisions in the basement and went over contingency plans with Casey. In the increasingly tense days approaching January 1, 2000, I alternated between buoyant optimism and distress.

It was hard to be creative and write. Instead, I focused on mountains. I told Cathy I would celebrate 2000 by climbing not two or three, but seven 4000-Footers, at least one during the winter. For half or more of those mountains, I expected to overnight in Appalachian Mountain Club huts, accompanied by a group of women I didn't know. I'd just learned about and signed up for a three-day venture in June called "Wilderness Heals." Each year thirty or so women hiked in the Presidentials as a fundraiser for the Elizabeth Stone House, a shelter and training center for women. Each hiker committed to raising $1000.

Mid-June would give Kate and me ample time to train. No matter which Presidential peaks Wilderness Heals chose to summit this year, Kate and I'd be able to bag at least two, maybe more 4000-Footers. Assuming I could persuade Kate. She said raising that much money intimidated her. I was pretty sure that, over time, I could convince her to come, especially if I fundraised for her too. She might also have wondered about carrying so much gear and hiking extra tall 4000-Footers three days in a row. I certainly did.

Remembering Frances bolstered my courage. Besides, by February we'd have mastered the ice axe. Surely axe-wielding, winter-hiking, mountain women could manage three days of climbing in summer. These prospects, after which I'd surely be an expert hiker, now had me leaping out of bed in the mornings. Despite the threat of Y2K, my mountain goals made the beginning of the new millennium feel momentous and marvelous. When I ordered our Christmas cards,

I splurged and had them printed with Casey's poem on the subject:

> *A Millennium of new things*
> *metallic paint and paper wings*
> *glitter gel, glow-in-the-dark braces*
> *new people and new faces*
> *new experiences and new places*
> *flying high in the cloudy sky*
> *in a silver suit with silver wings,*
> *thinking—a new beginning.*

10. HOPE IS A ROCK

When I complained to my therapist that my injured wrist could prevent my climbing Cardigan next month and then how would I ever learn to use an ice axe, he said, "Nothing stops you. You're unsinkable."

Over the next week, I turned his concept of me over in my mind, examining it like a strange object. I tried to apply it to myself, but I kept getting stuck on the things I hadn't accomplished, the times I'd curled up with a book because I couldn't face anything else, the places I was weak. I longed to see myself as he saw me, but when I leaned over the creek like Narcissus I found only rumpled, broken water.

I wondered if this sense of being invisible to myself was a common by-product of growing up in a home where everyone else's image filled the mirrors. Whatever the case, it left me feeling stupid, and ashamed. There were things I did like about myself, of course, positive traits I trusted, but they seemed situational rather than intrinsic. Whenever I attempted something new, I had to begin all over again building up confidence along with the new skills, one small chunk at a time.

Yet learning new things thrilled me. I was a change junkie, used to moving frequently and being offered a smorgasbord of *new*. My favorite phase of projects or relationships came at the beginning, when all was fresh and unknown and mysterious, full of possibility. Did this suggest I was, in some perverse way, addicted to proving, rebuilding, finding myself over and over just to lose confidence again with a new endeavor—like Sisyphus and his eternal effort with the rock? I hoped not. Anxiety was the uncomfortable underbelly of change, and the effort to find and prove myself repeatedly wasted both time and energy. Perhaps hiking would become the undertaking in which I learned to let go a little.

General management consulting, my first job out of graduate school, was, in ways I didn't understand at the time, perfect for a change junkie: always a new client, new company, new industry, new set of problems, new configuration of consulting teammates, and new position into which to fit myself.

I'd been a consultant only three months when we had to present findings and recommendations on my first consulting project to the CEO, President, and several Vice Presidents of a Fortune 500 corporation. I fretted the week before we flew to the client's headquarters, waking up in the wee hours, troubled and uneasy. I'd never given a presentation before. Heck, I'd never even seen one. The therapist I'd just started seeing, my first, asked, "What's the worst thing you can imagine happening?"

I thought for a minute. "My father jumps up from the back of the room and yells, 'Don't listen to her. She's just a wise-ass kid. She doesn't know anything!'" My father had taken a management consulting position when I was in high school, but quit in less than a year. A man with thirty years' experience at the time, he'd decided all consultants were charlatans.

My new boss, Ben, was younger than my father but still thirty years my senior and an ex-Marine. He insisted I give a large share of the presentation to our clients. As the cheapest team member, I'd done much of the work, but that didn't usually translate into getting to shine in front of clients. I hoped this meant he viewed me as good consultant material and by extension, if he thought so, maybe I could, too.

On the appointed day, he, the other team members, and I led the clients through our findings, conclusions, and recommendations. The presentation, even my part, went flawlessly and I was exultant. I could tell Ben was pleased, too. But after a few questions the CEO, a man my father's age, said, "Ben, this is terrific work. Why don't you come back next week by yourself to discuss it further so our language won't offend the ladies."

Ben spoke up on behalf of the "ladies," but the CEO was adamant. In one stroke, he had erased me and the other woman on the team. On the plane home afterward, Ben sat next to me. After we'd received our drinks, he asked if I felt deflated.

Cautiously, I shrugged.

He sipped his whisky. "You were hoping the CEO would be so impressed with how smart and talented you were he'd offer you a job on the spot—Vice President of Deep Problems."

I squirmed, but couldn't help smiling.

"Instead, the guy proves he's just another chauvinist." Ben made me laugh and we talked for the rest of the flight home, the most concentrated amount of time I'd spent with my boss in my three months. He said something else I never forgot. "The thing that most attracts me to people is not their strengths." He paused. "It's their vulnerabilities."

∽

After the death of my mother, who'd always been the communications hub through which news of my brother flowed to me and vice-versa, I had hoped he and I would talk more often and that his and my relationship would improve. Once we'd settled her estate, a miserable process that brought out my mistrust and his anger, I suggested my family travel to Texas for Thanksgiving to be with him and Mardy, their children, and grandkids. I'd offered to host, but my brother never wanted to fly north.

I hoped Bill and I could clear away the lifelong competition that rose like a wall between us. At night in our motel rooms, with some help from Mardy, we opened up enough to talk about the past. I thanked Bill for our breakfast conversation in Denny's eleven years before when he had confirmed Dad was an alcoholic. In response, he described how our father had stoked the competition between my brother and me by flinging any successes I had in Bill's face, asking why he couldn't do as well as his kid sister—something I'd never known.

As we recounted family stories to Mardy and Larry, I mentioned the time Bill had hit my dog Raffles with his car and broken Raff's leg to teach him a lesson about chasing cars. Bill looked stricken. "Jesus, I drove into your dog?"

"Don't you remember?"

He shook his head slowly. "I must have been drinking. What an awful thing to do. I'm so sorry."

Nor did he remember the time when I was seven and he sixteen when he'd set off firecrackers in the mailbox and the mail carrier had called the police. While my mother opened the door to them, I ran around the house making sure Cindy, who at ten had recently gotten her period, hadn't left any used pads lying around and wasn't walking around naked wearing just her sanitary pad and belt. I'd been afraid they'd arrest her along with my brother.

During one of those healing nighttime talks, Bill shared something that made me cry. My father had never told my brother he loved him. Not once. Bill and I still had worlds of difference between us. We still hurt each other, whether we meant to or not. But those visits, in which we tried to bridge the past, brought us closer.

~

The summer before college, I came into our living room in Oak Brook, Illinois, after a tennis match with Karl, a friend from my fourth and final high school. I was thrilled I'd found someone to play with. Though Karl hadn't played tennis for as long as I, he was a big guy and athletic. When my father put down the paper to ask me how the match went, I proudly announced, "It was great. I won!"

My father shot me a disgusted look. "For crissake, haven't you ever heard of winning the battle and losing the war?"

He and my mother fought with me constantly about politics, body hair, and the way to act with boys and men. By my late twenties, I'd had it. I wanted better relationships with these two people I loved. I wrote long, angry letters to my father. He wrote long, angry ones back. I'm not sure either of us understood the other any better, but at least we were trying. My mother and I didn't write, we talked on the phone. All our thorny, raging talks balanced on the fulcrum of hope, on my part, that I could be who I was rather than who she wanted me to be (a devout Catholic, celibate, conservative, and a woman whose chief goal in life was to marry well and bear successful children) and still have her love. I also hoped, unfairly and foolishly, to change her into the mother I wanted her to be (more self-aware, accepting, and liberal, less manipulative and more feminist.) Wrangling to understand and free myself from my parents' ideals led me into therapy and I wished they'd get therapy, too, a practice they believed was strictly for crazy people. But therapy, whatever else it might be, was based on the belief that people could take charge of themselves and change.

Just a few years before my father died my parents drove from Florida, where they'd retired, to visit me in Boston, stopping along the way to see friends. One of the dreams for their "golden years" was this kind of long, leisurely road trip to see the country and the friends they'd made living in all the places they had. They didn't know that after he retired at seventy, my father would live only two more years because—as I see it—his mother had finally died, he had set enough money aside for my mother and Cindy, and he no longer knew, without work, who exactly he was. When I'd congratulated him on his seventieth birthday, he turned on me. "What the hell for?" he said bitterly. "It's all downhill from here."

As was so often the case, that day my father taught me a great deal. He was the North Star against which I navigated.

And yet, in that last visit to Boston, he surprised me.

I had come to their hotel to collect my parents. For some reason, my mother wasn't with us when my father and I stepped into the elevator down to the lobby. There were four or five other people in the elevator and I don't remember anything about them except they were adults, and strangers. My father, who never did things like this, turned to the person next to him and said, beaming, with a nod in my direction, "That's my daughter."

The person smiled, I think.

Incredibly, my father went on. "She's almost twenty-nine. She went to Harvard Business School." And again, conversationally, as if the other person had responded, "She's a management consultant."

I had been stunned. Mortified. No one had said a word and the elevator doors had opened and everyone fled. Yet I could still see my white-haired father and his secretive little smile, as if he were holding back great peals of joy, shining with pride and telling me the only way he could.

❧

There was another side to hope. Hope was an annoying thing, the chip, the grit, the grainy irritant inside an oyster that bedeviled the mollusk until it created a pearl. Sometimes winged like an angel, yes, hope could also be tough and abrasive and controlling, and it wouldn't let you go until you trembled at your limits to make something beautiful inside the sharp shell of your life.

It was this nagging need to improve my life that had flown me down to Florida the second year after my father died. Being married to Larry had given me courage and a place to land if my world, as I feared, shattered.

It was spring. The back yard of the house my parents had built for their retirement, that my mother now lived in alone, danced with color. Cherry-colored blossoms covered the crepe myrtle trees. The slats of the back fence stood like awkward prom dates behind the long hedge of azaleas wearing hot-pink gowns. Hummingbirds flitted from blossom to blossom fanning themselves, drunk on nectar. It looked like Eden before the Fall.

"Mom," I said, "We need to talk."

My mother straightened her already straight spine in a way that meant she preferred to escape but wouldn't let herself. She opened the back door and walked outside. We sat down next to one another on the rattan love seat in the shade.

I'd prepared all kinds of gentle ways to lead up to the subject it had taken me so many years to broach. My mother snapped a dead branch full of dry leaves from one of the potted geraniums and now held it tightly. Her hands, with the huge arthritic knuckles and swollen fingers, were spotted with age. Now that the moment had come, I couldn't remember anything I'd rehearsed. The words scattered like bees.

Before I lost my courage, I plunged in. "Mom, if someone kept punching me in the stomach—" I jabbed my right fist hard into the air as if it were my body, rapid fire and grunting with the effort of each strike—"would you want me to tell them to stop?"

"Yes!" my mother said, her roan-colored eyes wide and frightened. "Of course I would."

"It's like that for me when you're drinking." It became so still not even a bird spoke.

I rushed on. "I never know exactly when you're going to say something that hurts me like a punch in the gut." My mother sucked in her breath, but I had to continue, to get it all out. "I don't know when, or why, or where, I just know that you will."

I forced myself to hold my mother's eye even as I heard the dead geranium leaves rattle and I despised myself. Who was throwing punches now? "I can't control what you do when we're not together, and I'm not trying to," I said. "That's your business."

My regal mother looked so small and fragile sitting there, a widow whose daughter attacked her on her own back porch.

"But if you call me when you've been drinking—and I can always tell—I'll hang up. If you're visiting me up in Boston, I'll ask you to leave." My voice shook, but I kept going. "If I'm here, at your house, I'll catch the next plane." I finished in a whisper. "I will. I'll leave you."

I was lucky. She never drank again in my presence.

11. ROADBLOCK

A week before Christmas, after we had finished our Winter Hiking classes and had to wait a month until Cardigan, Kate and I worked out in the subway. As we ascended our third Porter, she broke the news. "I've got a mass in my abdomen. One end is near my ovaries."

I stopped dead.

"They don't know for sure what it is. In early January, I'm having surgery to remove it."

"Oh, Kate, how awful!" I put my hand on her arm. "I'm so sorry."

She moved her arm gently to disengage my hand and kept going. I stood still. Jackie, my mother-in-law, was suffering through radiation for oral cancer as we spoke. Pancreatic cancer had killed my mother. Now Kate had a "mass?" I wanted to snatch her up and run away, throwing up barricades. I wanted to fight—anyone, anything. *Not my best friend, my hiking partner*, I thought. *Please, please, please, not Kate too.*

I stayed beside her, climbing the stairs, but my body was on autopilot while my mind leapt about like a squirrel. *This is why she's slower than I am. Was it affecting her on Lincoln and Lafayette? Sandwich Dome? What's her prognosis?*

She faced straight ahead, not looking at me. Perhaps the sympathy or the tears that clogged my throat would overwhelm her. How, then, could I help?

"I'm not pleasant to be around these days." She slid me a sideways glance that was apologetic. "The discomfort makes me cranky."

"Discomfort?" I knew the medical euphemism for pain. "You're having discomfort?"

She nodded. "Not all the time."

I wanted to yell at her to stop moving and look at me, to shake her out of her stoicism. *This is terrifying*, I wanted to say. *You have every right to be scared. To be angry, confused, lost.* But I was certain she didn't want an emotion-charged scene. Why else tell me in the subway?

Over the next two weeks, I asked Kate to train with me every day, not because we'd be climbing mountains this winter, but so she could go into surgery strong. It also helped me cope. When I asked her how she was doing, she said, "Mostly I just want to get this thing out of me. I can feel it growing." The day before she went to the hospital, we chugged through seven Porters carrying backpacks weighted with cans of soup.

⁓

Y2K never happened, a huge relief to the country and the world and everyone I knew, but four days into the new millennium, they operated on Kate. On the fifth day, I rode the elevator to her floor, gripping a long cardboard tube. The hospital smell, stale air laced with bleach, triggered unwanted memories. I had to remind myself several times that I was just visiting.

I took a steadying breath before knocking on Kate's open door.

She was not the robust woman with the flushed face and healthy sweat of two days before. She reclined against pillows, about the same color as her sheets. She didn't look pleased to see me.

Her husband rose from a chair by the bed and offered me the only seat in this half of the semi-private room. "No, thanks," I told Tom. "I'm fine." I walked up to the side of the bed, close to Kate. I wanted to take her hand, but didn't. "How are you feeling?"

"I'm all right," she said, grimacing. She shifted, moving her hips and legs, arching her back against the pillows. I recognized the restlessness from my own hospital stays. You tried to get comfortable enough to ignore the pain, enduring cheery visitors and waiting for them to leave so you could fret without an audience. I would keep my visit short but, perversely, now that I was with her in the cramped hospital room I wanted to stay. I was consumed with the desire to make things better for her. In fact, I was afraid to leave, as if my being here could keep something bad from happening.

Tom spoke up with forced cheer. "The operation itself went very well. We won't have the pathology results for a little while, of course. They believe they found ovarian cancer spread throughout the perineum. But they're quite confident they got it all. And with chemotherapy, the chances are very good, seventy-five percent, so we're looking on the bright side."

His full cheeks, naturally pink, insisted on health and optimism. If his smile seemed a little tight, I nonetheless got the message. I looked at him, a kind portly man in his fifties clinging to the bed rail and to hope, and felt the incipient sting of tears.

I blinked hastily. "Good, I'm glad they got it. Thank God, I mean. Good." I still held the cardboard tube. "I brought you something," I told Kate.

I unsheathed the poster and unrolled it. Between my hands stretched a stunning photograph of Half Dome Mountain in Yosemite National Park, its outline etched crisply against a cobalt sky. Sunlight sparked off the fountain of rock thrusting upward from the earth. "I thought you might want a mountain nearby."

For the first time, Kate smiled. "Ansel Adams?"

I nodded.

"It's fabulous." She reached out and squeezed my hand.

Tom asked to see. He took the poster and, after admiring it, rolled it up and held it in his hand. "Thanks so much, Cheryl, that's great. I'm sure Kate will really enjoy this. We'll find space for it in the study."

I didn't want to be pushy, but the point was for her to have it *now*, to remind her what the future held, to give her a vision that outshone the present. I turned to Kate. "Where shall I put it?"

"There where I can look at it." She pointed straight ahead to the pale green wall across from her bed.

I dug in my fanny pack for the roll of masking tape I'd brought. "Do you think it's okay? I mean, the nurses—"

"I'll deal with the nurses," Kate snapped, making me grin. Grabbing the poster from Tom, I reached up as high as I could and taped Half Dome to the wall. "Some day we'll climb this," I promised.

"Yes," Kate said.

12. INTO THE RAVINE

"When the rug gets pulled out from under you for an event—even without Kate's cancer—everyone feels crappy and depressed," Cathy said. She sat in the cinnamon-and-white-plaid armchair in her basement office, copying the week's workouts from my athletic log into her files.

I was sweating on the inclined treadmill. I'd just told her about Kate and how my un-healed wrist had canceled my ice-axe weekend at Cardigan. The fabulous new millennium had barely begun and already it had knocked the happy right out of me.

"Yet I see from your records that you kept doing Porters. Excellent!"

Doing Porters without Kate hurt. I went faster, sure. But she didn't wheeze along beside me or keep me up to date on articles in *The New York Times* or *Backpacker*. The only things that kept my anxiety and misery about her under control were training and thinking about mountains, insisting to myself that mountains were still in our future.

From the treadmill, I told Cathy that Kate would be laid up from surgery for six weeks. "Then chemotherapy for seven months. Seven months! Who knows when she'll be able to train again." I stuck to these smaller issues to keep my mind from sinking into deeper waters. Even so, tears prickled.

"What you need is a new training partner," Cathy declared. "Lots of my clients use the buddy system to stay motivated. On track."

"I don't want another training buddy. Besides, most of my friends would rather host a kindergarten sleepover than do a Porter."

None of her other clients was a hiker, but Cathy sent two women my way, a runner and a cyclist. They were each willing to do Porters once a week. I had to admit it helped to have company. As we trudged up and down the stairs, we talked. The runner also had a best friend with ovarian cancer and we rested our battered hearts in each other's company. The cyclist's mother was ill, as was my mother-in-law and we consoled one another. I began to think there might be other women out there I could rely on—not, like Kate, to research hikes, see movies, discuss gardens; not to be interested in what Casey was learning in fifth grade; not to talk politics or feminism and then stick a follow-up article in my mailbox; not to go to the sports store for yet another piece of hiking gear; not to have an obscure cooking instrument or ingredient I needed to borrow—but at least for a regular workout. I promised myself these were interim measures, that Kate would be back. I felt less guilty that way.

I visited Kate most days, leaving my massage table set up in her study so I could do Reiki energy work on her. I could hover my hands right above her abdomen without having to touch her stitches. I'd gotten trained to do Reiki years ago when troubled by shoulder pain. After I'd practiced on Kate, she felt so mellow and boneless she learned Reiki too so we could work on each other. We agreed Reiki was as mysterious as electricity or computers, two other things we didn't really understand but clearly worked.

One late January afternoon after we'd eaten lunch, she lay on the couch in her living room with the heat up and logs burning in the fireplace. Now that she'd started chemo, she always felt cold. She wore a flannel nightgown, sweatpants, and socks under a bathrobe Larry had lent her. Moxie, their orange tabby, sat next to her on the sofa and kneaded her chest with white paws. I made two cups of tea and carried them over.

"Chemo's going pretty well," Kate said. She insisted she didn't feel ill, just tired and cold. Most of the time she was up and about but had to rest for part of each day. She was waiting for her hair to fall out. "My skull hurts," she said. Soon she'd be telling me her head was freezing and it felt like needles were trying to push through her scalp, but she wasn't there yet.

After a pause, I confessed. "Cathy found me a couple of women to do Porters with."

Kate pulled a blanket from the back of the couch and spread it over her feet and legs. "Good," she said. "You need to be ready for Wilderness Heals in June. Three days in the Presidentials is big."

I unclenched my hands from the tea mug. "You're sure?" Looking forward to the expedition—despite my fear that I wouldn't be able to manage three consecutive days of 4000-Footers—was the happiest corner of my life right now.

Moxie padded down to nestle between Kate's blanket-covered feet. "In fact," she said, "let's do Porters this weekend. I'll be ready by then."

"Fantastic!" The heart and mind often play a strange duet. I was both certain Kate wouldn't have recovered enough yet to do Porters and immediately hopeful she could join me in June for Wilderness Heals.

She did, in fact, go with me for Porters that weekend. Her strength after major surgery and heavy doses of chemotherapy was nothing less than heroic. Throughout February and into early March, she accompanied me most weeks for a round of

Porters. When she tired, she strolled the plaza to catch her breath or chatted with the token taker while waiting for me.

I trained with the cyclist and runner, too. I had to. My annual mammogram the week before had picked up a change in the pattern of calcifications in my healthy breast, not the one with pre-cancerous cells. They'd scheduled me for an ultrasound the next day, to get a clearer picture. The ultrasound technician had taken one look at the screen and left me on the table to find a radiologist. My pulse had shifted into over-drive.

The radiologist was a friendly woman with dark hair who kept up a stream of pleasant chatter. She apologized for the cold gel she re-applied to my breast, for the pressure of the instrument against my skin. I didn't smile back. I watched her face. I saw the moment her focus sharpened. "What is it?"

She kept her eyes on the ultrasound screen. Her left hand continued to manipulate the ultrasound device in its pool of cold jelly, probing my breast. "There's a suspicious mass, about 3x4mm, surrounded by calcifications. You need to have it biopsied."

"But what do you think?"

"I can't really say without a biopsy."

"Come on. What are my odds?"

She made some kind of internal assessment and gave in. "Fifty-fifty."

I'd sucked air. Gotten dressed. Driven home. Called my dentist's office to cancel the afternoon's appointment and dismayed the kindly receptionist by sobbing when she asked me to reschedule.

The breast surgeon decided to operate in late February—two lumpectomies in the "healthy" breast, one to remove the mass and the other to excise a separate area of calcifications. I didn't ask her this time how my breast would look afterward. When I asked her the odds of finding cancer, she refused to comment.

Training kept my body strong and my attitude, at least while I pumped out endorphins, optimistic. Moreover, I could share my terror with the cyclist and runner in a way I couldn't with Kate, whom I didn't want to burden and whose fate I was desperate to avoid.

~

While waiting for my upcoming surgery, I invited Kate along on outings with Casey and me so often my daughter, who both loved and worried about her Auntie Kate, got annoyed. Everything we did had to be done at Kate's pace and end when Kate faded. Yet I had a frantic desire to include my friend in everything.

So when Casey the *fashionista* insisted she come with Kate and me to pick out a wig, I happily agreed. Had I known how long we would spend watching Kate try on wig after wig, the realities of her condition forcibly etched in our minds, I would have made Casey stay home.

After another early dinner at my house without our husbands and during which I scurried around the kitchen serving my debilitated best friend and my irritated daughter, I had to face facts and listen to Casey. I could no longer pretend that having Kate present did not change everything. She was no longer stalwart, strong, witty Kate, a charming woman who adored my daughter. She was, as anyone would be, needy. Conversation revolved around her disease. Trying to take care of her scared my daughter and drained me at an alarming rate. I teetered on the verge of resentment. Because Kate didn't ask for anything yet I felt compelled to support her, I had to think of things first and then offer them. Not only did I give her Reiki, I had to propose I do so. I felt as if I held up both ends of the seesaw, running from my end to her end and back again as fast as I could go.

Thinking such thoughts made me feel shallow and

petty. Besides, who forced me to give more than I should? Not Kate, certainly. She never wished to impose.

To further complicate things, since she had heard the results of my ultrasound, Kate actually had been thinking of me—she stuffed my mailbox with articles about women with breast cancer and medical reports on the disease that no one had actually said I had. Each of these gifts arrived in my hands like a time bomb. I knew she was trying to help, but it felt like she couldn't wait for me to join her on the other side of the cancer divide, and I wanted to shout, "Stop giving me cancer!"

One night I was sliding smoothly toward sleep when I remembered something I had dreamt in my late-twenties. In the dream I stood on a vast, empty field of withered brown grass, feeling very alone. I was, however, not alone. Over my shoulder I carried a braided rope thick enough to moor a sizeable ship. Behind me, the rope looped around my mother's waist and behind her, around my sister's. I pulled them forward with all my might, straining desperately to get them to a towering stone wall that bisected the field for as far as I could see. There was no going around, under, or over it. There was nowhere else to go but through it, through an oval, dark opening so black I couldn't see into or beyond it. The opening frightened me. I didn't know what waited on the other side. I only knew I had to go through—my life depended on it—and I was dragging my mother and sister with me. I could not, would not, leave them behind.

Laura, my therapist, pointed out the obvious symbol of the birth canal and my being reborn into that terrifying and thrilling unknown—life, my own adult life—on the other side of the wall. I wept telling her how heavy my mother and sister were, how hard it was to carry them, how I had done my utmost to save them both. She noted I took on a great deal of responsibility. She said that, in the dream, my mother and sister did not seem to want to come with me and that, perhaps, the struggle to get through the wall was my quest, not theirs. She wondered aloud if people who did not want to be *could* be saved.

I had not liked what Laura had to say. Her comments made me face a secret I'd kept from myself all the while I'd been busy taking emotional care of the two women I most loved: I was afraid to put the rope down, to march forward alone.

～

Seven days after I'd had the lumpectomies, the phone rang. I'd just come home from walking Casey to school on a brisk sunny morning, glad to be outside for the first time since surgery. She and I had admired the brave purple and yellow crocuses and green shoots of daffodils. I was headed up to my office to write, Juniper beside me and spring in my voice as I answered the phone.

It was the breast surgeon, three days before I expected to hear from her. I leaned my back against the kitchen wall wishing I could close my eyes, wishing I could breathe. She said, "The pathologist found invasive lobular carcinoma. Cancer. The good news is the tumor is on the small side. We caught it early, Stage 2."

I slid down the wall to sit on the floor.

Larry came home from work to be with me. We decided tonight was the night.

After dinner, he and I sat at the kitchen table while Casey lounged on the floor playing with Juniper. I took a mental snapshot of my ten-year-old while she cuddled her fluffy white pal, innocent in a way she would never be again. My daughter's body had grown fuller, I noticed, as if gathering itself for the stretch of height to come. I watched her ravenously, committing the moment to memory, wishing I could deposit her in the land of the fairies where years of our time passed in a blink so that she wouldn't have to live through all that came next.

I pushed my empty wineglass away. "Honey, Daddy and I have something to talk to you about." Behold your mother, about to become your newest lesson in the fragility of life. "I got a call from my doctor today."

She sat up, holding Juniper tightly enough that the dog squirmed. In a clear, solemn voice, my daughter said, "I know, Mommy. You have cancer."

Her face, open and brave as a flower, broke me. After a minute, I whispered, "How did you know, Bear?"

"I just knew." She sounded ageless, wise, and accepting as a priestess, a prophet. If only I could build a shield around her, clasp Wonder Woman's bracelets on her young arms. I couldn't say a thing. I looked over at my husband. Tears wet his face.

Still clutching Juniper, Casey climbed onto my lap. I closed my eyes, smelling puppy hair and fresh girl skin as we wrapped ourselves together. Larry came over to kneel on the floor beside my chair and add another layer of love, binding us into a close family knot, as if to ensure we would never come undone.

Four days later, I sat fully dressed on the edge of a padded examination table. Larry squeezed into a small plastic chair at my feet. The breast surgeon stood. She spoke ugly, unwanted words. "We didn't get clean margins on the biopsy. Since some of the tumor remains, you'll need another lumpectomy." Fleetingly, I wondered who "we" was, what part I had played in not getting the whole tumor. Then I wondered how many lumpectomies one breast could sustain.

"You might want to consider a partial radical mastectomy."

I picked up my head to stare at her. My mother had had a mastectomy. Her naked, lopsided chest appeared before me. I saw the deep red grooves where the straps of her bra dug into the tops of her shoulder from the weight of her prosthesis. I heard her lowered voice asking, *Do you mind if I wear my robe without my 'bosom?' By the end of the day I just can't wait to get the thing off.* I saw her hand drawn to the diagonal slash of scar across her chest, massaging circles into it while she winced and groaned.

Abruptly, I was back in the exam room, sitting on the table with the hygienic paper crinkling as my legs swung back and forth of their own volition and the doctor's voice approached and receded and slapped me like waves. "There's additional surgery—in the armpit area—to remove approximately a third of the lymph nodes so we can see if the cancer has spread."

Two more surgeries? My mind stumbled and got stuck. From then on, words swirled in and out of my hearing. *Possible radiation. Chemotherapy. Adjuvant therapy. Tamoxifen.* Larry's pen scratched furiously on the yellow pad in his lap. The surgeon wore a nervous smile. The room was very cold.

Eventually, she stopped talking. She and Larry looked at me. "This is bad," I whispered. "Isn't it."

Her smile disappeared. "Yes," my surgeon said. "This is bad."

That wasn't what I'd hoped she would say. Later, I'd be grateful for her honesty. After a beat, she said she needed to examine the wound site from the lumpectomies but kindly didn't make me change into a paper gown, just lifted my shirt. I watched her dark eyebrows contract. "I can't operate on that."

I looked down. Midnight purple bruises covered my chest and side from my collarbone to my waist.

"We'll have to wait at least two weeks. Probably three. You have to heal before I can go in again." She gently replaced my shirt.

Larry asked how long for each stage of treatment and when the surgeon answered, I added up weeks in my head. A minimum of thirty. Thirty weeks. My mind couldn't do the simple division that would tell me how many months that was, but I remembered pregnancy was close to forty weeks. Which made me think of Casey, but there all thinking stopped.

Once we were in the car on the way home, I managed the division of weeks into months. I turned to Larry, whom we had decided should do the driving. "Seven months, like Kate's chemo," I told him. "From now until October."

He reached over to put his hand on my thigh. His eyes were sad, shiny with tears. *He doesn't deserve this*, I thought. *His mother just died.*

After a while, I said, "I'll miss the whole spring. The summer. Most of the fall." I pressed my left fingertips lightly into my right hand, which still hadn't healed enough to wield an ice axe. "That's the entire hiking season for a whole year." I sat there, stupefied.

"We'll get through this, Suchs. We'll do it together."

But I was down a tunnel pursuing another thought. As abruptly as a switch flooding the darkness, I now saw that this meant I would miss my Wilderness Heals hiking trip. "Goddamn it!" I slammed both fists into the dashboard.

13. BERKSHIRES

Larry and Casey would spend spring break in Florida with his bereft father and brother. I knew Larry had to mourn with them, but I worried about Casey who'd never even met my father, had lost one grandmother at five and now the other at ten and, by the way, her mother had cancer too. Yet she was eager to go see her grandpa and uncle, swim in the sunshine, and, I guessed, get a break from the cancer and me. I missed my mother-in-law keenly, but now I had to deal with my own cancer. Instead of going with Larry and Casey, I retreated to a yoga center in the Berkshires, at the western edge of Massachusetts. Years before, I'd stayed at Kripalu for a weekend and remembered the fine vegetarian food and the 6:00 a.m. Gentle Yoga class. I had never done any yoga before Kripalu nor had I since, but attending that class was like getting up to see the sun rise. It left a lasting impression of ease and optimism, making Kripalu a good place to heal from one surgery and prepare for the next.

The Berkshire Mountains, sometimes called the Berkshire Hills, rose from the Western New England Upland, a plateau roughly 2,000 feet high that extended down from the Green Mountains of Vermont. The Berkshires were made up of three ranges and topped out at 3,491 feet with Mt.

Graylock, the highest point in Massachusetts. While my wrist couldn't wield an ice axe, hiking there at the end of April wouldn't require one and I was desperate to set my feet on a trail, even one that didn't lead up a 4000-Footer. Since my diagnosis, I'd been unable to concentrate on writing, but this I could do. Kate decided to drive out to join me after my weekend workshop ended.

The workshop was called "Healing through Grief." It helped to talk about mourning my mother-in-law, my fear of losing my best friend, and the grief I felt about amputating an intimate, visible part of my body—a tender part of my sexuality and womanhood that, though sliced open, gouged out, and sewn up too many times, I could not imagine my life without. I did not want to walk the cancer trail.

When the workshop ended, I grabbed my boots and drove off to Great Barrington for a quick hike. The three-mile loop trail of little Monument Mountain (1,710 feet) was both short enough to complete before dark and billed as the "signature hike of the Berkshires." I launched myself onto the path, my legs and back gradually loosening knots accumulated from two days of sitting on a metal folding chair hunched in grief. I sucked the chilled, piney air deep into my lungs.

Soon a "staircase" of quartzite rock appeared. Steps had been notched into the gorgeously veined white stone, and it felt like stepping up a hillside of Michelangelo's glowing Carrera marble, the bright quartzite offering sharp contrast to the spring greenery and brown soil.

I came upon a plaque beside the trail. This was called Monument Mountain because it honored a Mohican woman who had leapt from the cliff to her death rather than be forced to marry a man not of her choosing. I understood her desperation as I faced a future I hadn't chosen either.

Though it wasn't a peak on my list, too little to call getting to the top a challenge and therefore a success, I noticed that even this small hike calmed and soothed me. That night, deep in the meditative state of a Reiki session, I wondered where exactly my severed breast would go. Instantly, an image appeared. I didn't know where it came from or how much it was influenced by the story of the Mohican woman who gave up her life to save something more important to her, but a woman showed up. She was middle-aged and wore armor like the knights of old, a veteran warrior, battle-scarred and weary, limping along what appeared to be an empty road, carrying helmet and sword and—somehow I knew this—she was the personification of my breast.

Her dark hair was tangled, her face weathered and seamed, smeared with dirt and blood. Nevertheless, she answered my question. "Why, I'll go to the mountains, of course." Her warrior's voice sounded steady and certain. She seemed at peace with her fate. There was even a note of relief in her voice, as if she were glad she could stop fighting, at last, and rest.

I realized I could visit her. My breast wouldn't just be thrown onto the garbage heap and gone forever, I would be with her every time I climbed a mountain, every time I pressed my face to a rock, every time I saw a peak limned against the sky. Matanna would be there. That was the name I gave her. Whenever I was able, I could commune with Matanna, my lost part, in the mountains.

I had learned long ago as a management consultant that when clients started using your words to describe a problem or a solution, you were halfway to success. Diagnosing a health issue—naming it—opened the door to resolving it. Larry and I had named our daughter *Casey*, derived from the old Gaelic word meaning *courage*, long before she lost her beloved grandmothers, several great aunts and uncles and a cousin, and feared for her mother's life. Naming was power.

Right after breakfast, I set off so I could be back for Kate's arrival. I wanted more of the peace I'd felt on Monument Mountain. Eagerly, I drove to a state park nestled in the southwest corner of Massachusetts. Alander Mountain reached 2,238 feet making it, in my book, a big hill rather than a mountain, but it was secluded and woodsy. This wasn't about achieving mastery or control or success. I needed to be on a mountain so Matanna and I could have one last hike together before we were separated.

By 7:30 a.m., I strode along a gently rising trail with no one about. The day blustered, full of brazen wind and cold enough to tingle my nose and numb my hands the moment I stopped moving. High clouds covered the sky in a shiny blanket through which the sun glared whitely. I was happy.

But after half an hour, the close, dark woods began to call up horror movies and scary headlines of shooters and ax-murderers. I didn't consciously relive the several times I'd been accosted by drunken or lust-ridden men, but my body remembered. And I was completely alone. I shivered, trying not to look over my shoulder, yet unable to stop scanning the surrounding trees. I marched along rapidly to avoid looking like prey, worried about a kind of violence I could have ignored had my DNA differed by a chromosome—and it made me feel out-of-control and helpless. I preferred the kind of fear that came from challenges like 4000-Footers, situations I could plausibly work my way through.

It never occurred to me that day that I might be frightened of more than an encounter with an ill-intentioned person. I had not yet acknowledged that, because of cancer, death perched like Edgar Allen Poe's raven on my shoulder. Though as yet unknown to me, my fear of dying bled into the air.

I huffed along indignantly, refusing to quit, turning fright into anger and making better time than I expected.

After an hour slid by and no one had appeared, my fear of being alone dissolved. I'd warmed up and was moving fluidly. It's hard not to be optimistic when your body is working and you're breathing the cold, spicy air of woods and mountain. For a few precious hours, I forgot about cancer.

The next afternoon, after some yoga, Kate and I took off for a brief hike. Outside the dining room, we walked up a grassy hill where actual llamas roamed, creatures my animal-loving daughter would have flipped over. Glancing at Kate, I remembered the second time I'd met her, a few weeks after her open house. I noticed her in the audience of a feminist lecture and suggested we eat lunch together afterward. The next afternoon, she'd rung my doorbell. A few minutes later, I watched as she and Casey walked down the street, Kate holding my three-year-old's hand while she let Casey hold sweet Marla's leash. Casey had turned around to look at me, her little face suffused with rapture. That may have been the moment I started loving Kate.

Spring mud sucked at our boots as we headed up to a road high enough that, from its macadam surface, we gazed down over the sprawling wings of the main building and the small lake on which it fronted. There was something tender in the view, as if we could cup all of Kripalu and its gentle inhabitants who worked hard at offering us contemplation and healing, in the warm palms of our hands.

We entered a forest. Lime-colored ferns sprang from the ground. A few trees had begun to unfurl neon-bright baby leaves. The chilled air smelled juicy and young, full of sap. Musty bass notes from the sea of dead leaves beneath our feet merely underscored the freshness. Here was the cycle of life—we could not only see but smell it. Kate and I strolled and enjoyed, not finding much need for talk.

We arrived at a pond with a tiny brick shelter housing, we assumed, some kind of waterworks. Kate checked her watch and, after admiring the pond, turned back toward Kripalu for her Reiki appointment. Part of me wanted to go with her and nap before dinner, but somehow I stayed.

As I walked, my mood shifted. I was sick of calling up courage. Tired of stepping out and plodding forward. I thought of one of the yoga poses we'd been taught that morning: surrender. I hated it. I never wanted to surrender. Since diagnosis, my life had been a steady stream of disappointments and losses, large and small. Letting go? I couldn't plan anything further out than a day or two. Life as I knew it had fallen through my fingers like so many bread crumbs that I hoped, but was unsure, I'd be able to pick up again some misty time in the future.

I recalled that the yogini had taught us another pose—for nurturing. I snorted. Nurturing was the hardest thing of all to find. I had lots of support, from Larry, my therapist, my Reiki Masters, Cathy, and friends, but I yearned for nurturing. Nurturing was someone noticing you shivered and finding you a sweater without your having to ask. Nurturing was someone who, seeing you looked worn, urged you to go lie down, the way my sober mother used to do. Adults weren't watched over in that way, except as fragile elders, but here was where I *wanted* to surrender. I longed for someone else to make all the doctors' appointments, figure out what had to happen next, take loving care of my daughter, and sit next to me on the sofa when my emotional entrails hung out. I wanted, just for a little while, to give up responsibility.

I wanted my mother. Despite her flaws, despite her and my father's having raised me to be the kid who never needed help or betrayed a weakness, she had often been nurturing in her non-drinking years, and I missed it. My mother had been dead six years, but I wished the woman who had lived through cancer before me could show me the way. I hungered for her special chicken soup, the soft satin quilt she had covered my child self with when I was ill. If only I could hear her tell me, as she always had, that I did too much, that I needed to rest more, perhaps I'd be able to. Most of all, I longed for her to tell me it wasn't my fault I had cancer, that I hadn't, like Lizzie Tish, done something wrong.

I began to cry, not just the usual tears that came so frequently these days, but loud, shoulder-heaving sobs. I sunk onto a felled tree trunk, my face in my hands. When I began to shiver but couldn't stop sobbing, I got up and hiked as I wept, trusting my feet to find their way. Four miles later, I felt cleansed and, though exhausted, nurtured. Ready.

14. ANCHORS

A week after the mastectomy, I managed a Porter. I had to. I had looked in the mirror. There was a chest that appeared slender and curved on one side, broad and flat as a plain on the other. This creature in the mirror was half woman, half boy. Through the thin blue and purple skin all the ribs showed, many more than I was used to seeing. A long slash of black stitches ran from sternum to side like a jagged branch of lightning. Two worm tunnels crawled across the motley chest, one above the lightning, one below. They had to be the tubes to the internal drains left in place to sop up blood and fluid. A violet puff of tissue swelled like a toadstool by the armpit on the boy side. Beneath that several black Xs, stitches, drifted down toward the waist.

Pain streaked through the phantom breast. It would be ten months before those spasms ended. The lightning would, in time, fade to a bone-colored tattoo. But it would be years before I was never surprised when washing myself in the shower and it would take more than a decade before I appeared one-breasted in my dreams.

For now, I needed to get used to this new body, to make sure it still worked. I hoped to feel less like a victim and more like a woman who had chosen amputation to stay alive.

During the three-week interval after surgery and before che-motherapy began, I climbed one Porter on Mondays and another on Thursdays. Kate joined me for ten-minute walks around the block. Over the weeks we built up to thirty minutes, then forty and sixty.

In the same way I approached climbing mountains, I did everything I could to prepare for the massif of chemo-therapy. I researched the drugs used, their side effects, and tips on how to handle them. I read books by women with breast cancer.

After my oncologist mentioned a remarkable organiza-tion called The Wellness Community, a place that offered free therapy, yoga, lectures, and other services to cancer patients, I joined a therapist-led support group of twelve women and men who had various kinds of cancer, including mine. Most had been in the group for months, even years. They'd become experts on the physical, financial, and emo-tional effects of cancer, generously sharing their hard-won knowledge. I sank with relief into their frank company. Now, once a week, I could unpack myself emotionally and learn that I was not alone.

Hearing me rave prompted Kate to join a Wellness Community support group herself. She began to open up in a way she hadn't as yet about her illness, and mine. Soon, the times we got together, we spoke in a *lingua franca* character-ized by the honesty and depth, even black humor, of cancer patients willing to examine their experience.

For physical and energetic support, my big-hearted, deeply skilled Reiki master, Ulrike Dettling, promised to come to my first chemo appointment to give me Reiki. She also set me up with a gifted woman training to be a master, Lynne Roberson, who generously provided me Reiki at a reduced fee, an offering she continued for several years. When my support group recommended acupuncture to boost the immune system chemotherapy assaulted, I scheduled weekly acupuncture with Lili Cai, an intuitive, caring, expert practitioner.

In the same way it takes a village to raise a child, I learned, it takes a village to get a person through cancer. The disease forced me to ask for all kinds of help—*surrender* indeed. My village enabled me to face chemotherapy knowing that, no matter what my condition, they would keep my daughter on as normal a schedule as possible. Two friends organized a network of helpers for my family and me. Folks signed up to walk Juniper, bring us dinner, drive Casey to piano, have her over for play dates, and take me to appointments when Larry had to work and I wasn't capable of driving. At the exact time I felt unfairly targeted by cancer, health practitioners and caring friends made me feel undeservedly fortunate.

Just before my first round of chemotherapy, my family and I drove to Waterville Valley for Memorial Day weekend. Larry had added my responsibilities to his own. Casey worried about me. My work, my novel, was on hold. Since my diagnosis, I hadn't been able to do anything more creative than journal, cursing or weeping onto the page. We all needed a rest, and I needed to reassure myself on a mountain.

On Saturday we took Juniper and headed to Mts. Welch and Dickey. The 4.4-mile loop with its 1800-foot elevation gain and splendid views was a family favorite. On this blue-sky day, Casey and Junie climbed happily and Larry strode along in his usual fashion, as if his legs had been designed with elevation gain in mind. The trail up to the Welch ledges brought me close to Matanna and felt thrillingly doable.

But as I stood up following our lunch break, a wave of dizziness and exhaustion struck me, as if my blood had drained out onto the stone where I sat. I took a few breaths but didn't tell anyone, thinking that once calories from lunch reached my muscles, I'd be fine. Yet no matter how much I willed myself to, I just couldn't get up the steep, hot slabs of Welch's cone.

For the first time, on a mountain I normally used for training, I had to give up.

The next day Larry found us an easier hike. The Cascade Brook Trail ascended 2.8 miles to our destination, Lonesome Lake for a picnic, gaining 1350 feet of elevation. We parked at the same lot from which Kate and I had launched our climb up Lincoln and Lafayette last fall. With every step along the woodsy trail I shed a pound or two of worry, practically bouncing through the dense greenery. Larry led, setting a stiff pace on the gently sloping ground. Casey followed behind, while Juniper stitched in and out around our feet.

To my surprise, I fell farther and farther behind. Sweat slicked my skin and dampened the neck of my shirt. I was breathing hard. Was this my new fucking normal?

Mosquitoes and flies harassed us so thickly they could have hauled us off like the winged monkeys of Oz. By the sixth or seventh stream crossing, I didn't know how much more I could do. At the same time, I yearned toward the summits of North and South Kinsman, two 4000-Footers nearby. I imagined breathing their invigorating alpine air, inhaling hope. And accomplishment. I imagined telling Kate, "You'll never believe what I did over the weekend, just four weeks after a mastectomy!" I pictured sticking red pins numbered six and seven into my wall map of the Whites.

But there in the woods swatting at bugs, even the single mile remaining to Lonesome Lake boggled me. I'd managed the last half-mile on pure will power and that well was running dry. If I kept going, Larry might have to carry me out. At the next trail junction, I gritted my teeth, and admitted to my family that I needed to return to the car and that before I could manage even that, I had to rest.

I was grateful to be living, to have a plan with the medical help and alternative support to fight cancer. At the same time, I grieved the loss of the woman I used to be and I feared the journey to come, one that, ironically, I could have gotten through better had I been able to return to my 4000-Footers. I urged Larry and Casey to start back without me so I could have a few moments to myself. Alone in the forest, I allowed the swirl of emotions to flow. I leaned back against a large boulder and let the damp from the stone seep into my skin, hoping to soak up endurance as well. Who better than a rock to teach me?

15. THE CURE

On the sixth day after chemo, I crawled up the stairs on all fours. Reading a book or watching a video overtaxed me. It took all my force of will just to get out of bed. I had become a parasite, living off of Larry's endless, uncomplaining efforts both at work and at home. Besides lying in bed, the only thing I could do was eat. In a truly repugnant way, I felt pregnant. My belly stuck out and I was constantly nauseated. Though starving, the smell of cooking made me sick.

My scalp itched and hurt. I touched the hair I'd cut short so the falling-out period would be less dramatic and thought, *It won't be long now.* When I attempted a ten-minute walk with Juniper, I couldn't catch my breath. My skin turned sallow and broke out in nests of whiteheads. My mouth hurt enough from mouth sores that I avoided Larry's kisses. My teeth and breath never felt clean. Every part of me had problems. It was as if my body tried to combat the invasion of toxins not in a planned, orchestrated way but by each body part panicking. The result was like watching a cobra eel its way into a house with all the residents fleeing and screaming from each room in succession as the deadly snake slithered through.

I wanted to call up my friends and weep all over them. But when the telephone rang, I didn't answer because I didn't want to talk to anyone. I had reached, as one of the chemo nurses had promised I would, the "emotionally labile" stage. I hated my life. I hated my cancer. I hated myself.

Yet on day ten, I woke up exuberant. I enjoyed a forty-minute walk with Juniper and did the post-mastectomy exercises for my arm, went to the park with Casey to toss Junie her Frisbee, and had lunch with a friend. Maybe I'd be as strong as Kate. For the first several months of her chemo, she'd been able to do errands, cook dinner, and go walking. Even do Porters. Maybe I would have weeks in each chemo round where I could have a somewhat normal life, sort of like hiking a twenty-one day mountain on which, like the Whites, I perennially trekked up, down, up again, then down. If I knew that would be the path, I could plan ahead.

That afternoon Larry took me to my "nadir" oncology appointment, the lowest point in the cycle. My white and red cell counts had dropped precipitously, but not atypically, a nurse told us. Still, I should avoid getting close to people while my immune system was weak and should definitely avoid crowds. She said to return for testing in three days to be sure my counts hadn't gotten worse.

After Larry dropped me at home on his way back to work, I discovered that two dozen roses from Bill and Mardy had arrived, their old-world fragrance filling the first floor. I felt so lucky—so loved—I decided to get dinner ready to save Larry from having to. I set the table, fed and walked Juniper, and cleaned up the kitchen. One of the amazing parents from Casey's school had brought over a turkey dinner earlier in the day—it showed up like fairy food in the magic cooler on the porch—and I had it all ready and warmed up by the time Larry arrived, just like a healthy loving wife might. He fiddled with the mail, went upstairs to change his clothes, checked his email. I called him once. Twice. Casey sat patiently waiting at the kitchen table. I called upstairs a third time.

When he walked into the kitchen, I exploded. "Where the hell do you get off? What's so goddamned important up there you can't come down until everybody's dinner is cold!" But I didn't want an answer, I wanted to knife him. My hands shook with the urge to punch his face.

He pulled out a chair for me. "Suchs, this is obviously more than you should be doing."

I sat, deflated. I couldn't even be trusted to reheat dinner. Was it the steroids that were part of chemo? My daughter had to serve me my plate.

My blood counts plummeted. The oncologist put me on daily antibiotics to ward off infection, a prophylactic regime that, since my cells never did recover, would continue for the rest of my chemo regimen. These kinds of things didn't happen to everyone. Many women in support group didn't suffer the intensity and number of reactions and side effects that I did. Once again, as with anesthesia and pain killers, I proved unusually sensitive to drugs.

Despite the fact that I no longer trained, and our sessions sometimes felt like one more chore when I was already flattened, I continued to see Cathy. After five years of working together Cathy was dear to me, a source of emotional support who believed, especially on days when I couldn't, that I would survive cancer. Setting tiny goals with Cathy, like walking around the block or taking a nap, was a way of insisting I had control over something, that I *would* be well, that I would hike and work again.

Kate, having finished chemotherapy, rarely stopped by. She spent the summer traveling to their place in Maine, visiting family in Florida, or just having fun now that her cancer had gone into remission and she had her life back. She had a bulletproof excuse for avoiding cancer-land and making the most of her newfound freedom and health, which

I understood. Though I didn't want to drag her down, though other friends came forward to help me and my family, I missed her.

⌒

The weekend I'd have been hiking with Wilderness Heals, I prepared for the second round of chemo. For some reason, my balance was more affected this cycle and I pitched into walls. In steroid overdrive, I zoomed over to cancer support group, easing up on the accelerator only when I discovered I was twenty miles over the limit. In group, I wanted everyone to talk faster. One of the men warned me to expect a steroid crash, and when it came, he counseled, "Just let it happen. If you try to fight it, it will only last longer."

The third night without sleep I got back in bed at 5:00 a.m. to wait for Larry to wake up. When he did, he held me while I wept torrents onto his chest. The crash I'd been warned about had arrived, but I was too enmeshed to see it until he pointed it out.

"I feel so helpless," he said.

I knew if he could find something else to do for me he would somehow manage to do it, overstretched as he was. He seemed to believe that if I rested I would get better. He couldn't comprehend the emotional toll of my own helplessness, the feeling that I'd been taken over by an alien. I longed for him to join me emotionally though I couldn't explain to him how, and he, who was willing to do anything for me, was unable to simply sit and be present—too overburdened with tasks and too frightened, I suspected, to go there. We had polarized, as we sometimes did under stress. He *did*. I *felt*. The split left each of us lonesome and drained.

⌒

Halfway through the second round of chemo, I lay on my bed as if I were a fluid-filled bag of pain. The backs of my hands ached. My back was a haunting ground of old wars. The tops of my feet tingled and burned so much I couldn't wear shoes. The slightest touch on my skin seared me. I couldn't get dressed or walk the dog. At least the blisters on my "private parts," as Casey called them, had disappeared.

In support group, I complained about chemo brain. "I forget everything." Heads nodded around the circle. "My brain stutters. I'm stuck waiting for a thought to materialize."

One of the men said, "I can't concentrate long enough to finish a newspaper article."

"Me either!" I said. "And I interrupt people like a two year old because if I don't spew whatever thought I manage to have, I'll lose it by the time they finish their sentence."

Knowing laughs.

At home I felt like a slug who accomplished exactly nothing all day. So I wrote myself a job description. It included tasks like going for chemo and blood work, making doctors' and acupuncture and Reiki appointments, and attending them. Dealing with health insurance. Participating in support group. Seeing Cathy. Taking pills numerous times a day. Forcing myself to walk outside. To lie down. The job? To get healthy.

One day when the unpredictable fortunes of chemo brought my energy back, Juniper and I celebrated by meeting Sarah at Fresh Pond.

Fresh Pond Reservation included the reservoir that provided Cambridge with drinking water and featured a walking path around its two-and-a-half-mile perimeter. The Pond was actually a lake that a retreating glacier had left behind 15,000 years before. Native Americans and settlers alike had appreciated its unusually pure water, hence the name. A private ice-cutting company had flourished on its shores well into the mid-1800s, selling ice to countries as far away as India and China.

When training, Kate and I had circumnavigated Fresh Pond several times a week, often going twice around for five miles. Over a hundred acres of trees and meadow surrounded the lake, so much terrain there was a real live forest ranger to watch over it. Ranger Jean wore the dark green uniform and hard-brimmed hat that reminded me of Smokey the Bear, and the sight of her this morning cheered me.

Sarah and I encountered the usual mix of walkers, birders, runners, bikers, baby carriage pushers, and, happily for Junie, dogs. Summer wild flowers nestled in the brush and birds called from the trees, making me aware of how much I missed coming here. Everything about our walk together was a tonic—spending time with Sarah, listening to her and being able to attend to her words properly, being able to form cogent sentences, walking at a pace that, while not my usual, was only mildly embarrassing, and making it the whole way around.

16. TRUTH

After more than two months of chemotherapy, facing my final round, I was no longer a fighter. My chemo appointments were no longer *events* or *mountains* for which I prepared. The good days that had provided a sense of life between the troughs didn't arrive anymore. I felt a sudden empathy for the secretary of defense. It was as if I'd run out of troops and supplies and even the National Guard and police were all used up. I had nothing left with which to defend myself from this cancer or its treatment. The buried truth that I'd hidden from everyone, including myself, emerged. I didn't say so aloud, but I didn't care if I died. I'd rather not breathe again than endure any more.

Even bundled into a fleece robe in the summer sunshine of our backyard, I was cold, though I sweated and froze by turns. I rested on a lounge chair and wished I could tend to my garden. I had tried putting my face to a flower or two but they, like everything else, smelled wrong. Certain days my legs were too heavy to pick up and I lost my balance whenever I turned my head. I couldn't regulate my functions or my senses.

Some women in support group were able to work at their jobs during chemo, but my body had become a maddened bronco desperate to buck off an unwanted rider. My bones hurt. My organs hurt. Periodically, it felt as if something had just exploded inside my skull. Some nights I wanted to saw off the top of my head and leave it lying, like a Frisbee, on the nightstand.

My memory had packed up and gone. My brain was made of fuzz. Reading, even watching movies on television, demanded too much from me.

My skin blistered. I bruised everywhere. I bled from tender places. My teeth hurt and one cracked and had to be pulled. My mouth was full of sores. I didn't want to eat because of the nausea, and when I did, the acid pain in my abdomen afterward doubled me over. Each morning I found myself awake but unable to summon the energy to get out of bed. I accused Larry of having sucked my blood during the night.

Nothing could be planned. There was no future; there was only the endless, shallow now. I was dissolving, bit by bit. Not just my body, but my soul. My interest in life, my zest, my love for family, for hiking, for writing. My desire to be a good mother, to finish my novel, to care about anything bigger than the war zone of my body. I was no longer a whole person. I was no longer me.

I prepared a cache of leftover meds that I secreted away, a motley jumble of drugs carefully preserved in case the day came when I needed to swallow them all at once.

17. TRYING

I didn't know when my mother began drinking. Maybe after she married my father. She had told me that when my father got angry in those early days he wouldn't speak to her for weeks. I could only imagine those first years between them, complicated, no doubt, by his own upbringing. His parents had always told us grandkids they were farmers from Austria, an area that had been part of the Austro-Hungarian Empire, but today actually lay within the borders of Poland. They had little schooling and had emigrated separately in their late teens, met and married in the United States, my grandfather nine years the elder. I remembered eating dinner at my grandparents' small kitchen table when I was ten or eleven and hearing my grandfather ask Antonina, my grandmother, for the mashed potatoes. Though he could easily have reached them himself, I passed him the bowl. He shook his head and refused to take it. My grandmother had to get up from her chair, take the potatoes, walk around the table, and serve him.

My grandfather had ruled my grandmother as if she were his slave. Who knows if she agreed when he decided they would move away from their daughter in Pennsylvania to go live with their son and his bride in Florida. Though hale and only in his early fifties, my grandfather believed my father, still in his twenties, should support his parents. Maybe that's when my father started drinking.

Perhaps it was genetic and my parents were already active alcoholics when they met. If not, there were enough probable causes afterward: her three miscarriages; his WWII experience in the Pacific; her war at home with their young son, fending off would-be stand-ins for my father, wondering if and in what shape he would return; the dysentery that never quite left him when he did come back; his harshness toward Little Bill who was too much like the mother he knew and not enough like the strange man he didn't; their constant moves for his career; the birth of a daughter with Downs; my father's subsequent nervous breakdown; my mother's insistence that despite what the doctors said, she would keep Cindy at home instead of institutionalizing her; my mother's risking another Downs baby, again contrary to doctors' counsel. I didn't know whether my father had wanted to tempt fate with another child or not, but I do know her pregnancy resulted in my birth and my father's vasectomy, a procedure used at the time chiefly to prevent reproduction by the insane, criminal, or perverse.

Both my parents had guts and determination and brains, but they were far more afflicted by the difficulties in their lives than they allowed themselves to admit. I tried not to make the same mistake.

Ironically, though I didn't have alcoholism, I quit even my few glasses of wine each week. A wise old oncologist had recommended abstention because alcohol consisted of liquid sugar. Tumors loved sugar.

Cancer had taught me another thing. I needed to understand my body better. I had to *listen* and slow down rather than bull my way through pain. If I didn't, I knew hiking would become the next sport I'd have to cross off my list.

I felt gratitude, even some admiration, for the scarred, depleted, crooked body I inhabited. Chemo symptoms lingered and I faced five years of treatment with Tamoxifen, but even as I raged and despaired and foundered during the final weeks of chemotherapy, one thing saved me. It wasn't my love of life or work or the mountains or even Larry—I simply had not been able to abandon Casey. I could not consign my daughter to growing up without a mother.

Six years after her death, I still sometimes reached for the phone to call my own mother. But she was gone and the closest thing I could find to being mothered, the best way I had of nurturing myself after the battering rams of cancer and treatment, lay in the mountains. The White Mountains pulled at my heart. They would keep me alive for Casey. I relied on them now for much more than opportunities to find clarity, prove my worth, and succeed.

But no matter how much my spirit longed to be hiking, my body had other ideas. Tendons blasted by chemo and now Tamoxifen, dried up, grew brittle, and hurt. More importantly, they were a prescription for injury. Acupuncture, Reiki, and a monthly massage, despite their expense were no longer *alternative* treatments. When Cathy and I put together a program designed to get me back up a 4000-Footer, we added these visits to my strength and cardio workouts. We also included a daily regimen of stretching with icing afterward to reduce inflammation and pain.

I went to a Pain Management Center for my still-recovering wrist and hand. I joined Healthworks Fitness Center for women. I signed up for a class nearby, Yoga for Specific Needs, though I often lay on my mat with my eyes closed while class went on around me, too drained to do anything else. Once, an instructor leaned down to whisper kindly, "Don't worry." She smoothed my right shoulder onto the mat from where it curled forward. "It took me five years to fully recover from breast cancer." She meant well, I could feel her kindliness pour over me like a warm blanket, but her words felt like blows. I wouldn't survive if I had to wait five years to find myself atop a big mountain.

I kept doing all these things. I wasn't hopeful, exactly. I was just doing what Cathy kept me focused on, what one friend called "the Cheryl thing"—putting one foot in front of the other, trusting something good would emerge from the effort.

During a session with Cathy, I got back on the Nordic Track, a machine that mimicked the motions of cross-country skiing. As I stood on the wooden slats and stared down at my scrawny legs, I yelped, "I've lost muscle mass!"

"Never mind," Cathy said. "I'm going to train you like an Olympic athlete."

I whipped my head toward her. "I can't—"

"What I mean by that is we'll start out slow and easy." Not a concept I associated with Olympic athletes. "If ten means going as fast as you can go, aim for a level four. We'll do splits: a minute on then a thirty-second rest. Two minutes on, thirty-seconds rest. Three minutes, and so on. Got it?"

My chemo brain didn't get it at all. But I trusted Cathy to guide me through. I grabbed the hand straps. "Go," she told me.

After six minutes, sweating and shaking, I wanted to stop, but Cathy encouraged me to continue to ten. Though my legs and arms trembled, I was euphoric. "Major milestone," Cathy cheered. "Great job!"

After she left, my hands and wrists ached too much to journal on the computer. I had to ice my right arm, both wrists, and my right knee. I decided to do even shorter workouts. But I'd keep going.

The next day, I headed out for a Porter, just one. I needed to know what I could do. The smell of scorched steel and piney cleanser greeted me like an old friend. To my delight, I managed two slow Porters, the extra one really giving me a lift. I didn't let myself dwell on the days when I did nine Porters. I made up a little tune. *Healthy*, I sang to myself, *I'm getting oh so healthy.*

By March, Kate sometimes joined me for my four Porters, twice a week. When Junie and I went for Fresh Ponds, she sometimes came along, determined to keep up her strength. Besides my own fear of a recurrence, only one thing blighted the green world of my healing: Kate's news. A mass had appeared on her pelvis and she was back in chemotherapy. Ovarian cancer had returned.

We spent as much time together as we could manage, for both our sakes. Unlike most of her first time through, chemo now pummeled her to the ground. I began a slow upward spiral as she headed back into the maw. Facing cancer had changed us. We were much more direct with one another now. When I told her I wasn't like those amazing women who, after treatment, volunteered to help other cancer victims, Kate laughed and shook her head. She hadn't been either. "There's a part of me that wants to run from anyone with cancer," I confessed to my cancer-ridden best friend.

Kate understood. "I felt the same way. Everything about cancer took me back to a place I wanted to escape." We both nodded, rueful and sad. She leaned forward to put a hand on my knee, tears glazing her eyes. "I wish I'd been a better friend during your treatment. I wish I'd done more for you."

I couldn't lie. Those long months without her, I had missed her and gotten pissed off and then missed her again. But what I replied was also true. "It doesn't matter now. I'm okay." I didn't need to say the rest—that she was not okay, that there was no assurance I really was okay—we spoke cancer shorthand now. She knew what I meant. We smiled at each other, best we could, through the tears that still came too frequently.

Cancer affected my work. After chemo I tried to continue my novel, but it was as if my writing gears had been buried in sand. I couldn't find the right voice again, or the tone. Chemo brain was a problem, too. I stared at the piles of pages, several hundred of them, utterly overwhelmed. I didn't remember all the characters. I couldn't retain why they did what they did or why I'd invented them in the first place.

After weeks of trying to carry on with the book, I quit. I had never let myself give up on difficult tasks before cancer, but now I did. "We're out of here, Junie girl," I told the dog as we left my office. I grabbed plastic bags for her and water for me and headed over to Fresh Pond.

As my dominant arm and hand continued to be weak and swollen, I raised the issue with my physical therapist. She explained that losing lymph nodes in my armpit meant the lymph in that area moved sluggishly. She added that my arm—with its popped-out, stringy tendons and dimpled flesh—might never again be as strong as the other one.

The Wellness Center, where I still attended support group, hosted a lecture by a lymphedema expert. She advised women who'd had armpit lymph nodes removed not to lift heavy objects. Too much strain could lead to elephantine swelling. To prove her point, she showed us slides. Gasps rose from the audience.

She'd treated women who'd gotten lymphedema from a burn on the surgery arm, too many mosquito bites, or just a fever. Gardening, the thing that gave me such pleasure, was rife with thorns, bugs, and dirt that could trigger the condition. Her list of taboos went on: saunas, steam rooms, whirlpool; repetitive motions like swimming, tennis, and rowing. At least she didn't mention hiking. I sat there with my face frozen and my heart banging. My hand and arm had swelled off and on since surgery. I already wore a compression sleeve and glove at the computer. Was the Nordic Track machine verboten? Had cross-country skiing, my foremost winter delight, become the newest sport I had to give up?

I tuned back in to hear someone ask about breast prostheses. The speaker paused. "Some doctors think wearing the prosthesis is a good thing."

My surgeon did. She said, especially with scoliosis, I needed the weight of the prosthesis—and it was surprisingly heavy—to balance my spine.

"But," our expert continued, "if it were me, I would *not* wear a prosthesis or, for that matter, even a bra. There's another nest of lymph nodes near the top of the shoulder. Bra straps cut into them, especially with a prosthesis. I wouldn't risk it." The whole room stilled.

Wearing a prosthesis became an issue I never resolved. Much like zigzagging down Tecumseh to avoid lightning, no course seemed safe. As I had then, I alternated between two options, wearing the prosthesis and going without it, trying to escape the perils of either.

That night after Casey was in bed, I told Larry about the lecture. Only as I recited the litany of potential triggers did the penny drop. If a bra strap and prosthesis were risky, what about a backpack?

18. ICE BREAKER

Since cancer, I got anxious whenever Casey was too long out of sight, but I let her, now almost eleven, return to summer camp in Maine. When Larry and I arrived two weeks later to pick her up, we discovered a changed girl. She barely let me hug her before remonstrating, "Calm down, Mom!" As she ran around telling friends good-bye, she hugged not just girls but boys. I noticed a thin blond shadow of a boy following her. She told us, "I don't want to leave."

Whoa.

She'd written articles for the camp newspaper and started using antiperspirant. At home she loaded dishes into the dishwasher without being asked. She wanted to get her ears pierced. Even her tone changed. When I described the new plants I'd put in the garden, the person I still thought of as my little girl said politely, "That's great, Mom."

Just as I began to adjust to this surprisingly mature young person, I found her watching Disney's *The Aristocats* video. I sat next to her on the sofa as sweat dripped down my sides from a Tamoxifen-induced hot flash. "Honey, are you sad about not being at camp?"

She paused the video. "No-o."

I asked her how camp was different this summer, what she had liked about it and who were her new friends. She turned the movie off. Though she didn't say so, I could tell she was pleased the subject was being given its due. There was something weighty about camp this year. It had stirred something in her, something that loomed large. "Next summer," she declared, "I want to go for the whole month."

I told myself her independence was a good thing. Age appropriate. More importantly, it meant she no longer worried about me. During the school year, she confessed, she had watched the classroom door each day with her stomach aching, waiting for someone to walk in and tell her that her mother had just died.

I was glad she felt freer. But I still worried whenever Casey or Larry left me. Death might no longer sit on my shoulder, but it hadn't yet moved out of my house. It had also killed my novel. I could only write pieces I knew I had time to finish.

To celebrate my one-year anniversary of surviving cancer, my family, together with a friend of Casey's, took a trip. Northern Spain was every bit as wonderful as I remembered from my junior year abroad. I still needed a sleeping pill each night to be able to take on the next day, but the girls were my best medicine, cooking up wild fantasies and aligning themselves against Larry and me in what must have been wonderful relief for our only child. We ate tapas, enjoyed Miró's wacky images, and applauded Flamenco dancers. In the Pyrenees, we did a couple of short hikes, picnicking beside a royal-blue lake. We finished the trip on the beaches of the Costa Brava, soaking up the sun, the Mediterranean, and the healthy salt-laden air. For two weeks, I gave myself permission to feel completely cancer-free. I didn't wonder if my cancer had recurred and no one had yet found it. I didn't write post cards to my friends in support group. I didn't worry about Kate. I didn't shove the past sixteen months away as if they'd never happened, but I let myself move on.

This was part of the process, support group had insisted. This phase, of being alive and loving it, thinking about life questions rather than death questions, of going places and having fun instead of being ill—this, they said, I had earned. With courage, love, and generosity they pushed me gently out of the group. I had only to look around the circle of their faces, or into the eyes of my best friend next door, to seize hope with both hands and ride the wave of health as long as I could.

As summer waned, we took advantage of Waterville Valley for the Labor Day weekend. Saturday morning was glorious, dry and 60°F while the sun peeked in and out of happy white clouds. Since the day was so clearly designed for hiking, Larry and I chose a new trail to explore, a five-mile loop that led to East Pond and Little East Pond and gained only 1000 feet.

Except that 1000 feet was 1000 feet and, though the trail was lovely, I struggled. I huffed and puffed and slowed distressingly whenever we encountered a hill. After lunch beside East Pond, Casey continued her independent streak, taking Juniper and marching far ahead of Larry and me. Both ponds glittered like sapphires. Knowing the fabulous weather was predicted to continue, back at the car I blurted, "Let's do a 4000-Footer tomorrow!"

They'd never climbed a 4000-Footer before, but we'd been taking Casey up and down Welch and Dickey since she was five and she played soccer and skied. Larry worked out at the gym and ran, but the truth was he never had to train like I or other people did. Though I did work out now, two years and cancer had happened since I'd trained for a serious climb. I was nowhere near as strong as I'd been when Kate and I did our last 4000-Footers, Lincoln and Lafayette. Nor had I organized and prepared the way I always did. But, we'd done those hikes in the Pyrenees, two personal Sherpas stood in front of me, and the weather would be a climber's dream. How could I not seize the day?

Casey was initially disappointed to learn Mt. Osceola, the mountain I admired daily from our apartment windows, required only 6.4 miles round trip, a number that made me sink into the sofa. Ever since her friend had complained in Barcelona about a 10-mile hike with her parents the year before, Casey had gotten competitive about mileage. To pique my daughter's interest, I confessed Osceola had another summit, East Peak, that could increase the distance to 8.4 miles. I cautioned her that it was extremely unlikely I could manage two 4000-Footers.

But Casey wasn't the only competitive family member. The day before I'd been most put out to learn that our Waterville neighbors, Zoe (who had worried about Junie and me on Tecumseh) and her partner Lindsey had climbed Osceola a few weeks before. Though I knew it made no sense, I felt they'd left me behind.

I was tired of being left behind.

Especially regarding Osceola. I'd hankered after this mountain, the highest peak in the region, ever since we'd bought our place here. On the bus ride up to the ski area in winter, I gazed out at massive Osceola where two long slides on her flank formed a "V" that whitened with snow, branding the mountain with a very female cleft. To my eye, this made her the matriarch of Waterville Valley.

Osceola was the only 4000-Footer left in Waterville that I hadn't climbed. The bible described an "impressive . . . narrow, steep-sided ridge." Words like this, I'd learned the hard way, could be code for wicked damn hard. But the book also promised pretty good footing and moderate grades, with only "scattered steep pitches."

The next morning burned blue and clear, full of fall crispness. On Mt. Osceola Trail, Casey immediately took the lead. Being on the soccer team had improved her wind. Junie danced along just ahead of or behind her, sometimes even, much to Casey's annoyance, between her legs. I hadn't yet figured out how to avoid the risk of lymphedema carrying my gear, so Larry shouldered my load.

I wore a fleece but soon warmed up enough to yank it off and tie it around my waist. Once Casey was out of sight, I confided to Larry how much it galled me to have to give up East Peak, knowing someday I'd have to struggle up this trail again.

"You'll be stronger then," he said reasonably. Already I was asking him to slow down. My thighs had knotted into distraught bundles of overworked muscle from yesterday and my joints ached, despite all the ibuprofen I'd swallowed.

I gave Larry my water bottle to hold. After a mile, the camera in my pocket weighed as much as a bowling ball and I gave him that, too. Half a mile later, I stuffed the fleece from my waist into his pack. If I could have, I'd have climbed inside along with it.

The trail, but for a few lovely bits covered with pine needles, was rock-studded and root-tangled, typical for a 4000-Footer, but not what I had fantasized. We had to lift our legs up over stones and watch every step. My legs trembled. Sometimes I lurched along as if I'd drunk my breakfast. My muscles seemed to have forgotten how to catch and release. On this popular trail everybody passed me, even little kids. My left heel shot pain through my calf.

Larry climbed first so he could lean down, arms outstretched, to haul me up. I began to think the summit would never appear. I began to think if I achieved the summit I'd never make it back down. I began to think there was no summit.

By now I was grabbing onto trees to pull myself up. I quit stopping for breaks, too afraid I wouldn't get going again. For the last steep pitches, I had to yank my legs forward with my hands. Most of the time now, Larry kept an arm around me.

Fifteen agonizing minutes later, we found Casey coming down the trail carrying Juniper in her arms. "Where have you been? You took forever!" They'd reached the peak, waited, then come to look for us. Her palpable disgust with our slowness made me smile. She remembered the hiker I used to be.

Casey and Junie summited first, then Larry hauled me over the top. I stood there breathing and shaking. After I waved them on, they wandered off to explore the broad ledges and take in the view. I stood there recovering and thinking about Kate. Like thunderous Tecumseh with Junie, this was a 4000-Footer without her. I longed to hug her and high-five one another. Moreover, if she were here, for sure she would live.

Once my legs steadied, I crossed the summit to the nearest edge, expecting to see a pretty view of skinny Waterville Valley, like the views from Welch and Dickey, just from a different orientation. I was wrong, delightfully wrong. The vista was so much more than that. Gazing eastward, I marveled at Tripyramid, the brute size of it, the scar of the scary North Slide we'd avoided. Words rolled through my weary brain. *Majestic. Powerful. Humbling.* I turned slowly to soak up the landscape, allowing myself to believe that though sometimes nearly carried by Larry, I had actually summited Osceola. I'd made it. Without months of preparation and planning. Post cancer!

Well away from the edge, I absorbed the northeastern view, inhaling in wonder. Before me spread wave after wave of mountain. I counted no fewer than seven ranges, each surging behind another. They stretched to the horizon, emerald-blue, and, as they marched farther away, shadowy cerulean shapes that touched the deeper blue of sky. A puff of smoke rose above a peak that had to be Washington and the cog railway that chugged to its summit. I felt caught up in the motion of those rocky waves. I wanted to join Matanna there, in my true home. I could take off into those mountains, up and down and over until I knew each and every peak. I could let go of my complicated city life and live in the mountains, exploring them all day long and sleeping in them at night. The vast astonishing beauty caused, along with the joy, an ache. I was so small and there was so much to absorb, to feel, to be. The mountains called for grandeur and I was only one person and, at that, a lesser version of who I was before. If only I were a more tolerant, better person. I longed for everyone to experience this breaking open of the spirit that was at once nourishing, illuminating, and sweetly painful. Why couldn't everyone bathe in the heady, healthy liquor of this majesty we could take no credit for but could only lean into and applaud? Here a world existed in which all things small and large, mobile and rooted, oxygen giving and oxygen absorbing, had a place in a balanced, sacred whole.

I was on such a mountain high I didn't even know I was high. I felt certain that if everyone could spend time in the largesse of the mountains it would change the fabric of society. I was ready to hug all the strangers on Osceola, invoke their promise to safeguard this place, and take the lessons garnered here back home to share. We could organize . . .

"Mom!"

The sound of Casey's voice startled me. Deep in my mountain reverie, I'd forgotten she existed.

"We're starving!" She beckoned me to where she, Larry, and Juniper sat beside the open pack.

I creaked over, bent down, and kissed the top of her head, inhaling her sweaty girl smell. I picked up Juniper and held her curly warm body close. Dank with mud, she squirmed to get down. I sat by Larry and put my hand on his khaki-clad thigh. "I love you all," I said. "I just love you so much."

Larry kissed me. Casey rolled her eyes and bit into a sandwich. Juniper whined for her treats.

Until the food hit my system, I hadn't understood how low on fuel I was. In my indoor life, I'd grown away from the concept of food as fuel, but today the need to eat to keep the engines and ropes and pulleys of the body running, rocked me. Larry poured Junie kibble and a bowl of water. As the rest of us munched chicken sandwiches, cookies, and apples, Casey pointed. "Look, Mom. East Peak isn't so far."

I looked. "I'm too tired, sweetheart. Thanks." Now that I'd sat down, a heavy blanket of exhaustion descended. I wanted to lie down and sleep until a helicopter came. "I know you're trying to help, but I just can't do it."

"Yes, you can. You know you can. You got up here, didn't you?"

I kept chewing. Swallowed water. I hated appearing weak, especially to my daughter. I'd done it too often these last eighteen months.

"You know when we get down you'll wish you'd gone. Just think. You could put *two* pins on your map." She flung an arm around Juniper who lay by her side. "Junie and I'll help you."

I took my lunch pills. Tamoxifen, of course. Also Effexor, an anti-depressant that in low doses helped combat the Tamoxifen-induced sweats and temperature swings. The anti-depressant part didn't hurt either. Then I took a handful of supplements recommended by the nurses who called from my health insurer, each of whom had also survived breast cancer: a baby aspirin a day because chemotherapy tended to weaken the heart, multi-vitamins because after chemo the body had trouble absorbing nutrients from food, calcium pills and Vitamin D because the bones got whacked, fish oils for the heart, and coenzyme Q10 and chromium picolinate, for reasons I couldn't recall. As I gulped them all down in one swallow, it occurred to me that if I didn't make it as a writer I could work for drug runners as a mule.

I glanced speculatively at Casey. Maybe she was right. Certainly she was right that I would hate not doing East Peak.

My ambivalence irked Larry. He knew how I'd struggled on the way up. "This is a really bad idea," he said, pulling out the map to show us, his finger tracing the trail. "This is not some easy ridge walk. See that steep descent from where we are now? Look at those contours! Then we climb up for a whole mile. Afterward, you have to do all that in reverse just to get back here. After which there will still be 3.2 miles down to the car!"

I levered myself up. I had to bounce my knees up and down a bit before I was sure they'd hold. The hump of East Peak stood a little below us and disconcertingly far away. My jaw clenched. He was right it was too much, but what straightened my spine was that Casey believed in me. "Let's give it a shot," I said. "It'll be an experiment. We can always turn around and come back."

Larry blew out a breath, exasperated. He was both concerned for me and too rational to understand that, from the moment I decided the state of the universe would improve if everyone could visit mountains, I'd left reason behind. It was never reason that got me up, or down, a mountain. Sometimes it had been willpower or obstinacy. But today, it was heart.

Almost immediately after we set off for East Peak, the trail dove sharply downward in a rocky scramble that— I didn't admit to my family—triggered my fear of heights. I took deep, slow breaths. When Larry descended in front of me, he didn't say so but I knew he figured from there he could catch me if I fell. I discovered it helped. His height blocked my view of the sheer drop.

He and Casey alternated carrying Juniper over boulders that her legs weren't long enough to leap. Mercifully, a few flat stretches appeared on the trail between the vertical descents. Then we arrived at the chimney. Another V-shaped cleft, a narrow one, long and steep, that we somehow had to get down. The back of the cleft and the two rock faces of the V came together like three sides of a fireplace chimney and were nearly smooth, with few rocks or roots to grab hold of. My throat tightened. Just peering into the chimney gave me vertigo. Climbing down would require hands, knees, elbows, toeholds, a strong back, and balance. A trip or a fall would be serious.

A spur trail around the chimney was well travelled. This looked pretty inviting to me, but Casey refused. She wanted to test herself. "You go around if you want," she told me.

But then I'd be separated from her and I'd gnaw myself to bits worrying about her. Besides, how could I be less brave than my baby? There was nothing for it but to stick my legs into the chimney that I wished we could magically pop through like Santa Claus. The three of us eased ourselves downward searching for toe and handholds. Larry went first, carrying the backpack and tucking Junie under one arm like a football. I jumped into second place so that if necessary I could cushion Casey's fall. We slowly made our way down the steep sides of the chimney in a crouch, clinging to rock with our fingers when we could, pressing against the opposite rocky face with forearms or hands when the V narrowed.

I was no longer exhausted and weak—I was scared witless. Invigorated by terror. Perhaps Casey was too. She started to laugh. Then I laughed. We kept laughing, at the sheer thrill of the thing. And, in my case, laughing was better than crying. At the bottom of the chimney, we collapsed onto rocks until our hilarity subsided.

Next we climbed upward. Catching my breath was hard.

Raising my legs was hard. I told myself, *Any idiot can do a mile.* I didn't think about getting to the top. I didn't think about how I'd have to retrace these steps. I ventured no further into the future than picking out the next spot to land one boot, then the other. It was a very long mile.

We arrived at our second summit of the day, the apex of East Peak. There wasn't much there. We stood in woods with no view, at a point in the trail no different from any other but for the cairn that marked the top. For me, it was monumental. Larry snapped a picture of Casey and me standing by the cairn holding hands. Casey, my inspiration, gazed seriously into the camera, but I exulted, my face split by an enormous grin.

And then, as suddenly as the uplift of victory washed through me, it evaporated. I stood at the summit with no view and looked back across two years of fear and the slow, confused beginnings of recovery. I held Kate and Matanna with me in spirit, as well as the women in support group whom I loved and probably were dying. I was the lucky one, unbearably blessed. I'd traveled down into the abyss and back out again. Though battered and frailer than I liked to admit, here I stood, on a summit. I had to believe that if I'd made it this far, surely there was more life—more mountains—in my future.

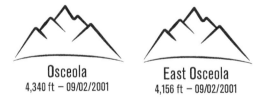

Osceola
4,340 ft – 09/02/2001

East Osceola
4,156 ft – 09/02/2001

19. HIGH AND LOW

It took weeks to recover from adding red pins number six and seven to my map of the Whites. Both calves developed tendonitis and I was depleted enough to spend half of each day in bed, where I daydreamed about the following spring's hiking. Kate, deep in chemotherapy, couldn't plan ahead. She lost weight and required blood transfusions. We told each other that the new drugs would do the trick, we just didn't know when.

Kate's decline and the zest from my Osceola victory forced me at last to look for a hiking partner, even a temporary one. At a parents' meeting at school, I studied Ginny, mother of one of Casey's classmates. Ginny was eight inches taller than I, athletic, and from California, all of which seemed promising. Over the years, I'd heard her identify herself as a feminist and talk about taking kids on hikes when she was a teacher. After the meeting, I sidled up to her and made small talk as I steeled myself to pop the question. As soon as I asked if she'd be my exercise buddy, my mouth went dry. What if she said *no?* What if she said *yes* but we didn't get along and were stuck with each other? And how would Kate react?

"Sounds like fun," Ginny said in her open California way. "What do we do?"

She liked the form for training buddies that Cathy gave me and committed right away to working out together for six weeks. We began to meet on Monday afternoons, my weekday mornings being reserved for writing and writing classes. Up in my guestroom under the eaves, I sweated away on the Nordic Track while Ginny did yoga poses I wished I could imitate.

I told Kate I'd found a workout buddy. She didn't say much in response. I was surprised, but then, we were on different channels. During cancer, a person dialed to the death channel and the small things that mattered so much when tuned into the life channel lost importance. She may have been relieved I'd found someone else, or simply too sick to care.

Since my tendonitis precluded Porters, Cathy sent me to cross-train in the pool, a place I hadn't been for six years. Twice a week I swam laps again, though only twelve at a time. My arm and chest couldn't take any more. I added an aquatics class to the regimen.

When I described to Ginny my quest for The 48 and how Cathy and I set goals, Ginny said we should create an event for ourselves. So vital herself, she encouraged me to focus on vitality rather than mere recovery. We decided to attempt a 4000-Footer in May, blasting months past the six-week term of our buddy contract.

Did I feel guilty moving on, training for a hike without Kate? Down to my toes. As I used to tell Casey when she was a toddler, "I feel two things at once." Ginny couldn't be Kate, the woman who tackled the 4000-Footers with me shoulder-to-shoulder, who had taken the winter hiking course, and who sweated through Porters and training and planning. Ginny and I weren't deep friends with years of shared confidences. She hadn't gone with me to pick out my grand-dog. My daughter didn't love her like an aunt. But she was hale and available and willing, and she would get me back to bagging peaks for success and to the mountains that gave me so much more.

Though my age, Ginny didn't have a single gray hair. She skied double-black diamond trails. Now she wanted to get back into hiking and I was grateful. Ginny worked out daily, rising at 5:00 a.m. to squeeze exercise into her busy life as a choral conductor, musician, singer, wife, and mother. I didn't have to cajole her into exercising—she was the direction in which I needed to go. In fact, I aimed to be just like her, strong and hearty. Had she been the least bit snooty about her prowess, our buddy training wouldn't have worked. It was only her generosity and upbeat attitude that made an alliance possible.

∼

My choice of Mt. Moosilauke, a 4000-Footer that stood west of the main pack of the Whites, pleased Ginny. The views from the top were reputed to be magnificent. I picked a loop trail 7.2 miles long with 2450 feet of elevation gain, twice the height of the Empire State Building. This didn't bother Ginny, but I gulped, hoping the hike wouldn't be too hard without Larry to haul me along. I needed to make serious use of the winter to get my body ready.

Yet despite weekly acupuncture for my immune system, I caught every virus. Continuing tendonitis required PT appointments during which Dexamethasone, the same steroid used during chemo, got pushed into my calves by electrolysis. The physical therapist gave me a stretching regimen that I added to the exercises I still did for my chest and right arm. Some weeks, pain forced me to ice arm, chest, and legs four times a day.

At least my writing life had revived. At a writer's workshop on Cape Cod, I met a woman who used a placement agency to help her get published. Once they accepted her as a client—they first needed to approve a sample of work—she paid them a fee every two months. Along with her check, she sent a short story that they proofread and formatted, then returned to her with a bunch of labels, each addressed to a different literary journal. Using the labels, she mailed a copy of her piece to each publication.

Why not? I asked myself. Winter and spring could be a time to rebuild not only my hiking, but also my writing muscles.

When the agency accepted me, the 2002 goals I set with Cathy included Ginny's and my hiking event, Moosilauke, and six writing events. Every two months, I had to ship off a piece of work—a piece of my soul—to a bunch of hard-eyed strangers. My goal was to make 2002 the year I became a published author, something I'd never attempted before and made my heart flutter.

My first writing event occurred February in the post office. Into the large-knuckled hands of a friendly postal clerk with brown sideburns, I deposited a pile of magazine-sized envelopes, each containing my short story, a cover letter, and a self-addressed, stamped envelope. At the last moment, when I should have been feeling excited and victorious, I couldn't let them go. "This is my first short story," I blurted. "I'm hoping one of these editors will publish it."

"Hey, good luck," he said, a benediction that allowed me to release the envelopes. I watched as he weighed each one and calculated the postage. Was I imagining it or was he treating them tenderly? I immediately developed a superstition that meant he had to be the one to receive every future batch.

Each day around lunchtime I lurked by the front door telling myself I was not waiting for the mail to arrive. The submission agency counseled patience, explaining that under-staffed and over-submitted literary magazines could take up to six months to respond. They advised me to expect a lot of impersonal rejection forms. Acceptance of a story that was decently written depended on whether it suited an editor's taste, her/his mood that day, what they had published on the subject in the last year, the size of their slush (unsolicited) pile, and whatever piece they might have read just before mine. Also sunspots. I didn't need an MBA to understand I sent out multiple submissions at once because we were playing a numbers game.

Roughly four weeks after my first writing event, my mailbox began to produce thin envelopes addressed to me in my own hand. The first five rejections were form letters, but one editor had scrawled, "Well-told story. Hope you'll submit again." The agency told me to treasure the comment; editors rarely took time to write anything and these two sentences could be the foundation of a great relationship. I tried to bend my mind around being glad to receive a rejection with seven hand-written words.

My self-addressed envelopes bearing rejection letters continued to arrive throughout April. Cathy, an athletic coach who understood and reinforced how success in one part of life encouraged success in other parts, reminded me this was just my first attempt at getting published, like a first race. I agreed, telling myself I'd have better luck with the next piece. But I was just blowing smoke. I knew I'd sent out my strongest story.

⟳

My sister had been deteriorating for a while, but I hadn't had the strength to face her. Now I was ready. In Texas, we'd visit with Bill and Mardy, their kids, and their families for a few days but first, Larry, Casey, and I travelled to Piney Ponds.

"Is that her?" Casey whispered. Cindy looked like a dried apple, wrinkled and hunched. Her hair needed cutting and had gone from salt and pepper to a shaggy silver mane. She had few teeth left that she had not ground to nubs or that hadn't been pulled to make room for the false teeth that Bill said she refused to wear. She ate only soft foods now, and her cheeks caved in.

Cindy smiled to see me and I hugged her fiercely as I kissed the top of her head. Then she asked, "What's your name again?"

The whole afternoon went like that. I kept touching her and hugging her and telling her I loved her, as if I could make up for the two years cancer had kept me away, as if she could remember me by feel.

When we took her out to dinner at a chain restaurant that her favorite caretaker said Cindy liked, the place and the idea of food seemed to revive her. By the time she finished eating, however, she looked bewildered. "Where's my home? Take me home." When her caretaker greeted Cindy at Piney Ponds after dinner, my sister rushed over and clung to her. From beneath the woman's arms, Cindy's faded brown eyes peered out at me as if afraid I would tear her away.

Kate, too, wasted away. The flesh melted from her bones the way my mother's had. When I visited her, I saw the two skeletal images, Kate and my mother, side by side. The whitened hair, the skin hanging from arms. The calves that were nothing but bone walking. The hollows beneath cheekbones, the enlargement of eyes. The fading. The pain. Losing Kate brought back the loss of my mother, the loss of my mother-in-law, of my father, as if each separate grief were tied to the next like the silk handkerchiefs magicians pulled from their pockets, a stream of sorrow that would only grow longer.

Sometimes I stood in my office and felt the slow pulse of Kate's presence from her house, fifty feet away. I wondered how it could possibly be right for me to feel joy when I knew that she was next door dying. Had I not been through cancer myself, had I not learned from the wise ones in support group who had survived so much how fleeting health could be and how precious, I could not have kept trying to relish my life as Kate lost hold of hers.

On a day she felt strong enough, we walked arm-in-arm to our favorite cozy restaurant down the street for lunch. She told me that, despite her condition, she wanted one last trip to Florida to see her siblings and their families, to say good-bye to her mother. Her dying wasn't a separate topic; it was folded up into our conversation like the pleats in our napkins. She wanted my opinion on which cemetery to be buried in. I learned that my best friend who had researched for years before writing a word of her children's book, had her epitaph nailed. *Lucky mother, wife, writer, hiker, friend.*

After wiping my face, I said I was glad she felt free to talk with me about death. It made me feel closer to her than ever.

"Cancer does that," she said. "Doesn't it?" Her face, despite being emaciated, shone. Kate was no longer the quiet, aloof woman who resorted to witticism or changed the subject when the emotional content got heavy. She was accepting and unafraid. She was transformed.

"A high school friend came over yesterday," she continued. "She helped me sort through stuff to give away." She poured both of us more chai. "I've got a pile of hiking things I want to go through with you."

I absorbed this as the body blow—and the gift—that it was. We walked home with our arms around each other. At her driveway, I mustered the courage to ask something I'd been avoiding for weeks.

My pulse beat in my throat. It was one thing to listen to her talk about it and quite another to broach her death myself, especially when I, another cancer person, would remain after her. Alive. "I have a request." I got that far and stopped. We faced each other in the shade of the big pine beside her driveway. I swallowed. "I don't know if you can do it or not. It's . . . big."

She waited calmly, as if to say, *Like our conversation at lunch wasn't?*

"If you can . . . only if it's okay with you . . . I'd really like to hear you say . . . if it's true . . . say it's all right for me to keep doing The 48, even though—" I broke off to search her face, terrified in equal measure that I was hurting her and that she wouldn't be able to give me her permission.

She started to cry, and I hated myself. I reached out for her and we hugged, our stomachs and chests bumping.

Her voice trembled into the hair above my ear. "Yes. Yes, of course, I want you to go on hiking." She sobbed outright now, her shoulders shaking. "I need you to take me with you." We held one another so tightly I could feel the sobs move her ribs up and down. "I want you to do it. Hike so it can keep you healthy and strong . . . like you've kept me."

———

In early May, when I harvested the day's catch of the thin envelopes I'd grown to abhor, I was prepared for the usual rejection. I had to read the letter twice. *The Distillery*, a handsome literary journal published in Tennessee, wanted my story! It didn't matter that neither I, nor anyone I knew, had ever heard of them or that the payment for my untold hours of work would be two free copies of the journal. I screamed with delight, jumping up and down in a circle in the front hallway.

———

For our anniversary, Larry had reserved an inn in Princeton, Massachusetts, for the weekend, knowing I wouldn't want to be more than an hour's drive from Kate, but neither of us had expected her to fail so quickly. Since she insisted we keep our reservation, we cut our stay to one night.

As soon as we got back to Cambridge the next evening, I rushed next door, anxious to see Kate. Though it wasn't yet dark, Tom told me she'd already gone to bed. It was all I could do not to ask if I could peep in, make sure she was breathing. I had trouble sleeping that night, knowing I'd missed one of the precious days Kate and I had left together.

Sunday morning, Casey was still at a friend's where she'd spent the weekend and I was headed to my car to pick her up when Tom walked down their driveway to put trash in their barrel. He came over and put his arm around my shoulder. "When you're ready, you should come see Kate. She's taken a turn for the worse."

Standing there on a sunny day in May, I asked what that meant. Because I couldn't ask *How much time does she have?*

He explained that because of organ failure she now had septicemia. Their sons had flown in that morning. I started to run to my car and he added, "And Cheryl? Just come in."

Wide-eyed, I started the car. I could have called Larry at his office and asked him to get Casey. I could have asked her friend's mom to keep Casey longer, but my hands shook and my mind wasn't working. I just knew I had to hurry. I drove very carefully, very fast.

After dropping Casey at home, I raced up Kate's porch steps, my footsteps on the wood announcing me as they had so many times before. Tom rushed down the hall from their bedroom. "The boys are in with her, " he said.

"Should I wait?"

"No. I don't think you can."

Kate's other best friend, Pauline, stood by Kate's feet and her two sons filled the narrow aisle between the hospital bed and the bed their mother could no longer lie in.

I'd never done this before, been near someone so close to death. I joined Pauline at the foot of the bed and we silently did Reiki on Kate, touching her feet. Tom came in and moved his sons away to make room for me. I was aghast and appreciative at once. Surely they belonged there more than I? But I stepped forward into the space they'd opened. I leaned down. In the bed, her eyes were half-open, her fingers drawn back like claws. She twitched restlessly. I wasn't sure she knew I was there. I reached out to lightly hold her hand.

Everyone else could hear me and I longed for privacy, but this was my one chance. I knelt down on the floor beside her to be closer to eye level. "Kate," I said urgently. "It's me, Cheryl. I'm here. Oh, God, Kate." I hadn't prepared for this moment. My words should have been precious, perfect, eternal. I couldn't think at all.

"I'm so grateful you're my friend," I told her. "So deeply grateful. I've learned so much from you. I will miss you . . . so much." I tried to stifle sobs so I could get the words out. "I'll take you with me on the 4000-Footers. I promise. I'm praying for you to have an easy crossing. I won't ever forget you, my friend." I squeezed her hand. "Kate. I love you, Kate."

As distracted by pain and as far inside herself as she was, she turned her head to me. She looked right at me, maybe seeing me, aware now of who I was, at least I thought so. From her throat came this sound I'd never heard before, something worse than a gurgle or a groan. *Arrrggh*, she told me. Three times.

"I know," I whispered. "I know you love me." Her effort was so enormous it suggested she had waited for me to say good-bye.

I kissed her cheek. Kissed her hand. Forced myself to let go of her hand. Touched her shoulder. Moved back to her feet so her boys and husband had room to be with her.

Minutes later, blood spurted from her mouth and she was gone.

PART TWO

"The best remedy for those who are afraid, lonely or unhappy is to go outside . . . nature brings solace in all troubles."

—Anne Frank

20. BALD PLACE

No one is home when I walk over to Kate's yard and sit on one of the weathered Adirondack chairs where we so often collapsed after Porters. The tender June morning smells sweet. Bees hum. It's sixteen days since Kate died and the hurting goes on.

In half an hour, Ginny, who has become my steadfast workout partner and friend, will pick me up to drive to New Hampshire. We'll spend the night in Waterville Valley, like Kate and I used to, so we can start early tomorrow on Moosilauke, our 4000-Footer.

I get up from the chair and wander the yard. Remembering how carefully Kate designed the plantings a few years back, I touch the pink dogwood that was one of her favorites, press my cheek against the peeling bark of the birch trees that reminded her of Maine and New Hampshire. I don't realize I'm searching for anything in particular until I squat down and pick two purple violets, sweet and lightly scented. I twine their stems together and tuck them into a pocket.

〜

Ginny drives to spare my right knee and desiccated tendons. Because she's not Kate, I take out a yellow pad and a pen. I need to know what Ginny wants from this hike. Remembering the goals and fears I'd talked over with Cathy, I begin. "I want to get to the top and complete my eighth 4000-Footer."

Ginny leans back in the driver's seat. "Wow," she says. Her awed look makes me laugh. With her skiing, daily workouts, and western hiking experience, she'll most likely climb circles around me.

I reel off my other goals. *Avoid new injuries. Enjoy Ginny's company.* That last one is a bit of a question mark. I like Ginny, but we've never hiked together. I pause. "When we talked about it last week you—remarkably—said we'd be taking Kate with us. I'm not sure what that means to you, but for me, well, I'd like some time to hike alone to think about her. Talk to her."

"I get that." Ginny reaches over to turn down Mozart. "I could think about my Dad then." She glances at me in the passenger seat. "You know, it's really helpful for me to hear about your journey with Kate." Her father is dying of cancer.

The insides of my nose sting. Since cancer, everything— surprises, generosity, even relief—incites tears. Nothing like asking someone to hike with you, carry extra stuff, and then leave them alone on the trail. "Thank you, buddy." We have slipped into calling each other "buddy" ever since we filled out Cathy's buddy forms.

Now it's Ginny's turn. Her foremost goal is to enjoy the splendor from the top. "Views are my favorite thing."

I mull that over. Views are gifts, but I also like the woods, wild flowers, wildlife or signs of them, creeks, streams, rocks, lichen, even mushrooms and other fungi. In fact, I'm hard pressed to think of any scenery I'm not interested in on a hike.

Ginny continues. "I'd like us to do a silent meditation together, too. Maybe ten minutes? Just to be in the moment, aware of everything around us. When I'm talking, it's hard to appreciate where I am."

Next I scribble down our fears. My biggest worries are that my Achilles' tendons won't allow me to make it to the top, that the hike will damage them further, and that I'll fall and break something again. I admit, aloud, that I'm afraid Ginny will jet past me and that both she and I will lose patience with my slowness. Weather is my final concern. I really don't want to get shut out of this hike that will help me bear my grief.

Despite the fact that this is her first 4000-Footer and her first hike in the Whites, Ginny's only fear is bad weather. I admire her confidence.

We relax into silence, more connected to one another now and more alert, I hope, to potential issues. I've forewarned Ginny that we'll return to our list to debrief post hike. She applauds the idea. I'm thrilled that using my individual process with another hiker is going so well.

After dinner, in the living room of my apartment in Waterville Valley, Ginny arrays her hiking clothes and gear on the sofa. She's brought some things on the list I gave her, but she's also missing some. I'm perplexed. If somebody figures out a list of stuff necessary for a trip and gives it to me, I follow the list. Who doesn't follow a list? The electricity of our mutual irritation charges the air.

I mumble that I can probably loan her stuff. I go into my bedroom closet and dig through the bag of gear I accumulated with Kate. I pull out a Mylar emergency blanket, a small flashlight, a 96-ounce water bottle, blister prevention pads, a long-sleeved polypro shirt, and a whistle for blowing the three blasts that signal an emergency in the mountains. With these things piled around me on the floor, I sit back on my heels. Is it fear that makes me follow lists? Probably. They make me feel safer, more in control. It dawns on me that I tend to plan for the worst and then expect the best. Ginny appears to expect the best, too, but where's her margin for error? I can't help thinking Kate never shirked from packing our list.

In the living room, I hand Ginny the gear. She asks several times if I'm sure she can borrow it. Does she not want to add weight or is she being nice? Then comes the moment I've dreaded. To avoid risking lymphedema carrying a backpack, I've bought a hip pack and will wear a khaki fishing vest loaded with pockets. Both vest and pack are filled to bursting. I hand Ginny my rain jacket, extra water bottle, and the First Aid kit.

At the look on my face, she says gently, "I know you hate not being able to carry them yourself. But I'd rather hike with you and carry a little extra than have you not be able to come."

I hug her hard, and blink a lot. I don't want her to feel she has to comfort me in addition to shouldering my load.

⁓

Moosilauke Ravine Lodge was built as a ski lodge when competitive skiing began and is large enough to house fifty people. Later acquired by Dartmouth College, it's now a place where people can sleep and eat while they enjoy the mountain and surrounding woods. With its dark paneling, the place has the feel of an upscale hunting lodge, more gentlemanly than rustic.

We find the women's room, bundle into fleeces and long pants, and start out on the Gorge Brook Trail, named for the eponymous brook that chatters beside it. When I chose this hike, we agreed we'd take the easy route up and the challenging one down. Were I to do it again, I'd reverse that.

We turn onto Snapper Trail to begin our upward climb. For the next mile, we speed from one side of the trail to the other, admiring patches of painted trillium, their creamy white petals faintly striped with maroon that radiates out from a cranberry triangle in the center. "Three petals, three leaves, a center triangle," Ginny says. "I like number patterns."

"They do say things come in threes." I think of the threes in my life: three children in my lottery family; the intense bond between my mother, sister, and me; the family I have created with Larry and Casey. My first 4000-Footer, Tripyramid. And today, though only two are alive, there are clearly three of us on this hike.

Soon Ginny and I shed our fleeces. I wince when they, too, go into her pack. Though not steep, the steadily increasing elevation hurts my left heel and calf. Half an hour later, I sit on rocks by the side of the brook to immerse swollen tendons. "Icy!" I gasp. But the irony—Achilles developed his weak heel because he was held by it when dipped in a stream, whereas I salve mine by dipping it in a stream—appeals to me. By the time I lace on my boot, my foot has gone numb and I'm invigorated, ready to gambol up the trail. Only Ginny's picture taking slows me down.

I've introduced Ginny to a runners' strategy Cathy taught me, one that Kate and I tried out on Lincoln and Lafayette. To help with our pacing and mental attitude today, I've divided the trail into four sections or "quarters" though they aren't necessarily equal. For each quarter, I've created an affirmation to counter negative, downward-dragging thoughts like *I'll never make it to the top.*

Our first quarter, with a book time of eighty minutes, will take us 1.7 miles to where we join the Moosilauke Carriage Road. *I'm just warming up* is our affirmation because when I tell myself *I'm just warming up,* my shoulders relax. Warming up is something you do before you actually exercise, something easy. Loose. Fun. Every time I ask Ginny how she's doing, she trills, "Just warming up," and we laugh.

We turn onto the Moosilauke Carriage Road, a path built wide enough for a carriage to ferry tourists to the summit for the view or to stay at the small hotel that once perched on the rocky cone. It must have been popular; tolls were collected on the Carriage Road until 1919, though no signs of such traffic remain.

After a couple of miles, with only a mild Achilles burn and not much complaint from knee and hip, I'm able to warble our second quarter affirmation. This quarter, 2.1 miles and a lot steeper, takes us to the top and, if we manage to go as fast as book time, will last for two hours—exactly the kind of challenge that kindles my self-doubt. So I sing out *I feel surprisingly strong!*

I even hike a little faster than Ginny who is burdened with the bigger pack. When we reverse positions, her height blocks my view. I'm waiting for the trail to get hard, but so far it's been wonderfully doable. With my mind freed from anxiety about summiting, my thoughts default to Kate. Ginny listens as I describe our climbs together.

"You were true hiking buddies," she says.

I smile. "Even before we knew what a 4000-Footer was." A few paces later, I tell her how lucky I feel to have been present at Kate's death. "I've never experienced that before. It was difficult but . . . an honor. I wish I could've been there for my mother."

"I know what you mean. Chances are I'll be at home, not the Midwest, when my dad dies."

Minutes pass. "It's spooky," I say, "your maiden name and Kate's married name being the same." We recently figured this out. "It seems prophetic. Like Kate blesses your being my buddy. Like she really meant it when she said she wanted me to keep hiking." I pause in the trail as my eyes fill. Ginny folds me into a hug. We stand there like a strange beetle, our packs poking out behind us.

After blowing our noses, we hike in silence for a while. This happens naturally, and it feels to me as if the spirits of Kate and of Ginny's dad accompany us. I talk to Kate in my head, trying to come to terms with the impossible reality that I will never again see her scarlet face on the trail or hear her point out something I've missed. I take out the twined violets, wilted now, and hold them in my hand as I hike. On this glorious spring day surrounded by trees and plants thrumming with life, I am certain Kate is glad to be here any way she can.

I shouldn't compare Ginny with Kate, but I can't seem to stop. Ginny expects this, raising comparisons herself when I carefully do not. She amazes me. Kate was a cool, invigorating day in spring—like today—her many buds partially furled. Ginny walks around as open and sunny as a mid-summer day. Yet neither burdens others with their sorrows and, when possible, both prefer to avoid sinking too deeply into emotions. At least, Kate was that way on our hikes. Cancer changed her.

We arrive at the broad, boulder-strewn summit. The name "Moosilauke" derives from Native American words for "bald place." When I read that, having been bald myself I grimaced, but the treeless plateau delights me. Ginny shrugs off the pack, throws her arms out to the side and spins in a slow circle. "This is the most fabulous view! What a hike!"

Besides velvety swaths of New Hampshire, we can see Vermont's Green Mountains swell to the west. In the Northeast, the Franconia Ridge hulks proudly in front of stand after stand of mountains, including the tall Presidentials. I point out to Ginny Little Haystack, Lincoln and Lafayette, Kate's and my last climb, now two-and-a-half years ago.

Near us on the summit, the remains of the hotel's foundation create an L-shaped shelter from the winds that I imagine, on less balmy noons, whistle across the stones. No one else is here. We explore the panorama, Ginny with her camera clicking, before settling on sun-warmed rocks for lunch. As we eat, an enormous black bird alights on a pile of stones a few feet away to stare at us boldly. The bird's a good two feet tall, with a wingspan double that. There's a certain shagginess around the throat that lends it a rakish air, as if to say, *I am who I am, I needn't keep my feathers neat.*

"I think that's a raven," I whisper. I've seen one stuffed at the Harvard Museum of Natural History. Humans and raven remain motionless for a long minute. Moments later, it spreads its inky wings and lifts off with a few powerful flaps.

"That was really something," Ginny says.

I nod. "Some Native peoples believe ravens and crows guard the spirit world."

Ginny leans back against some rock. "Seems pretty fitting for us." She looks at me. "You okay?"

I am. Nothing about death frightens me now, not my own anyway. In fact, I feel as if I have just met the raven of death that sat on my shoulder during cancer. What still gets me like a punch in the gut is the thought of losing someone I love. Like I just have.

As we begin our descent. Ginny recites, "Third quarter, our 'focus piece.' *I have a lot of energy left.*" The affirmation would have been more convincing if she hadn't interrupted it with a huge, sun-drowsy yawn.

I'm counting on the exaggerated affirmation to help me through the next 2.1 miles, the steepest part of our descent. The third is the hardest quarter, Cathy says. Mind and body tire. The Appalachian Mountain Club trains hike leaders to be particularly vigilant in the third quarter because in most endurance sports, people get injured when they begin to wear out.

I lead as we rock-hop down the Gorge Brook Trail. Before long, my Achilles tendon blazes fire and pain shoots from knee and hip. I begin to understand why people come up rather than down this way. After the carriage road, Gorge

Brook Trail feels like the rocky bottom of a dry streambed running downhill, endless and steep. Our joints are jolted without respite. I mutter our affirmation under my breath.

We've gone one interminable mile, still in the third quarter, when I hear a *snap* and Ginny cries out. I whip around in time to see her face-plant into scrubby brush and rocks beside the trail, terrified she'll roll over the edge.

"Gin!" I run over to grab her. I help lever her up to sitting, impeded as she is by the turtle shell of her pack. Her shin's scraped, as are both palms. A bruise from a broken branch already purples the top of one arm.

She wobbles up to stand. "I'm okay," she says. "I'm okay." Her face is white.

"Give yourself a minute, buddy. Why don't you sit down?"

She sinks onto the trail.

I dig out her water bottle and put it in her hand.

She stares at it. Seconds later, she starts to cry. "I'm sorry," she says, her blue eyes wide. "That just really scared me."

"You pitched face-first down the side of a mountain! Of course you're scared." I feel rotten. Maybe her balance was off because she carried my stuff. "I think you're in shock, buddy." I move her hand with the water bottle toward her mouth. "Water will help."

As she drinks, I search my vest pockets for ibuprofen and arnica cream. I give her two pills and ask if I can rub arnica on her bruises. "It's homeopathic stuff that reduces swelling. I use it all the time."

She nods.

After the arnica, I slather antibacterial ointment on her shins and apply Band-Aids. By now Ginny's shaking. We bundle her into her fleece and I feed her trail mix for quick sugar. "Take your time, Gin. No rush. We'll just enjoy the view for a while."

"I've never fallen like that."

I'm glad to see color come back to her face. "Everybody falls sometime. I fall at least once every hike. Hey, last time I tripped, I broke my wrist." I attempt a grin. "You've got a ways to go to catch up."

After that, we descend slowly. I wonder how much farther before we reach the McKenney Forest plaque that's our next milestone. The accident wiped out my sense of distance. My feet burn and I feel like there's no padding between my soles and the rocks. Taking care of Ginny drained me more than I realized, or maybe it's the aftermath of adrenaline rush. I plod along with my knee howling and wish we were done.

Since we still have the mountain to ourselves, I suggest we sing. Kate and I sometimes did. At the thought of singing, Ginny's head lifts. She's a musician, after all. We belt out show tunes from *The Sound of Music, South Pacific, Oliver,* and *My Fair Lady.* I even prance a bit on the trail. Ginny teaches me a chant she learned when she led her choral group to South Africa. We end by clapping hands to *Rise and Shine,* a favorite at our kids' school.

Back in the woods and near water again, we take a break. Ginny dips carrots and celery into hummus while I dip heels and knees into the chilly stream. With numb, refreshed feet, I strike out gleefully. I don't notice the growing gap between us until she calls after me, "Wait up, rabbit!" I do, then set a slower pace. As my feet warm up, the burning and stabbing return. My energy has ebbed and I'm fresh out of ideas to bolster us. Ginny's quiet, too.

As we round a bend I spy a middle-aged woman ahead of us on the trail, the first person we've seen. There's something curious about her gait. When I catch up to her, she says she began at the other end of the mountain. "I've got a degenerative disease. Going uphill my muscles lock every few steps. But hiking helps hold my hip in place. I'm so slow only a few of my friends can stand it so I hike alone a lot. Sometimes I get lost." She smiles. "Hey, I'm faster going down."

I admire her pluck. But if this pace is faster, I empathize with her friends.

We exchange names. She's Ruth, and the three of us chat about the mountain and the day. By now my sore self itches to go around Ruth, but I can't abandon a struggling woman on the trail. Not that Ruth has asked for my help. Far from it. She's hiked all day by herself. I figure that just makes her more tired and injury prone. I glance back at Ginny and shrug a question to her. She nods, seeming content to stay.

"Are you peak bagging?" Ruth asks.

"Cheryl is." Ginny can literally talk over my head. "This is my first. It's sure harder than I thought it would be."

Ruth tells us she's done thirty-three of The 48. In her condition? I ask how long it's taken her.

"Oh, ten to fourteen years, depending on how you figure. And I'm fifty-five," she adds with visible pride. Three years older than us. Her drive and determination in the face of appalling physical difficulty are inspiring.

Ruth asks me which mountains I've done. It doesn't take long to tell her.

"Wonderful," she responds. "I had to do Osceola twice because the first time I didn't do East Peak."

I silently bless Casey.

We reminisce about hikes we have in common while our feet slowly carry us closer to the Lodge and Ruth's hiking poles ping off of rocks. Ginny asks her which 4000-Footers are the easiest.

I turn my head to look at my buddy. "Good to know, don't you think?" she says.

Ruth rattles off, "Mounts Tom, Hale, Willey, and Field."

"Any tips you care to pass along?" I'm too tired to come up anything more than the catchall query I ended interviews with as a consultant.

Ruth's response surprises me. She holds up her hiking poles. "Get yourself a pair of these."

Sure, I think, she needs them, but I'm not disabled. Hiking poles are for winter hiking and old people. My silence must betray me, for Ruth adds, "They take a lot of weight and pressure off your knees, especially on the descent."

She has my attention.

"They're great for balance, testing the stability of your next step, fording streams, and such. It's like having a longer pair of legs. Or arms," she says thoughtfully.

I follow her trying to imagine using hiking poles. She continues, "They're also good as crutches."

Crutches?

After we see Ruth to her car, Ginny and I linger in the Lodge. We slump into bright green Adirondack chairs, gazing across a grassy yard at Moosilauke, and munching cherry tomatoes left over from lunch. It's 4:30 in the afternoon and we just hiked for eight hours. I'm wiped. Ginny says she aches all over from her fall. "What's book time?" she asks.

"Five hours."

Ginny drops a tomato. "You've got to be kidding!"

"It doesn't include rest stops, an hour and a half on the summit, picture-taking—"

"My fall."

"—slowing down for Ruth, any of that."

Ginny shakes her head. "I can't imagine." A few minutes later, she perks up. "We forgot the last quarter affirmation, buddy. *We've done it!*"

Driving back to Cambridge the next morning, Ginny and I debrief. We've achieved all our goals. With my left calf propped on the dashboard to reduce swelling, I take notes on a little square pad with a wee little pen, both of which she magicked out of her glove compartment.

"Put down for me to buy my own shirt. I shouldn't have to borrow yours."

I like this new attitude.

"Also bring fewer tomatoes and less trail mix. They weigh too much."

We pass a few miles in silence. Then I scribble on the pad. "I'm going to buy hiking poles."

We drive for a while just listening to Haydn. She leans back in the driver's seat, her long arms reaching out to the wheel. She tends to drive over the speed limit, but she changes lanes calmly and smoothly. Just like Kate. They never seemed to rush, nor did they trance out and forget where they were going like I do. "Hey, Gin?"

She looks over at me.

"Thanks for carrying my gear. And for listening about Kate. And telling me about your dad." My voice shakes a little, but I don't cry. "You're a good friend. A good hiking buddy."

Moosilauke
4,802 ft — 06/04/2002

21. SURRENDER

Ten days later at Gem Pool on the Ammonoosuc Ravine Trail up to Mt. Monroe, I take off my left boot to relieve throbbing tendons. In the Presidential Range, the woods sing with rushing water from rain and, even though it's July, snowmelt. Lush mosses cover rocks in capes of emerald. To my right plummets a narrow three-tiered cataract of frothing white water. Even the cold air tastes like water. Gem Pool is aptly named, a sea-green jewel so clear bits of mica sparkle up from the bottom. As I sink my foot into the icy liquid, Sarah snaps a picture of me yelping.

Where would I be without Sarah, who knew Kate, the most fitting and only one I wanted on today's hike. She carries our two lunches, the First Aid kit, my fleece, rain jacket, and second water bottle. My hip pack brims with extra socks, wool hat and leather gloves, a chemical pack that turns cold when punched, and an ace bandage; a water bottle, flashlight, whistle; blister packs, emergency blanket, and bandana. And a pound or two of Kate's ashes.

Most of Kate's remains are buried in Mt. Auburn Cemetery, an arboretum and botanical garden nearly two centuries old that sprawls through Cambridge and Watertown, one of the most beautiful places in New England.

Migrating birds harbor there in spring and fall to enjoy the abundance of trees and ponds. While pregnant I lumbered through the cemetery considering names etched into tombstones for my baby. Infant Casey got pushed along the paths in her stroller, and later she raced up the steps of the stone tower for views of Boston. Kate and I had frequently enjoyed the arboretum as part of our training.

I'm going to buy a spot near Kate for Larry and me. He thinks I'm crazy to spend our money on this when I'm not yet fifty-two. Maybe he worries I'm taunting fate. But after cancer and losing Kate, mortality feels as real as my right hand. I need to know where my ashes will rest. I want Casey to be able to mourn her parents in a place she already loves. Besides, I like the view.

It was at Mt. Auburn Cemetery with Kate's family that her sister-in-law leaned into me to whisper the story of Kate and the hospice nurse. The nurse arrived the Friday before Kate died, just after Larry and I left for our anniversary overnight. She was introduced to Kate while my friend lay in the hospital bed in her bedroom, too frail to make it out to the living room couch anymore. The nurse, her sister-in-law said, was cold and brisk. "She's going on and on about gruesome details of how the body fails and what Kate will need, catheters and such, when Kate rears up in bed and looks the woman right in the eye. 'I just want you to know I've climbed 4000-Footers in the Whites.'"

⌒〜

The hike up to Gem Pool with Sarah has already tested the boundaries of what I can manage. Despite the hiking poles I'm using, thanks to Ruth, my right knee aches as if a tiny drummer practiced with a hammer on my patella. Even after frigid stream dunkings, my left heel and calf have required a handful of ibuprofen.

Though it's mid-summer, not October, today's misty, chilly weather reminds me of Kate's and my last 4000-Footers. I miss her so acutely I move in a fog of Kate.

Sarah never hesitated about this hike. She wanted to honor Kate, she said, and she didn't want me to go alone—as if I could. She added that it gave her another way to grieve her mother, whom she'd lost the year before. As we climb, each story she relates about her mom teaches me something new about my friend of over thirty years.

We talk about Kate, of course. I tell her, "In some ways, Kate filled in after my mother died. Just—sending me articles. Loving Casey and Juniper. Caring about my new chairs. You know?"

Sarah nods. "Few people are close enough to care about both the little things and the big."

I'm so grateful Sarah is here, that she knew Kate, that she's known me so long, that she met my parents and sister, that she is the compassionate woman she is. I experience a moment of terror at the thought of losing her, too. I push the thought away, but fear twists my thoughts to my sister. "Cindy's at a nursing home now. She needed more care than Piney Ponds could give. Mardy's her guardian angel, going over there every week. Bill doesn't want to see Cindy like that. They both tell me not to visit her. They think it will break my heart."

"That's really generous of them." Sarah's voice is warm with understanding. "The whole situation's so sad."

After Gem Pool, the trail morphs from a manageable though rooty path into nothing but rocks and ledges that progress from no-joke steep to even steeper. As we haul ourselves upward, Sarah and I meet a few people coming down. They are not happy. They couldn't summit Washington or even its neighbor and our destination, Monroe. Wind chill cut the temperature to 12°F and winds blew 60-70 miles per hour. The fog was so thick they couldn't see Lakes of the Clouds Hut right in front of them. They're still wearing hats and mittens, their faces pinched and pale.

Still, Sarah and I climb. A few more people descend, but no one else besides us goes up. I stare at the gray-bellied clouds and murmur, "Kate, could use a little help here."

Sarah adds, "Getting rid of the fog would be good."

The trail goes straight up slabs. To maintain optimum traction, we step around mud and puddles to keep our boots dry. Though it hasn't exactly rained, the ledges are slippery with moisture. We have to bend down sometimes and use our hands in a kind of grown up crawl.

Suddenly Sarah slips and scrapes her shin, just like she did when the three of us hiked Tripyramid four years ago. I stop to wait while she doctors herself with the First Aid kit, my legs trembling from the morning's effort. As we draw closer to Lakes of the Clouds Hut, there's an ache deep in my chest. On the summit of Monroe I will lose the last physical manifestation of Kate.

Four-and-a-half hours after we began, we arrive at the hut, one hour and forty minutes slower than book time. At 5,050 feet, it's cloudy and the wind is bitter, but the thick fog we heard about has disappeared. Kate's doing? Inside the large wooden hut, which looks a lot like Greenleaf Hut that Kate and I saw on our last climb together, we buy soup and hot cider. Even inside it's so cold and damp our breath forms tiny clouds.

Twenty minutes later, I'm still sitting across from Sarah, my hands wrapped around an empty but still-warm mug and she's still taking tiny sips of what's left of her soup. We're avoiding what comes next.

I take a deep breath, blow it out. Say we should get going. From Sarah's backpack we dig out all our extra clothing and put it on.

From the hut, the trail up Monroe is an easy half-mile, rocky with occasional patches of soft dirt, nothing like what we faced this morning. Nobody joins us. I turn around three-quarters of the way up and snap a picture of Sarah on the path below me. Beyond her the stony, olive-colored flank of Washington tilts sharply into Ammonoosuc Ravine at an angle so dizzying it seems active—as if the skin and shoulder of Washington were flowing downward, and the hut must surely be swept from its perch along with the rest of the heaving mountainside.

The sky glares silver and in that tinny light, shreds of fog bleach the short grasses and plants that can find purchase against the whipping wind. Though my legs have gone numb, my nose and fingertips tingle with cold. The wind slaps at our hoods, erasing other sounds. We move in a loud but speechless world.

From the top of Monroe, we gaze out at thick banks of cloud and, beneath them, mountains darkened by cloud shadow. The wind pushes so strongly that I climb over a knob on the summit and scramble ten feet down the northeastern side for shelter. I find a rocky slip where the bulk of the mountain offers a windbreak and there's a narrow ledge. Sarah clambers down next to me. There's just room enough for the two of us and our packs. With our backs against the mountain, we look out over a ravine that is wide, deep, and riotously green: Oakes Gulf. A wildness swells from this mountainous cleft. It surges up and blasts us with raw life—powerful, harsh, real—and I know it's the right place to set Kate free.

I haven't thought of it this way before, but there is nothing peaceful about scattering her ashes here. Her spirit can find peace back at Mt. Auburn Cemetery. Here, she will fly. Roam. Roar. I want that for her, fiercely. I want my quiet friend to blast her way through death, to be fettered no more by hesitation or constraint or any kind of pain. Here she can be the mountain woman who always lived inside her.

Among the boulders I set up something like an altar, something like a shrine. I spread out the white bandana covered with the green female symbols that Kate brought me from an ovarian cancer fundraiser. On top of the bandana go photos of Kate hiking, Kate grinning arm in arm with Casey, and Kate holding all four pounds of Juniper on that trip to New Hampshire together to pick out a puppy. Sarah finds and places pebbles on the pictures so they don't blow away.

As best we can, Sarah and I kneel on the wet, grassy ledge while fog settles on our shoulders. We are silent a while, looking at the images of Kate, the woman who left a hollow in me that threatens never to be filled. Then we talk in quiet bursts, sharing memories of Kate as they come to us, our voices breaking. We end by my reading aloud a poem I wrote for her the day after her death.

"You ready?" I ask Sarah, who nods. We stand and turn carefully to face the deep ravine.

Holding the stuff sack that contains Kate's ashes, I dip my hand in. Surrounded by crumbly, dusty beige ashes, sharp bits of white that can only be bone needle my palm. I close my fingers around what's left of Kate and wonder if touching her so intimately is invasive, perhaps even sacrilegious, followed by a shameful moment in which I wonder if it's sanitary.

I steady myself by leaning into Sarah at my side and hold my fist out into the heaving air as far as I can without falling off. I whisper to Kate that Matanna is waiting for her, that the warrior woman of my lost breast will keep her company, then open my hand. The ashes and bits of bone are whipped away over Oakes Gulf. Sarah and I watch them soar above the tangled, dense wilderness below. Despite my wet cheeks, I feel a searing joy knowing that Kate will in some way inhabit this untamed, untainted place. Sarah flings some ashes and then motions me to do the rest. I like that the wind tears the ashes from my hands, as if Kate flies away eagerly to crags and corners and treetops where living people could never go.

When there's nothing left to set free, Sarah and I gaze into the gulf while the wind burns our faces. After a long while, Sarah admits her feet are numb. I tuck hair that's frosted and dripping with fog under my hood and swipe tears from my cheeks as we pack up Kate's shrine.

As soon as we climb up over the knob to the summit, two young men arrive. They tell us they are brothers, the exact same ages as Kate's sons. Sarah and I exchange glances. We take their picture and they take ours. As we turn to begin our descent, the sun slices through the matted clouds, spilling buttery yellow light on our path.

"That's Kate," Sarah says.

Monroe
5,384 ft – 07/11/2002

22. SHIFTING TERRAIN

Mt. Hancock's namesake was the first to sign the Declaration of Independence, using large, bold strokes. Like that signature, Hancock sprawls, a whole ridge unto itself. In Waterville Valley the night before we hike Hancock North and South, Ginny and I fill water bottles, organize trail food, and load up my hip pack and her backpack. She hoists her pack and clomps around the condo wearing it, looking anxious and defeated already.

I'm surprised. I'm the one with physical problems, still recovering from cancer. She trains every day, even carrying her pack on our Porters. She hefted gallon water jugs two to a hand from the car up to the apartment. Yet she's muttering under her breath. It's worrisome watching someone so strong feel anxious. *Kate never acted like this*, I think but don't say. Though I've scrupulously reduced my stuff for Ginny, I am the weak link who can't carry all she needs.

I check Ginny's pack to see what can be jettisoned, astounded to find our lunch in an insulated food bag with a heavy frozen icepack. I ditch bag and icepack, ditto a rigid camera case. I transfer granola bars from her pack to the back of my fishing vest and exchange my fleece jacket for a lighter pullover. If I get cold, I'll hike faster.

She still looks nervous. I don't get it. She's atypically anxious and I'm atypically not. Must one of us get the jitters before a 4000-Footer? Is that how we work? Having been so fearful myself before climbs, I should be more compassionate, but I'm not. For once, my guts aren't twisted up and I'd like to keep them that way.

After we part for the night, I tell myself Ginny will feel better once we hit the trail. Riding this wave of optimism, I phone my brother. When I ask how Cindy's doing, Bill says she's no better, her doctor prescribes different medications but nothing helps. I find myself pacing the bedroom. To change the subject, I tell him where I am and my plan for the next day. He exclaims, "I went to camp in New Hampshire!"

"Really?" I find it hard to picture my brother in these woods. He'd much rather swing a golf club.

"Yeah, you were little. What's the name of that big lake?"

"Winnipesaukee?"

"That's it. We used to call it Camp One-Up-Your-Sockee." He chortles like a twelve-year-old.

At 5:00 a.m., I slurp green tea while Ginny darts around the apartment. She thinks the headlamp is heavier than the mini flashlight we're leaving behind and goes into the windowless bathroom to test them. She comes out preferring the flashlight to the headlamp I inherited from Kate, but I acquiesce. Then she wonders about the small tube of sunscreen. If only I could carry more myself.

Ginny wasn't like this a year ago, before Moosilauke. It doesn't occur to me that now she knows what she's in for. Our elevation gain today—2650 feet—is several hundred feet higher than for Moosilauke and the loop trail is two-and-a-half miles longer. Maybe I should be anxious.

Ginny takes the wheel to spare my knee and tendons, saying she actually prefers to drive. I know what she means because I prefer to drive, too. As we speed along, my dependence and the desire to stand on my own, my gratitude to Ginny and my unreasonable aggravation that she's not behaving like Kate, tick back and forth inside me like a metronome.

We park at the lot off the Kancamagus Highway, an American Scenic Byway named for Chief Kancamagus, leader of several tribes. The Kanc, as it's known, is the only road that cuts through the heart of the White Mountain National Forest and it's famous for spectacular views.

Outside the car, a 45°F chill clings to our skin and we're afraid it may rain. I stare at a many-peaked giant of a mountain south of us, pulling out my map to identify it. I'm just getting oriented when Ginny, leaning over my shoulder, taps Osceola. Before I can react, she says, "Can I borrow this?" and whisks the map away. I have to put my hands in my pockets to keep from snatching it back.

We spar politely about which mountain is which, part of me noting Kate and I never argued like this. Eventually, I agree that Ginny's right. We are admiring Osceola's impressive north side, a new perspective on the mountain whose south façade I sigh over from my windows in Waterville Valley. Osceola looms across a ravine from us, frighteningly massive and scarred. I'm amazed to think I know the feel of her rough skin, that I've climbed across those shoulders. Embarrassed that I didn't immediately identify her, I decide mountains are like people that way. Sometimes it's hard to recognize them from the back.

We spray our clothes with noxious Deet, the most effective weapon against mosquitoes and the black flies that show up in late May. I've tried everything else. My latest purchase, which strains even my own credulity, is a watch. Strapped to my wrist, it emits a low buzz I can barely hear but which mimics the wings of the female dragonfly, predator of my nemeses. Very Dick Tracy.

After buckling her pack, Ginny goes quiet. I try not to notice, worried that it's 7:35 a.m. already. Yet when my boots hit the woodsy Hancock Notch Trail at last, all concern about time or Ginny and me fades away. "Let's rock and root!" I cry.

No hiker could ask for a better warm up on a cool spring morning. The first 1.8 miles, an old logging road, gain only 400 feet of elevation. Pine needles and dirt, actual dirt, soften the footing. When my Achilles tendons begin to smart, I don't care. I can't help but feel joyous as we march along, breathing in spring. We see bunches of hobblebush, a shrub that doesn't excite me until Ginny exclaims over them and I take a fresh look. The round pods of white blossom, somewhat like a hydrangea and as large as my hand, glow against the tender green of new leaves, lacy and cool. I have to admit that, to eyes grown accustomed to a forest palate of grays and browns, they offer visual refreshment.

Ginny is good for me. The thought pops into my head unbidden. I recall that every cup holder in her car boasted a pristine bottle of mineral water to keep us hydrated before we even got to the trail. Stocking the water wasn't on Kate's and my hiking list; my new buddy had come up with it on her own.

We walk at a comfortable pace, eyes roving to take in everything at once. Ginny admires plants as much as I do, as much as Kate did. Dang! I order myself to stop comparing the two women. It's stupid. It's unjust. How can Ginny compete with St. Kate? Besides, it's pointless. With a sigh, I let myself expand slowly into the larger frame of nature. Then Ginny jumps in front of me, saying, "I'll lead for a while."

I know it's only fair, but Kate never . . . I end that thought. We hike for a while. I notice Ginny is just slower enough than me that I have to pull myself up short to avoid treading on her heels. I pause in the trail. Wait. Start up again. Repeat. Feel constantly restrained. And her height blocks my view. Was being so attuned to one another on Moosilauke an aberration? A low-grade headache simmers behind my eyes.

A half hour later, we pass a verdant alcove encircled by small stones. Ginny continues on, but I call her back to the tiny glen in hopes of rekindling our connection. We face each other holding hands, forming a human circle within the circle of stones. Taking a risk, I whisper: "Close your eyes." Ginny complies. Her willingness to explore the unusual is one of the things I most enjoy about her.

For a minute, we just stand and breathe. The air tastes delicate, sweet. I am flooded with awareness of my good fortune: lucky to be alive, lucky to have a friend like Ginny, lucky to be in these woods today. I feel pretentious, even silly, standing there with my eyes shut but I want to follow my intuition, to open myself to the mountain and see what happens. I realize I've come for more than bagging a peak. We listen to the active silence of a living forest, still holding each other's hands. After a few minutes, Ginny whispers, "Amen." It does feel like prayer, what we're doing. I whisper, "Let's sing *Om*," something we do at the end of yoga class, *Om* having been the one-word prayer of people on the other side of the world for thousands of years. Standing on the leafy edge of Hancock, Ginny and I inhale deeply and breathe out "*O-o-o-m-m-m*," her trained voice humming on long after mine. We slowly open our eyes into each other's.

We're together again. I'm moved nearly to tears and at the same time—I don't know if Ginny feels this too—I blush with self-consciousness.

We're tramping companionably along the gentle rise of Hancock Notch Trail when Ginny, leading, yips in surprise. "I see a frog!" She bends down to peer into the mat of fallen leaves.

"Where?" All I see is forest detritus.

She points, slowly bringing her hand closer and closer to the ground.

"I see it! Is it a toad?"

A lock of her dark hair swings forward as she turns her head to me. "What's the difference?"

I don't know. After our hike I learn that frogs in the Northeast tend to live near water and, as a consequence, are green. Toads live in the woods, are marked by patterns of brown and beige, and have a line down the middle of their backs.

As we stare, the toad decides to make a run for it. *Run* isn't quite accurate. From the size of its hind legs I expect a great, startling leap, and I pull my head back to make room. What occurs looks more like stumbling. Shambling. Enduring chemo. "Maybe it's just waking up from hibernation," I say. "Or it's drunk on spring?"

"Or old," Ginny says. We keep staring. Some of the warty knobbles on the toad's back gleam copper. I would never have expected to find a toad so interesting, but now I understand why so many children's stories include them. Standing, they look humanoid and rather wise in a friendly, humble, ugly sort of way. Toads are the Abraham Lincolns of the forest.

We reach our first milestone, a weathered wooden signpost that directs us onto Cedar Brook Trail. In spite of our picture taking and flower ogling and toad inspection, we've reached the junction in seventy-one minutes. A mere six minutes over book time.

"And we're *just warming up!*" Ginny says.

We arrive at Cedar Brook, roughly fifteen feet across with all kinds of boulders strewn about. The dark water slides over submerged ledges flat as sliced bread and laid out in a crazy quilt of triangles, rectangles, rhomboids. Bronze patches gleam beneath flowing water. The whole area looks like an art installation. While dipping my heels in the brook, I snap photos that, even as the shutter clicks, I know will never capture the grandeur.

When we hike on we're silent again. Perhaps Ginny has water music playing in her head, too. Rain falls off and on like hesitant tears and the trail gets steeper and rockier, but I'm still waiting for it to get hard. Waiting for my breath to burn in my throat, for the time I am reduced to one slow, throbbing mass of pain, the time when only my will keeps me moving. I am waiting for that thin steel time.

Yet as our silence endures, I'm forced to notice that I must restrain myself from rushing past Ginny out of sheer exuberance. Who is this woman wearing my clothes?

Ahead of me, Ginny freezes. "Another toad," she whispers, pointing with her hiking pole. We're still looking down when voices rumble behind us. We haven't seen anyone since we parked two hours ago, a benefit of Hancock I was unaware of when I chose it. Bordering the Pemigewesset Wilderness, the Hancocks provide a sense of isolation that, all by itself, is a treasure. We step off the trail as two men hustle up. One looks to be in his early thirties, the other a bit older. Both are muscled, fit, and, despite the cold, wearing short sleeves and shorts.

"Beautiful trail," I offer.

They agree. The younger one asks which way we'll do the Hancock Loop. After I say we're climbing North Peak first, he responds, "Yeah, I thought about that. But I checked the Internet and last week a guy reported three feet of snow up there. If that steep run on South peak gets icy, I'd rather be going up it than down." He grins.

I do not look at Ginny. Snow? Ice? Internet? Shit.

"You must be peak bagging," I say.

The younger guy leans back as if I've slapped him. He settles his face into a heavy, serious look. "We're just out enjoying the scenery," he says. "Nature. You know."

What's so bad about peak bagging? An awkward silence ensues as I stare at him in obvious disbelief.

Ginny rescues us. "The wildflowers are lovely." We all smile.

"Well," the younger guy says, "Gotta hoof it if we expect to finish by 1:30."

Ginny and I hike in silence until the two men disappear. I'm in the lead now so Ginny's low voice behind me is easy to hear. "1:30?" she says. "That can't be right." We expect to be lunching atop North Peak as they finish up one entire hour *less* than book time. No wonder they were practically running.

"They're younger," I say. "And bigger. Did you see those knee caps?"

"Not that we're competing."

"Heck, no. We're just out enjoying the scenery. Nature. You know."

We laugh wickedly.

Ginny waits until we've crossed the next stream. "Do you think there will be ice?"

"Don't think so." I reach for my water bottle. "There's been a lot of rain."

The rain stops and the sky shimmers silver. Occasional splashes of gold drift through the fluttering green of new leaves. I can't believe how good I feel. Nothing hurts, not even my knee. I could scamper up this mountain. Without intending to, I draw far ahead of Ginny. She yells for me to wait up. When she approaches, I trill, "*Still just warming up!*"

She looks up at me from a few feet below, her face haggard. She gamely repeats the affirmation, but heaves her pack to the ground. "I really need to do more upper body work." Despite the cold, the back of her shirt shows dark patches of sweat.

"How about a granola bar?" I toss her one. Exhilarated, I'm not even hungry. While she eats, I consider my friend. She seems less excited than on Moosilauke, but she must be enjoying herself, spotting flowers and toads as she has. An unseen chickadee calls.

"Hear that?" Ginny holds up her index finger. "It's a major third." She whistles the notes back. For the next several minutes I'm treated to a duet as the chickadee and Ginny sing to each other, each repetition growing fainter as the bird flies to more distant branches. I decide I'd like to live inside Ginny's head for a while to hear the world the way she does. As she packs up I suggest we hike apart, like we did on Moosilauke.

"Fifteen minutes?" Ginny says. She checks her watch.

"I was thinking half an hour."

Her face loses all expression.

"Twenty?"

She nods. She decides to rest before following me, so I rocket off. I can't figure it. As we've gained altitude, Ginny has slowed way down. On Moosilauke, I lagged when she lagged. Her pack didn't seem to make much difference between us then. Maybe I am becoming an expert hiker!

From worrying about Ginny, I move on to worry about Cindy. Should I call her doctor myself? Do more research? Working the worry beads, I wonder if Larry got Casey to school on time and why, after my first acceptance, my next two short stories keep getting rejected. Am I a fool to think I can be a writer?

I blow a loud raspberry and give myself up to simply listening. The silence differs from the quiet when Ginny and I are together but not talking. It's deeper. I could be the only person on the planet. The only human sounds I hear—the tick-tock of hiking poles, the scrape of boot against rock, the hush of breath—are my own. The trees, however, speak.

They creak and moan. Their green leaves rush together, whispering secrets. Wind passes a tinkling hand through the leaves turning them underside up and pale, also plastering wisps of hair onto my cheek. Small creatures rustle in the dry leaves on the forest floor. Mosquitos whine. I find myself slapping at a bite on my leg and lift my Dick Tracy watch to my ear. It's still making an almost imperceptible sound. Should I wear it around my ankle?

Hiking on, I press my toes down against the soles of my boots. I literally feel my way into the physical connection between Hancock and me, pulling energy up from the earth's molten core through the mantle of rock into my feet and legs. I breathe. I walk. I breathe.

Reluctantly, I check the time, the whole concept of time feeling intrusive. Though I'd like to go on for hours, I stop to wait for Ginny.

So why don't I do my next 4000-Footer alone? The idea makes me grin. Then I remember the pack. The dangers of injury, getting lost, unexpected weather. I'd probably focus too much on pain. Time, that troublesome construct, would be my unrelenting companion. No, I decide. Hiking with someone else brings a deep human connection—and offers me the luxury of yearning to hike alone.

Five minutes pass. I wonder where Ginny is. I remind myself she has the whistle I lent her and she knows to blow three times for help. But what if she tripped like on Moosilauke? Maybe hit her head on a rock and is lying on the trail unconscious? I backtrack downward until I spot her fifteen yards below, climbing slowly uphill. "Hey, buddy!" Relief warms my voice.

She looks up. Stops. As soon as I get close, she dumps her pack and sits on the ground, her face shiny with sweat. I'm not used to seeing her sweat. "You okay? How about some water?" She nods. We drink in silence, maybe because we've grown used to it. I feel cheerful and serene from my time alone.

Ginny turns to me. "This is a lot harder than Moosilauke."

"Really?" I remember the bible called it "steep and rough," but what can I say when I'm still waiting to be challenged?

"Oh, yeah. This is the hardest hike I've ever done."

That doesn't sound good.

"Are you saying you *don't* find this difficult? Are you telling me this isn't *hard?* All these *rocks?*"

Truth or strategy? I don't want to discourage her, but I don't want to lie. I mumble, "It's kind of typical 4000-Footer stuff." Truth and strategy: I don't add that other 4000-Footers have been worse. Or that I'm pretty sure Hancock will *get* worse.

"So Moosilauke was *easy?*"

"Well . . . " This confuses me because I remember parts of Moosilauke felt easy, but coming down was hard and the whole hike depleted me. So is it me or Hancock that's different? "I'm not sure, Gin," I admit. "How about a sucky?"

I hand her a butterscotch candy. I pop one into my own mouth as well, hoping the sugar will shoot inspiration to my brain. Ginny shoulders the pack and we hike slowly on. I focus on staying just a bit ahead of her with the hope that she'll be able to draft, like a cyclist, from my momentum.

After a while, she says, "You're in great shape."

"You have the pack, buddy."

"No, you're really strong."

Could that be true? I'd like to hear more, but the wonder and envy in her voice embarrass me. "I guess it's those other 4000-Footers."

"Absolutely," she says. "You've got nine mountains in your legs."

⌒

Ginny sits on a log stretching her arms overhead, rotating her head and neck in slow circles. She pulls a bag of celery from her pack and offers me some. Crunchy, sweet, and wet, they are perfect.

"I hate hikes like this," Ginny says.

"Buddy! Why?"

"Where are the views? The sun? That feeling of being on top of the world?" She swipes her forehead with a bandana. "I feel suffocated by all these trees."

Rolling a stalk of celery between my fingers, I don't know what to say.

"And the trail!" she continues. "Ridiculous rocks everywhere. I'm constantly stepping up or over one. And it just gets steeper. We never get a break!"

We reload our packs and hike on. Ginny's heavy boot steps seem to accuse me. Finally, I say, "I guess I don't see it that way."

"Well, how do you see it?" she snaps. "You're happy the minute your boots hit the trail!"

At the acid in her voice, I half-turn to her. I'm startled, but what she says is true. Now, mingled with any anxiety and anticipation I feel, there's a sense of landing, of coming home. I *am* happy the minute my boots hit the trail.

I step off trail and wave her onward. "You go first, and I'll try to explain." I talk about the many hues of birch bark, the sounds the trees make, the thousands of varieties of ferns and how their soft leaves against my hand feel like the touch of a friend. I describe the colors and textures of lichen. How each combination of minerals, water, air, and sunlight has the same origin as us: a pinch or two of stardust. How some Native Americans call things in nature *sister, brother, mother,* or *father.* This is what I've learned while bagging peaks.

Ginny turns to me. She looks more alert, less drawn. "Keep talking," she says.

"Good distraction?"

"Yes. And the more you say, the more I see. If I can view the forest like you do, I'll probably like it better."

At the turnoff to the Hancock Loop Trail, a little less than a mile remains to North Hancock, our first of the two summits. We face our hardest section yet, and Ginny asks me to lead. Even with my mouth open to suck air and sweat slipping down my neck into my shirt, I'm happy.

We climb for another ten minutes then halt to zip off our pant legs. Despite the chill, the sun has come out and we're sweating. As we haul ourselves upward, I point out two more drunken toads.

Ginny says, "How much farther to the summit?"

There is only one answer to this question. Ever. "Almost there."

Having said the words, I realize they must be true. And I'm still waiting for things to get impossibly hard. I smile hugely. "Hey, Gin. This is as hard as it gets, buddy! And guess what?"

She matches my grin. "*We're just warming up!*"

I want to sprint the last few tenths of a mile. I have never felt this good scaling a 4000-Footer. I really *am* just warming up. In a burst of exuberance, I start singing "Seventy-Six Trombones." I turn around to serenade Ginny as she slogs up the trail, singing as loudly as I can and blowing an imaginary trombone. I'd play a cornet too, like the song says, if I knew what it was.

We find the side path just below the summit that leads through small conifers to open ledges filled with sunlight and warmth. I stop singing to gape. We drop our packs and admire the view. The trees blend into a huge blanket of green hugging the bony shoulders of the nearest mountains. Farther off, mountain ranges surge in three directions, row after row. I'd like to leap from the rocks and fly, soaring out over the glory spread before me. Instead, I stand and smile. I could have died and missed this.

I kick out my feet and wave my arms and wiggle my hips, aware I look absurd, that being precisely the point of this dance. I invent a song with complex lyrics that go: *Peak dancin' / Peak dancin' / Woo / Woo / Woo / Woo*. Repeat. Ginny joins in and soon we're howling our heads off. When we finally stop, she says, "You just created a summit tradition."

~

After lunch in the warm pocket of rocks and trees, in the midst of applying moleskin to my feet, I look up to see Ginny pointing the camera my way. Suddenly aware that I'm not wearing my prosthetic breast, I grab the hiking sock I've just taken off and stuff it down my sports bra, feeling like I'm back in sixth grade.

The human mind is capable of infinite contradiction. I can at once be in the midst of mourning Kate and find myself dialing her phone number to tell her how sad I am. I can be frightened of steep, high places and crave climbing. I can hike all day Amazon-breasted and not want a photograph of what I look like.

My feminist self sighs. Immediately after the trauma of cancer, I didn't care that my shirts hung askew. I told friends that if women with mastectomies camouflaged the fact, we wouldn't be able to recognize and support one another. If we didn't use prostheses, the epidemic of breast cancer would become painfully obvious, might even stimulate more research funding. Suddenly, I long for a movement to free women from prostheses the way we liberated ourselves in the '70s from girdles and pointy-cupped bras.

Ginny stretches out across a couple of boulders and closes her eyes. Now *that* is confidence. I'm afraid if I lie down I'll get tired, so I wander off to explore the summit, touching evergreens as I pass.

When I return, a navy blue bandana covers Ginny's sleeping face and ripples as she breathes. I check my watch and calculate remaining daylight. "Uh, Gin," I say softly. "We should get going."

"Sure," she mumbles, but it's ten minutes before she sits up. Once she does, she moves with stunning efficiency. We devour the 1.4 miles of pleasant ridge trail to South Hancock.

Descending South Hancock is another matter: a knee-buster, relentlessly steep. We pick our way down through rocks and slippery masses of fallen leaves. It's the treacherous third quarter. I quote our affirmation, *"We have a lot of energy left!"* When Ginny echoes me, it seems to be true.

∾

I'm first to see the snow. It fills the trail and winds down, down, down. I clomp into the white stuff for several feet before I slip. I catch myself with a pole and continue on. The second slip happens so fast I slide sideways off the trail into some brush, saved from a fall by a convenient sapling.

I warn Ginny, "Be careful!" Looking ahead, I see that the snow on the trail piles high in the middle and slopes down on the sides, forming an elevated, skinny, *icy* mound in the center that is wide enough for only one boot. This monorail is what results when a snowy trail gets packed down in the center by winter hikers. The top layer of crystals melts by day but freezes at night, creating a slippery path just waiting to twist an ankle or throw out a knee. The monorail covers the steepest part of our descent. I'm getting vertigo just watching it disappear over the side.

No more surgeries, I caution myself.

Ginny slides off the monorail about where I did. "So this is why they went up South Peak instead of down." Intentional or innocent, her comment slices through me. Meantime, a band of iron has begun to compress my diaphragm. If I don't get back on that trail soon, I'll start to tremble. My fear of heights is fully awake.

I dig in a hiking pole. Test it. Force myself to let go of the sapling. Jam the other pole in. Kick the toe of my right boot into the hardened snow, then the left. Turn myself down trail—scary, scary, scary—thrusting both poles into the sides of the monorail ahead of me. I could slide and roll a long way before banging up against a rock or tree.

My breathing quickens. I crab-walk forward and down the trail in small, mincing steps, one boot awkwardly angled on either side of the monorail, my weight all wrong. I'm leaning forward but holding back because I'm too scared to commit to the trail, my legs tense as sticks. With each slip, I nearly topple over. My boots slide in all directions, uncontrolled. My heart bangs my ribs as I force myself down, clutching the poles hard enough my wrists ache.

"This is nasty," Ginny says.

Merely the sound of her voice breaks my concentration. A boot slithers completely off trail and I hurtle and hop for twenty feet trying to keep my balance, until I pitch up against a big rock. I'm so glad to have been stopped, I don't care about the bruises.

"You okay, buddy?" Ginny calls.

I risk a glance up at her, standing with her knees bent, her poles pitched just right, perfectly balanced, as if she might ski down. The anxiety that wrinkled her forehead on the way up North Hancock has vanished. She may not like this vertiginous ice slide, but she isn't terrified. She's used to steep icy shit.

"Want to lead for a while?" It's as close as I can come to voicing my terror, and in that terror I turn to Ginny the way

I turned to Kate on the South Slide. Ginny's height in front of me is now a good thing. The drop that sets my stomach churning can't be seen and I'm not quite so dizzy. I follow the welcome, solid reality of my friend.

~

After the monorail, I have greater empathy for the way the toads lurch and stumble. My feet ache all the way to my knees, my bruised thigh throbs, and my Achilles tendons burn. My focus has evaporated and, though two more miles remain, we're out of food and water. We finish near dark, turning onto the Kancamagus highway at 7:15 p.m. We've been exercising for almost twelve hours and I'm not only wrung out, I'm ready to eat the dashboard. I suggest we cancel our dinner reservations in Waterville Valley and stop in Lincoln instead, forty-five minutes closer.

Ginny shakes her head. "I'm sweaty and disgusting. I need to shower and change."

"But it'll be an hour before we reach Waterville, even longer if you wash." My stomach rumbles. "You seriously want to eat at nine o'clock? I don't. I'll be asleep by then."

Ginny's stomach growls, too, but she doesn't respond. We drive for a while, the silence sharp between us.

We're both worn to a ragged edge but I can't see that. I tell myself Ginny is stubborn and unreasonable, that Kate never cared about her appearance after a 4000-Footer, that Sarah doesn't. I'm so hungry I feel hollow, but I do see we need to compromise. "All right, let's go to the apartment. You can shower and go out while I shower and get in my pajamas."

"But then we won't have our celebratory dinner!"

I thunk my head back against the headrest. Twice. I am not a nice person when I'm tired and hungry. Ginny's arms stiffen. She glares at the road.

I press my lips together and resign myself to watching all the restaurants in Lincoln whiz by.

A few minutes later, Ginny checks her watch. "I suppose I could wash up in the restroom."

My whole face softens. "Thank you, buddy," I say. I could kiss her.

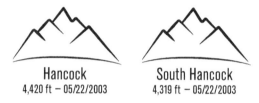

Hancock
4,420 ft – 05/22/2003

South Hancock
4,319 ft – 05/22/2003

23. DARING

From Waterville Valley to Interstate 93, I fiddle with my hair. The morning after the Hancocks, Ginny drives us back to Boston. Despite a satisfying hike, I'm remembering she wouldn't let me make our sandwiches the night before to save time in the morning, insisting they'd dry out. She repacked our lunch after I packed it. While we'd had sweet, close times on the Hancocks, often I felt like she was telling me what to do and how to do it, things that lit my fuse. But I *like* her. We could become really close. Which means I've got to risk confronting her so my resentment doesn't spoil either our hikes or our relationship. Talking about the dissatisfactions that colonize any real relationship scares me. I lick dry lips. "Hey, buddy, there's something I'd like to discuss." I look at the road. "Sometimes I find you a little controlling."

A heartbeat after the words leave my lips, I want to take them back. Ginny has gone still as a deer. What did I hope would happen? She'd chuckle, promise it would never happen again, and everything would be fine?

She still doesn't say anything and it's getting uncomfortably hot. I crack my window, stick my fingers out into the cold, and feel a little less trapped—until I remember the sound of the wind irritates her musician's ears. I pull my hand back in and close the window.

"That's funny," Ginny finally says, staring straight ahead. "I find you a little controlling, too."

Kate and I never had these conversations, even when we should have, even when I tried to. It suddenly dawns on me that refusing to engage in a conversation, however kindly, is controlling in its own way, but I don't have time to ponder that now. Kate certainly never ricocheted a comment back at me. If only I could say something funny or laugh, but I can't. My jaws are clenched tight. I suggest the only thing that comes to mind. "Maybe we should tell each other what makes us feel controlled and try to work it out from there."

I wish I'd thought this conversation through. Tentatively I offer, "When we were trying to figure out which mountain was south of the parking lot, you snatched the map out of my hands."

"I was just trying to show you." She turns to me in her earnestness. "You were looking at it wrong."

I raise an eyebrow.

"I can see how that would feel," she concedes.

My shoulders drop a fraction of an inch. I nod. "Your turn."

"Your packing list is over the top. Way over! I can't believe you want me to bring every little thing on it. It makes me anxious when I'm packing. And my backpack gets too heavy."

Knife to the heart. I can't thank her again for carrying my things; she'll feel like she has to reassure me when we're in the middle of arguing. I take a breath. "I hate packing, too. Finding and checking off all those items makes me crazy. I put it off till the last minute." I pause. "But in all the books I've read and in the AMC hiking course, experts insisted you need these things to be safe in the Whites." I pause again. "On the other hand, I do think we bring too much food, at least for me, and food is heavy." Then something pops into my head. "Maybe I can find a bigger hip pack so I can carry more stuff."

"Could you?"

And so we struggle through our list of complaints, working hard to be honest but not mean, to take in what we're being told. We go slowly and cautiously, thinking our way through. At some point, I admit my need to be in control and how pissed off I get if I feel someone else is trying to control me, though I don't tell her—yet—that it springs from a childhood where it seemed I had no control and few, if any, rights. Ginny and I confess that our husbands complain about how controlling we are, and that makes us laugh. Then we admit we've tried for years to let go more. And each of us thinks she has made tremendous strides in doing so. We laugh again, after which we sigh at how hard it is to change. "It's a spiral," I finally say. "You work on yourself. You go to therapy. You graduate from therapy. You think you're done but, really, you've just dropped a rung closer to the core and pretty soon you're circling the same damned mess all over again."

"True," Ginny says. "But still, it's progress."

"At least in the mountains I don't have to control things. The mountain is *there*. The weather is *there*. The forest, the animals, the flowers are *there*. I can't change a thing."

Ginny nods. "It's scary, too, but I see what you mean."

"It's a respite. A control-freak's vacation."

She reaches out across the seat to squeeze my hand. "It was brave of you to start this conversation, buddy."

I squeeze back. What an amazing person she is to say that. "I was scared spitless," I tell her. I rarely confess fear, but apparently I do with Ginny.

She switches CDs from Hayden to Brahms. Then she admits her period started yesterday morning. "It really sapped my energy on the hike."

Being post-menopausal from chemotherapy, I forget women my age still menstruate. "Why didn't you tell me?"

"I didn't want to be a whiner."

I mull this over as we cross into Massachusetts. I know exactly what she means. I never want to be a whiner either. But is it whining to say you're struggling? Where does this suck-it-up attitude come from?

In the gender workshops I sometimes facilitated when I had my consulting business, we talked about the fact that in our country, men aren't supposed to appear weak or afraid. This standard for male behavior tended to get imposed on women, too, because men created the norms, especially in places like business or sports. Like hiking. Yet psychologically it was healthier to be able to express, within civilized limits, what one felt. Group performance, I knew, suffered when men or women were required to stuff their true feelings.

"I've just invented Cheryl's First Rule For Hiking." *Uh-oh.* "Does that sound too controlling?"

Ginny grins. "What is it?"

"*Speak Up.* You and I promise to tell each other our weaknesses, our needs, our suggestions. It's good for the one speaking up, of course, but group theory says it's good for both of us."

I explain how everyone in a group represents some aspect of the whole. "When I complain, it means I'm express-ing whiny feelings for the group. You may get to be the voice of reason. Somebody else voices the group's fear. Anger. Longing. Excitement." I say that's why sometimes we get so outraged at the one in the group who wants to quit. Because a part of all of us would like to quit. Speaking up also enables other members of the group to help resolve one's dilemma. "Besides," I add, "if you don't tell me you're hurt or anxious or your period is wearing you out, then that's something else—a secret weight—you have to carry."

"And with each mile," Ginny nods, "it gets heavier. Harder to carry."

We make a pact that from now on we'll try not to be

afraid of how wimpy or weak we sound, we'll tell each other what's going on with us. We'll break the macho mold, by speaking up. We'll become a different kind of hiker.

I should have known Ginny would achieve this goal more quickly than I.

⌒∾

At our weekly training session, I tell Cathy about the climb, how differently Ginny and I experienced it, and ruminate about why. Since the Moosilauke hike, I've gotten a massage every three weeks instead of four to aid the muscles, ligaments, and tendons—the sweet stretchy things—that remained rigid and brittle three years after chemo. Taking Tamoxifen has worsened the problem, so I've added more leg stretches. "Paying attention to what my body needs must be working," I grunt, as I lie on the floor doing a set of chest presses with three-pound weights.

From her chair, Cathy nods. "Don't lock your elbows." She purses her lips, thinking. "You've successfully climbed eleven challenging mountains. Also sounds like you were the leader again even though Ginny's an experienced hiker."

I rest the weights by my sides to stare up at her. I'm working to become a better hiker, obviously, but the notion that I might have already arrived somewhere on the journey when so many more climbs remain surprises me.

Cathy continues. "Most people don't accomplish what they set out to do. Not all my clients do the workouts they set themselves each week. Not everyone embraces a sport, keeps trying to learn more about it. You do."

I frown.

She laughs at me. "Cheryl, you're an elite athlete."

Now I laugh. "Right. I'm an Olympian."

"Olympians aren't the only real athletes." She quotes me one of her favorite lines from that wise person, Anonymous.

"'Champions in any field make a habit of doing frequently what others find boring or uncomfortable.'"

I make a mental note to use that sometime as a fourth quarter affirmation. I know Cathy exaggerates to encourage me, but still, I can't get the words *elite athlete* out of my head. They pepper my thoughts throughout the next week while I try to understand what they have to do with me. Probably exactly as Cathy intended, the possibility of being an elite hiker sparks a rush of eagerness. Wouldn't Kate have loved the idea of our being elite athletes?

When Ginny and I meet next, I say, "Buddy, we hiked two 4000-Footers the earliest in spring I've ever climbed, when there was still snow. We're getting to be elite hikers." I watch from the corner of my eye to see how she takes the honorific that makes me feel like an imposter.

She raises her eyebrows. "Elite hikers." Then she bends down to tighten the laces of her running shoes. "I like it."

24. PATH FINDING

Two weeks after the Hancocks, I consider my wall map of New Hampshire. Crawford Notch, I notice, bristles with blue pins marking 4000-Footers I haven't climbed. My hiking goal for 2003, pledged to myself and to Cathy, has ramped up to seven peaks. Ginny and I just bagged two of them. Sitting at my desk, I study the bible and pick out treks in the Notch that will net five 4000-Footers this summer and fall.

The concrete evidence of mountains climbed—from scraped-up hiking boots to eleven red pins on my map—reassures me that I am alive, strong, and mastering something, particularly as my mailbox continues to produce rejection letters from literary magazines. Though I can't carry a backpack, I'm almost as fit as I was for Tripyramid five years ago, before I knew I carried cancer with me up and down each peak. I've got almost three years of Tamoxifen left, but much of the time I can predict and adjust to the continuing side effects. I know how to work with my body better, when to yield and when to push. I crave the proof each mountain provides that I am a woman gone through the crucible of cancer, a woman now engaged in pursuing her heart's desires. Each climb offers multiple rewards now.

For the next hike, I choose Mt. Jackson. Sarah, my stalwart mountain *hermana*, will join me. We haven't hiked together since we scattered Kate's ashes on Monroe last summer and I look forward to her company in an untried section of the Whites.

I also invite someone new: my friend Alexandra. We met seven years before in Mexico, at a Club Med for families. Since then our families usually spend Thanksgiving together at her rambling house with her four kids, two dogs, and assorted relatives. Alexandra is ten years younger than I, an unflappable mother with a powerhouse job buying books for a publishing house. Everything interests her and she knows something about everything. She's five inches taller than I with shoulder length, honey-brown hair, slender, and fit. She walks nine miles a day.

She's not used to hiking mountains however, so Jackson strikes me as a good first experience. Though Jackson is part of the Southern Presidential range, the Webster-Jackson Trail runs only a bit over five miles round trip and remains pretty moderate except for half a mile near the beginning and then again, as is so often true in the Whites, near the top. The summit promises views. The icing on this mountain cake is something called Elephant Head, a rock formation I'm curious to see, one that carries associations to the elephantine shape of Tripyramid five years ago.

If we follow a loop trail—my preference—we can include Mt. Webster, almost a 4000-Footer at 3,910 feet. We'd enjoy different views on the way down and the whole trip would only be 6.5 miles. Best of all, we don't have to make the decision about Webster until we reach the top of Jackson and can gauge Alexandra's level of interest and energy. I don't doubt Sarah's ability to do both peaks and, refreshingly, I'm pretty sure of my own.

The evening before our hike, Alexandra drives from Massachusetts to Waterville Valley. As we catch up during the dinner I've prepared, questions about the hike tug at me. *What about the prep talk? What are her goals? Her fears? What are your own goals?* But I didn't explain my hiking process when I invited her and the right moment to broach the subject never seems to come along. The evening speeds by and just as we're ready to go to bed, Sarah arrives, unsure until the last minute that she'd be able to make it. She and Alexandra take to each other like twins separated at birth. I'm relieved. Thrilled. They're so immersed in conversation, I have to shoo them off to bed.

Before we leave the next morning, they generously divide between them my extra water bottle, rain jacket, fleece, and the group First Aid kit. We start up the Webster-Jackson Trail on a lovely, sun-filled summer day. We soon leave the trail to follow a side spur for two-tenths of a mile to Elephant Head, and there she is. As surely as if carved, before us looms the regal gray head and trunk of an elephant jutting from the green mountainside as if surveying her domain.

"I like that you're calling it 'her,'" Alexandra says.

"You're such a feminist," Sarah chimes in.

I prickle a little, unsure of Sarah's tone. "Well, elephant herds are matriarchal. The eldest female leads and the rest tend the young collectively. They all band together against predators."

"Cool," says Alexandra. "What do the males do?"

"Drink beer and watch sports," Sarah responds.

We hike to the top of the slightly rounded dome between the ears of Elephant Head to gaze up and down the valley of Crawford Notch State Park. A small highway, US 302, runs through it, a skinny asphalt snake winding north and south as far as the eye can see, cutting between the brawny Southern Presidentials on one side and the Willey Range on the other. After enjoying the view, we apply more bug juice. Even the short, woodsy walk here plastered us with mosquitoes.

Before I leave, I touch the elephant's head, one female to another. I've gone a little ways down the trail when I realize Sarah and Alexandra are not behind me. They're still on Elephant Head talking. I wait politely for them to notice that I've started off. I wait some more. Finally, I call, "Hey, you two. Hike's a-waitin'!"

We march on, the trail alternating between moderate rambles and steeper pitches. The day turns hot. I mop my face with a bandana to keep sweat and bug juice from stinging my eyes. I can't decide if going faster reduces the number of bugs because I'm creating a breeze or increases them because of my copious sweat. Though I suspect my friends could go faster, they match my pace, enabling me to march along without having to break my rhythm.

Periodically, I join the conversation that buzzes between Sarah and Alexandra. I wedge in a few comments, but I'm too hot to sustain the effort. Then I spy a large, healthy bed of low-growing plants that look like but are not clover—wood sorrel. The delicate little pinky-white flowers have long since gone by, but the leaves still offer a lemony tang, a nice change from the salty sweat on my lips. I interrupt Alexandra and Sarah to pass around a few small green leaves.

"Nice," says Sarah, chewing.

"Mmm," says Alexandra.

They go back to talking about school systems and children, how each of their kids differs from their siblings, about learning and attention issues at different ages, what makes a good teacher, how sports can be helpful to kids but also incite competitiveness and feelings of inadequacy. I hang back, letting them stride ahead. I don't want to talk about kids. I want, just for today, not to be responsible for anyone else.

I nod to patches of bunchberry, small plants whose ivory flowers are shaped like dogwood blossoms and glow in the greenery. Then, over to the right of the trail, I spy tall Indian cucumber. "Hey, look!"

At the urgency in my voice my friends turn around, blinking a bit as if roused from another consciousness. I wave them over. "This is so exciting!" I touch the two layers of pointed whorls of green leaves that radiate from the stem like pinwheels. "If you dig these up, the roots taste crunchy and wet. Like cucumber. So if you're ever lost and desperate, you can eat them and also slake your thirst." Did I really just say *slake?*

"Speaking of cucumbers, how about a snack?" Sarah says. She plops down on a nearby log, promptly joined by Alexandra. Sarah passes around a bag of salt-and-vinegar potato chips. I'm too busy swatting bugs to be interested in either food or sitting. I stand, waiting for them to finish. Now they're talking about someone in Alexandra's office while Sarah the psychiatrist suggests potential reasons for his obnoxious behavior. I would find this interesting, too, if I were somewhere else.

I apply more bug juice, sip water, and wait for them to be ready to go. Only they don't seem to be getting ready to go. They are immersed, wrapped, cocooned in conversation so dense it even seems to keep the bugs away. I watch them for a while, shifting my weight from boot to boot. Then I look around at the trees. They smell good, these conifers. They look like blue spruce but I could be wrong. I've read this is old growth forest and I wonder if bugs prefer old to new growth. Can I feel a difference between this wise old forest and younger, fresher forests? I try, but mostly what I feel is the irritation of waiting when I'm eager to see more. I find myself wishing Juniper were here instead of back home with Casey. Junie would have been happy to hike on.

When it appears that neither of my two friends will ever stand up again, I effect the necessary interruption. We hike for a while and soon come to the short side path to Bugle Cliff. "What do you think?" I ask. "Shall we take it?"

They look at me blankly. "What's there?" Sarah asks. Turns out both were too busy to look at the Personal Hiking Log (PHL) I sent them weeks ago. The PHL is a tool, a matrix I developed that breaks trails into observable milestones with elevation gains or losses between each. With a PHL we can follow where we are without having to check the map constantly. We can know when a hard section's coming up.

After I explain about Bugle Cliff, Sarah says, "Sure. Whatever you think."

"I'm happy to go either way," Alexandra agrees.

I feel a sharp pang of missing Kate's and Ginny's interest in PHLs and trail choices.

At Bugle Cliff, about 400 feet higher than Elephant Head, the rocky ledge juts out facing the same direction but with the expanded view that more altitude provides. Wow. Both my friends promptly sit down. Why are they sitting down? We just had a break. Sarah gets out an orange and offers sections all around. When she's finished, she hurls the peel over the ledge into the foliage below.

"Hey!" I cry. "We're supposed to Leave No Trace. You know, as if we were never here." The Winter Hiking Course must really have had an impact on me, because I'm scandalized.

Sarah frowns at me. "It's biodegradable."

I parrot the course instructors. "It takes years and years for something like that to disintegrate. In the meantime, it's ugly. Wildlife eat it and then they come to depend on our garbage for food. Sometimes they'll delay hibernating or moving on. And some of the garbage isn't even good for them. The AMC's totally against it."

Alexandra hasn't said a word.

Sarah pauses with pieces of a hard-boiled eggshell in her

hand. "Okay," she says. "Just for you." She drops the bits of shell into a plastic bag.

Have I become the hike's tyrant? I'm aware I sound like a textbook, but the feeling that wells up inside me is the same that I had each of the million times I read *The Lorax*, Casey's favorite story when she was three. Using a scratchy old man voice for the Lorax, a homely, sad looking creature who accosted people begging them to take care of the forest, I would croak: *I am the Lorax. I speak for the trees.*

I think about apologizing to Sarah, but she and Alexandra are deep in conversation about where each grew up. I look at my watch. Ten minutes later, feeling like a Girl Scout leader, I rally the troops to move out. I don't know how I landed the den mother role. Nor do I know how to get out of it. It doesn't occur to me to employ my new first rule of hiking. I don't Speak Up. Instead, I stomp along, muddled and irritated, no longer noticing wildflowers. This is not how I expected this hike to go. I wanted it to be more . . . what? I don't know what my hopes were. I didn't write them down the way I usually do. Sarah arrived too late for our pre-hike talk, but why didn't I discuss stuff with Alexandra? We had the time.

I'm forced to admit that I felt too self-conscious, too uncertain that Alexandra would go along with making our hike more intentional, more intimate than a day's outing. After all, I wasn't officially in charge the way I had been of people who reported to me in my former career. No one had to do what I suggested, nor did I want to appear bossy or business-like to two cherished friends. I chickened out. But here I am, the de facto leader anyway.

We've come to the fork in the trail where we must decide to climb Jackson or Webster. Sarah asks me, "Right or left?"

I point her toward the Jackson branch, not bothering to explain that in case we can manage only one peak, it will be the one that's a 4000-Footer. I now understand that what we actually do doesn't matter to them. They're here to get away from stressors in their lives, as I am, but somebody has to know where we're going. I find myself recalling Sarah's and my phone conversation years back when I invited her to Tripyramid. After she said yes, I told her, "Awesome! I'll send you a map and trail descriptions."

"Don't bother," she replied. "I'll just follow you."

"Don't you want to scope it out? Know what you're in for?"

"Nope. Nolan does all that. The girls and I just go where he points us."

At the time, I'd been shocked into silence. How could my ambitious, intelligent friend sound so passive, so little like a feminist? Her comment had rankled for days—until I realized that following mindlessly was precisely what I used to do. Whenever I hiked before, I always followed a man. No wonder I hadn't liked to hear it. It wasn't until Tripyramid that I felt compelled to plan, prepare, and be informed. Tripyramid had been *my* hike, my test of myself, and I hadn't wanted to follow anybody.

Now here I am with Sarah and Alexandra, feeling like I'm a tour guide when I want our adventure to be the three of us exploring, discovering, and figuring things out together. Like Kate and me. Like Ginny and I are doing more and more. I didn't sign up to be the only one keeping time and following the map. Nor, obviously, had my pals signed up to make this climb the kind of experience I prefer. Meantime, I feel cut off from my tribe and—increasingly, as I stew about these things—from the mountain I came to get to know. I still don't Speak Up.

We creep our way up ledges near the cone of Jackson to the top. Once there we're treated to blue sky and green-clad views of the valley that lies in the fold opened up by Carter Notch, even catching a glimpse of Washington a string of mountains away. Sarah and Alexandra settle down to eat lunch and I join them. Alexandra pulls out a skimpy peanut-butter-and-jelly sandwich. No snacks. No trail mix or other goodies to share, and suddenly I miss the sharing. Of course, I didn't ask Alexandra to bring food to share. If I'd done my usual thing, I'd have requested she bring something for dinner the night before or contribute to breakfast the next morning, as Sarah did. I hadn't wanted to impose on Alexandra, figuring it would be a treat for a mother of four not to concern herself with meals. Now it occurs to me that when someone brings food, it not only creates a bond, it shares the responsibility for our time together.

We talk as we eat. I try so hard to connect with my friends that lunch goes on for an hour. I'm getting antsy, but I don't want to kill the party. Nobody else notices the passage of time. Reluctantly, I intervene and propose we add Webster to the hike rather than descend the same trail. I remind them Webster offers terrific views and that the ridge trail up to it is supposed to be an easy ramble. They leave the decision to me. As a controlling person, I should like that, right? Instead, I feel lonely.

After checking the sky, blue with only a few small, stable clouds, I opt for Webster. I figure I might never see it again, having so many 4000-Footers to climb. A clock ticks inside me composed of one part age and three parts fear of cancer returning, a clock that presses me to finish The 48 as quickly as I'm able. I don't have time to go back and re-do anything.

As we march along the woods-enclosed ridge, Sarah and Alexandra exchange stories of how they chose their careers and their first jobs. I lob in an occasional comment and pick up the pace. I thought things would feel different after our long, convivial lunch, but they don't. As my pals remain deep in conversation, I admire the trees, mushing my team onto the Webster trail to begin our descent.

An idea blooms. "Do you mind if I go on ahead for awhile? I just need some silence to feel the mountain." I try to say this without an edge.

They don't appear the least bit offended. I've finally gotten the gumption to Speak Up, and it works! I scuttle off as fast as I can go until I no longer hear a human voice. We haven't passed anyone else all day, so I'm quite alone. The trail grows rough underfoot, rockier, rootier, wetter. Harder on the feet. So steep my right knee, which has been silent thus far, protests. I have to concentrate on the footing enough that I can't look around and enjoy nature, so I need something else to focus on besides my knee and feet.

I begin to parse what's gone wrong for me on this hike, casting back to a conference I attended in 1980 on the nature of authority and leadership. Rather than listening to experts lecture and show slides, we learned directly from what we ourselves experienced being in groups: small groups, large groups, assigned groups, groups we created ourselves, groups with consultants in them, groups without. No one told us what to do. There was no agenda. We sat and looked at each other until somebody said something. Over the course of a couple of days, people started crying and admitting how afraid they were in a group of strangers or how they were attracted to other participants. The normal barriers disintegrated and the underlying emotions of humans in a group—the feelings usually denied or hidden—erupted.

What happened in those five days gave me my deepest understanding of how groups behave. I saw how easy it was for most of us, including me, to grow passive when there was an assumed or appointed leader—even if that leader wasn't actually leading or, in fact, saying a word. The hardest thing of all was not leading a group, but being a participant who retained her or his responsibility and authority.

After a particularly wobbly rock, I stop to tighten my

bootlaces. Hiking on, I promise to remember the challenges of being a responsible group member when I ask folks to hike with me, vowing to be clear with friends ahead of time about sharing the work of sticking to the right trails and making key decisions. I realize I have to decide, once and for all, if I am or am not leading these hikes. I don't assume I'll be the leader but, since Kate, everyone else does. Am I kidding myself? Avoiding my own responsibilities? And if I am the leader what kind of leader do I want to be? Two women I love and admire are enjoying the heck out of each other on this mountain. Why aren't I?

It's clear as the water in Gem Pool that too much talking pulls me out of the moment, away from the mountain. I need to do exactly that—talk—sometimes, especially at the beginning of a hike to connect with people and again in the final quarter when it's all about endurance. But I don't want to be drawn away from the natural wonders surrounding us the whole time. I need to engage with nature, too.

Something else I learned in that long ago conference I need to remember. As I explained to Ginny, every person in a group speaks for the group. A part of each of us wants to cause trouble at the same time another part wants to be kind. One part wants to lead while another part wants to be led. Each voice, each person, deserves to be honored. I haven't been honoring my two good friends.

I stop thinking when I see a tall wildflower staring me eye-to-eye from the side of the trail. The huge, delicate white flower resembles Queen Anne's Lace, but broken into segments and radiated out along thin green branches, like planets in a spiral galaxy. I'm enchanted. I touch the soft nodding head, the sturdy purplish stem. Its name, Angelica, seems apt both in appearance and application—Angelica was used to treat the black plague and continues to be an ingredient in herbal remedies.

With the acquaintance of Angelica, with the silence in which I hear only the softest clapping of leaves overhead or an occasional mountain chickadee calling *chick-a-dee-dee-dee*, I am back on the mountain again. I pat passing tree limbs and trunks. I'm aware my body hurts, but I'm also aware that the pain is a small thing, one voice in the web of voices heard and unheard all around me. I, too, am a small thing in the web. Home. For this little while, at least, I am part of the family of Mountain, and I no longer feel alone.

Jackson
4,052 ft – 06/28/2003

25. SPEED KILLS

On a bright Saturday in October, I am the first one up. We didn't get to Waterville Valley until after midnight, because Casey's now in high school. Her schedule of activities after class is daunting. Besides that, Red Sox fever has infected us. We've stayed up late night after night watching playoff games that didn't get decided until the ninth or went into extra innings. For the last five years, the Boston Red Sox have been stymied by the New York Yankees, an organization the Boston media never hesitate to call "The Evil Empire." Normally, I am the kind of baseball fan who accompanies my family to Fenway Park armed with a book, but the tension of this week's games has me grinding my teeth at night. A hike, I figure, will work off the stress of watching our home team, the team Larry has loved since law school, fuel the wild hope that this could be *it*—the year the Sox shatter the Curse of the Bambino and win the World Series for the first time since 1918.

The climb today will also be a welcome respite from writing disappointments. My year of sending a piece out to literary magazines every two months has gotten some results, but fewer than I'd hoped. After that first short story, a handful of poems made it into print but subsequent short stories have attracted a landfill's worth of rejections. A few editors scribbled enthusiastic comments in the margins along with requests to send in more work, which was encouraging. Except I had no more work and I couldn't write fast enough to think up, develop, and polish a new short story in two months. A story needed time to breathe, to age—to create enough distance between me and the words on the page that I could do a proper edit. Unlike the business work I had produced, my writing progressed at a sedate, downright sluggish pace. No matter how I urged myself to speed up, either on the hiking trail or, apparently, at the keyboard, I could only go as fast as I could go. I stopped using the submission agency.

I refuse to think about that on the hike. Instead, I remember the three of us clambering up Mt. Tom together before Casey went off to summer camp. While she was away, Larry and I summited Mts. Pierce and Eisenhower. At the top of Pierce, we were so absorbed by watching black thunder clouds race directly toward us, that only at the last minute did we tear ourselves away to hide in the trees below to escape the downpour and lightning and prevent Casey's becoming an orphan. After it blew over, we moseyed on to the summit of Eisenhower and wowed ourselves with the 360° panorama.

Today, I promise myself I will simply enjoy being together as a family. We hardly see Casey anymore. Her prep school in the suburbs is known for both academic rigor and sports intensity. Each day she commutes nearly an hour to her new school, traveling an even greater metaphorical distance from her small Quaker grade school in the People's Republic of Cambridge, but the prep school was her choice.

So far, she seems to be making the transition without a hiccup. Which is exactly what worries Larry and me. On the drive to New Hampshire the night before, we asked her how things were going. She'd kept her thoughts to herself thus far, but being trapped in a car in the dark with Juniper settled on her lap loosened her teenaged tongue. What she revealed surprised us. She had a *strategy* for her first semester, one in which she focused on making friends and settling in rather than worrying about schoolwork. Despite the oppressive amount of homework assigned each night, she refused to work too hard. She figured the faculty would cut kids some slack the first semester as they adapted to high school. It was so sensible a plan it left us speechless.

As I sit on the screened porch wrapped in a blanket and gaze out at Tecumseh and Osceola, their autumn flanks blazing with ruby, amber, and gold, I sip tea and spoon up yogurt, enjoying fall perfection. The sky glistens cobalt. The air coming through the screens has a snap to it, fresh and crisp. The temperature is predicted to hit the high 60s with a slight breeze. Hiking conditions don't come any better.

Larry wakes up and eats breakfast on the porch with me. Casey sleeps on. I've already walked Juniper, prepared lunch and snacks for four, filled the water bottles, and packed up my hip pack and two daypacks. Every half hour, Larry and I revise our departure time. We get how exhausted our teen is from all her activities and from the transition itself, so we wait. The three of us leave the apartment a bit past 11:00 a.m.

We plan to hike Mt. Hale, my sixteenth 4000-Footer. Hiking with my family, I'm coming to understand, changes everything. No quandaries for me here about leading or not leading. They refuse to talk about their hopes and fears beforehand. They won't participate in any aspect of my process. How am I related to such anarchists?

Hale lies about twenty miles northeast as the crow flies, but there's no such road through the mountains. Instead, we drive north through Franconia Notch, circle the southwestern clump of the Whites, and return south along their eastern side to Crawford Notch, my hunting ground these days. Many of these 4000-Footers, like Jackson that Sarah, Alexandra, and I hiked, offer more gentle peak bagging than their bigger granite siblings. As I drive, Larry, the only one who never gets carsick, sits in the back seat and reads aloud the newspaper's description of the duel to take place this afternoon between two pitching legends: Red Sox Pedro Martinez and the treasonous former-Red-Sox-now-Yankee, Roger Clemens. Occasionally, I interrupt him to point out a burst of pumpkin-colored trees or luminous patches of claret mountainside. I also suggest, since we're running so late and need to get back in time for the game, that he and Casey put on their hiking boots.

"It'll only take a minute," Casey mumbles. She nods off again in the passenger seat. Neither of them makes a move toward their boots.

When my stomach growls the noon hour, I suggest we eat some of the lunch intended, based on a much earlier start time, for the summit.

"We can eat when we get to the parking area. It'll only take a minute," Larry responds.

I urge them to drink a lot of water, like I'm doing, to hydrate before we start off. Unlike my friends, they ignore me. Any moment I expect one of them to snap, "Stop micro-managing!"

At the trailhead parking lot they get their boots on while I stalk into the woods to get rid of all that helpful hydration. Casey loads a roll of film into her newly purchased 35mm camera. She's found a new passion: Photography 101. Larry laces his boots. Back at the car, I shift weight from one foot to the other.

At last we start up the path to Hale. After ten minutes of hiking, Larry looks at his watch. "I'm going to miss the whole game."

I stop in the middle of the trail, Casey nearly stepping

on my heels. "Let's go back," I say. "Forget this." I can't bear to keep him from his game.

"No, no. We're here now," he insists, unable to bear keeping me from my mountain.

"I can do Hale another time. It's short. I can even do it by myself."

He shakes his head and lunges up the trail.

I continue to urge him to quit and he continues to refuse. Casey wisely remains silent. "I'll listen to the game in the car," he finally declares, and I give up.

But during the disagreement our pace increased and after we stop arguing, we really start to kick it. I prefer to warm up gently in the beginning of a hike, taking things at a leisurely pace until I've worked the driving kinks out of my knee and hip. No dice. We need to *move* to catch the game on the radio. Casey says nothing, but I can feel the waves of her displeasure strike the back of my neck. The only one who's thrilled with our speed is Juniper, who now doesn't have to dash back and forth on the trail waiting for us to catch up.

Fifteen minutes go by where the only sounds are my huffing, somebody's boot side-slipping, or my poles striking a rock. Then Casey says, "I can't take pictures racing along like this! The only reason I came was to photograph."

What? I thought she came because she liked hiking. I thought this would be a time for us to hear more about kids in her class, her teachers, the whole high school scene. Instead she admonishes us about f-stops and focus and lighting, delicate matters that apparently can't be rushed.

"Okay," I say, torn between her needs and her father's. "Fine." We slow down a tad. But she's made me remember I'm carrying a camcorder, something I've never done before but figured for only 4.4 miles round trip, it was worth lugging to memorialize my happy family out hiking together on a fabulous fall day. Now there's no time to stop and record, but no great loss, my family is not happy anyway.

I pummel the trail, leaning on my hiking poles to go faster. At some point, Casey yells up to me that her ankles hurt from soccer practice and she can't keep up this pace. As Larry zooms onward, I head back down the trail to her. Thinking fast, I suggest she take her time and enjoy shooting all the pictures she wants. Since we follow the same trail up and down, we'll meet up with her on the way back. The plan receives teenaged approval.

I abandon my daughter and race upward, sweating massively. The dense forest has captured enough humidity that I fantasize multi-colored parrots flitting through the trees. I catch up to Larry at a brook crossing, but don't stop. I know he can always catch me. As I bolt ahead, he yells he'll wait for Casey to see if she wants help crossing the slippery rocks. "Fine!" I yell back. Nobody needs to reach the summit except me. Juniper stays with him, lapping up water from the stream and wading in up to her chest to cool off. Though I wish she'd decided to come along, I tell myself it's just the mountain and me, and I start to enjoy hiking alone.

I blow past a milestone I recognize from my PHL. How did I get here so quickly? I wonder what time it is, but Larry has the watch. I pass a family speaking German and cross a wide stream. I stop for only as long as it takes to unzip the bottoms of my combo pants and hurl them into my hip pack. Sweat runs down my neck, chest, and back. Even my hiking vest, my second layer over a sleeveless wicking shirt, splotches with sweat. Still, dread of making Larry miss the game forces me to push harder. My lungs labor and my legs burn from the bottoms of my feet to the tops of my thighs. My shoulders quiver from leaning so much weight on my poles.

I'm about half way up "little" Hale when I realize I hate this hike. I want to quit. Anyway, I can't do it. I can't make it in time. I didn't get much sleep last night and I'm exhausted, lightheaded, and dizzy. What am I doing this for?

Still, I'm embarrassed to be defeated by a mountain so inconsequential that no one ever mentions it. I slow down, minimally, and start to think. Now that I'm thinking I realize that this little trail gains 2300 feet in elevation in 2.2 miles. Moosilauke gained just a bit over that in 3.8 miles. Jeez Louise. No wonder my hair is dripping and I can't seem to catch a full breath. From now on, I will treat every 4000-Footer with respect.

I start to worry I'll be the slowest person next weekend when I hike Mt. Whiteface with Ginny and two other women I hardly know. Maybe, despite my training, I've gotten out of shape since Webster and Jackson in July. In August, our family vacation took us to Cape Cod for two weeks. No mountains there. As I'm fretting, the German family passes me. Juniper arrives, following their enormous black dog that shambles along like a bear with a perm. A family with kids has bested me? No effing way. I gather myself, manufacture saliva for my desiccated mouth, and lurch by them. Junie sprints ahead, showing her tail feathers to their curly black brute.

From the corner of my eye, I note waterfalls, cataracts, little rivulets of sparkling water. No time to stop and appreciate them. I pass spectacular fall colors in a blur, blaze past a stand of yellow birch half-fallen that I'd like to record with the camcorder that bangs continually against my hip. No time. I don't converse with Juniper the way I usually do. I haven't the breath. My stomach grumbles nonstop, and I'm so parched the walls of my throat seem to stick together. Larry has all the water and food in his pack. Searching my vest pockets as I careen along, I discover three hard candies. Maybe I'd better ration them. I chuck one in my mouth, unwrap it with my tongue, and spit the cellophane into my top vest pocket.

I hear someone coming up fast behind me, and turn. I've never seen Larry breathe so hard or sweat so much. He gasps that he waited fifteen minutes by the bug-infested creek for Casey, only to learn she didn't need his help and was insulted by the offer.

We press on to the summit. Often I compose descriptions of summits and their views in my head as a kind of writer's exercise, but at the top I don't even look around. And forget my usual peak dance, I'm too busy choking down food and water.

I glance at Larry's watch. While chewing, I calculate. Re-check the watch. It seems to be true. After fifteen 4000-Footers, I have at long last beaten book time. By a boatload. I don't write down by how much—and probably due to shock, never will remember—because game time speeds relentlessly closer. Still swallowing the last mouthfuls of sandwich, we charge back down the rocky trail.

I swing on my poles like Tarzan. It's not yet 3:00 p.m. I figure if we continue to race we can just reach the car in time for the first inning and Larry won't miss a moment. He'll arrive home to see at least an hour of the pitching duel on television. Casey will have captured her nature shots. I will have summited my sixteenth peak. Everyone will be happy.

We meet up with Casey who's moseying down the trail. She greets us with, "You've been gone for hours!" Protective of her new camera, she's more cautious than I am descending the wet and leaf-slippery rocks and I chafe at the delay. Praise God, at least she's out of film.

We get to the parking area at last. I run to the car, start it up, turn on the radio.

Blatz! Shrisk ! Scrrr! Static. Nothing but static.

We hurtle out of the lot while Larry reaches over from the back seat to spin the radio dial to station after station. I obliterate the speed limit. Despite our best efforts, we can't tune into the game until we hit Route 3 and all we can find is a New York station where the announcers are clearly prejudiced and delusional. Once in Waterville Valley, I nearly miss the turn into our apartment as the whole Red Sox bench leaps up and rushes onto the field where a brawl ensues. Larry and Casey run ahead into the apartment while I park. I make it in time to watch the final inning. The Sox carry the day, one game closer to winning the pennant.

As for the hike, I can't form a clear image of Hale. It's all rushing water and rocks, wet leaves and sweat as I bagged a 4000-Footer in record time.

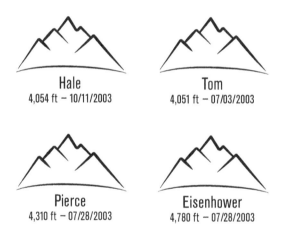

Hale
4,054 ft — 10/11/2003

Tom
4,051 ft — 07/03/2003

Pierce
4,310 ft — 07/28/2003

Eisenhower
4,780 ft — 07/28/2003

26. WIZARDRY

The four of us have finished dinner, the potluck that I hope has increased a sense of shared responsibility. We adjourn to the living area. A fire dances in the small fireplace in Waterville Valley and candles glow on the mantelpiece and on the coffee table spread with maps. I've set the tone for this hike every way I can. I suggested Lee and Clara drive up to Waterville together to save on gas and spare the environment, yes, but also to get to know one another. I'm hoping they formed a bond. I drove up earlier in the day with Ginny to conserve the energy that, post cancer, I still need to hoard before a climb. Tomorrow we tackle 8.4 miles and 2900 feet of elevation change up and down Mt. Whiteface.

For the past few weeks, I've organized like a leader, planned like a leader, sounded in emails and phone calls like a leader. Inside, I'm waiting for one of the group to pull back the curtain and call the wizard a fraud. I fear they will find my process absurd, my guidelines ridiculous, and my hiking pace glacial. In short, maybe one of them should lead.

Clara is the only one besides me who is peak bagging, with five 4000-Footers under her belt. She's a decade younger and 5'7" tall, a sturdy outdoorswoman from Maine who probably hikes a lot faster than I. She has managed political campaigns, which is how she and Larry became such good friends, and both facts tell me she's savvy and bright. I barely know the woman, but I'm guessing she can organize a group.

Lee, a quiet woman my age, I met in book group a month ago, drawn to her shining cap of silver hair and her thoughtful comments. She has traveled the world, which I admire, and I think we'll get along, but people can surprise you on a hike. She's only a little taller than me but packs a lot more muscle. For each of the past twelve years, she's climbed in the Himalayas and I'm more than a tad intimidated. Besides, Lee is an executive coach, a paid expert in leadership.

Why should either of these women follow me or my approach to facing a mountain? I'm grateful for Ginny's presence. She likes my style of hiking. Since our conversation about being controlling, I'm confident that even if she thinks I'm behaving like a jerk, she'll find a caring way to tell me so.

I dreaded calling Lee. To ask her to carry some of my things, I'd have to tell her why. I'd rather face a precipice. I want cancer firmly behind me, in the past. Not buried exactly, but not in my face either.

After my explanation, Lee said her sister had died from breast cancer. I closed my eyes, holding the phone tightly. "Oh, Lee. I'm so sorry. How awful." Why her sister and not me? Was Lee asking herself the same question? And how long would I, who felt so vibrant now, remain safe? These feelings were promptly followed by fear that Lee might want to talk about cancer on the trail. These days, I only wanted to discuss my cancer experience when I was overwhelmed by it—and I wanted to run from everyone else's.

I tuned back in to our conversation to hear Lee say "—following your example of saying you need to feel emotionally free on the hike, I want to tell you, even though she died a long time ago, I still have trouble with extended conversations about breast cancer. It makes me so sad."

I was happy to reassure her. After we hung up, maybe because we'd gone so deep so quickly, I felt vulnerable. Most people didn't drag out their emotional laundry to go hiking. Did she think I was too sensitive? Still too labile from cancer? I tried to picture a group of men going through similar conversations. Failed. Perhaps this very moment Lee and Clara were rolling their eyes thinking, *How tedious can she make a hike?*

These same questions flutter at the back of my throat as I sit on the loveseat in Waterville Valley and open the manila folder containing my notes. I stuff a pillow behind my back to try to still the spasms from the drive up. The intensity of Clara's, Lee's, and Ginny's attention makes my cheeks burn. The hike up Whiteface together begins right now.

Gripping my pen, I go straight to the hardest part before I can weasel out. I've told them to expect to state goals and fears, and I volunteer my own to start. "I'm afraid you'll all go faster than me. I worry I'll be a drag on everyone, and I'll feel not only like a slug but, on top of that, pressured to keep up. I hate hiking for speed." Four days ago, Hale schooled me on that.

I don't want to think—much less tell them—about the constant anemia or the low white cell count that persists. I don't mention Tamoxifen's effect on my tendons. I hold back when soon I will urge them to be forthcoming, maintaining a higher standard for myself that is as automatic and unconscious as breathing.

I admit my conscious fears. "I worry that the Blueberry Ledge Trail and those ledges will scare me witless. And I'm supposed to be the leader!"

They laugh, but the air vibrates with tension. The bible warns that the steep ledges require scrambling and are perilous if wet or icy. Even under the best conditions, I'm scared my fear of heights will freeze me the way it did on the South Slide.

I look down at my notes then pause, feeling my way to get right something the Jackson and Webster hike taught me. "Leading a group of hikers is new for me, and I'm a responsibility sponge. If there's any unclaimed responsibility floating around, I'll take it on even when I shouldn't. Needn't. I'm worried that my own sense of responsibility will do me in and I won't enjoy the adventure I've looked forward to." After my last two climbs, I need to enjoy this hike. I walk over to the fireplace to throw on another log. "It's kind of like when you have a party at your house and you're so busy making sure there's enough napkins and everyone's plate is filled that you don't have fun yourself."

"Performance anxiety," Ginny says. "That's why I never have people over for dinner." Everyone laughs.

"Yes." I return the poker to its stand. "It's also taking care of others beyond the point where it's good for you. How many women over-give? Aren't we raised to do just that?" Vehement nods from Clara and Ginny. Lee looks intent. Since cancer, I'm keeping an eye on my responsibility intake the way diabetics watch their sugar.

"How will we know?" Lee cocks her head. "I mean, if you're feeling too responsible."

I think for a minute, remembering the times on Jackson when I felt disconnected from Sarah and Alexandra. "I guess I'll just go real quiet." I give Lee an admiring glance. What an intelligent, useful question.

I take my place back on the loveseat. Now comes the moment I dread. "Next?" Will they ante up or will I be the only one with skin in the game, a failed leader before we leave the living room?

It gets so quiet the hissing of a log seems loud. The silence lingers. My heart beats in my ears. Then my buddy steps into the void. Clasping one knee, Ginny admits, "Like Cheryl, I fear that I'll be the slowest. I'm afraid I'm in the worst shape of everyone and I'll be all by myself at the end of the line."

Clara and I nod.

Ginny continues. "And I'm also afraid of the ledges." She lifts a tea mug up to her mouth, but lowers it again without sipping. "I'm afraid the ledges will be so steep my pack will pull me over backwards like an upturned turtle."

"Right." I scribble down her words. "We can take turns going last, can't we?" I turn to Clara and Lee. They agree. Now what have I done? Going last makes me anxious, too. Have I just over-given?

This time Ginny actually drinks her tea. "It's also good to distract me with talk. And it really helps to sing," says the choral conductor.

"Which is a treat," I say, "because Ginny has a beautiful voice."

When Ginny finishes, another silence falls and my nerves prickle. I can only hope and wait, and wait some more, stomach muscles tensing. I can't force Lee and Clara to share, but it will make such a difference if they do. Or don't.

I'm just about to give up and suggest we break for Lee's homemade apple pie when Clara, the youngster amidst us fifty-three-year-olds, leans forward twirling a strand of long honey-colored hair. "Well, we're three for three," she says. "My biggest fear is that I'll be the slowest."

The rest of us grin and, for me at least, it's pure relief.

"I worry I won't be able to keep up with you guys. Especially on the steep parts. I do feel some trepidation there. Sometimes the only way I can get down is to slide on my butt." She pushes her shoulders back almost defiantly. "The truth is, I'm fifty percent afraid I'll fall off the mountain and fifty percent afraid I'll look like a doofus."

Everyone bursts into laughter. I find the frankness of the woman from Maine admirable and downright endearing. I promise Clara she won't be last all the time either. She amazes me by responding she'd rather be last than feel pushed to go faster. Fabulous! "What can we do when you're scared at the steep parts?" I ask.

Clara tosses the now-wavy strand of hair she's been twisting back over her shoulder. "It helps if I can watch someone else go first to see how they do it."

"I'm just the opposite," I say. "When I'm nervous I prefer going first." Clara and I look at each other and shake our heads in wonder. It's like we're from different but complementary planets. I turn to Lee and Ginny. "What do you prefer?"

"I like somebody else to scope it out while I observe," Ginny says.

"And I like to go first," says Lee.

I feel like Noah. My ark has been conveniently populated in pairs.

Everyone waits patiently for Lee to take her turn. As I'm about to call on her, she finally speaks. She doesn't say she's afraid she'll be last or look foolish or take on too much responsibility or fall over. She says only one thing. "For the past dozen years, I've hiked in one place, Nepal. Those trails have become part of my life. Part of me." She pauses. "I'm starting to feel some anxiety over what I'm getting into here."

I'm taken aback, but I write it down. How can Whiteface possibly concern a Himalayan veteran? When Lee says no more, I prompt her. "Because of the ledges?"

She nods. "The rest of you know these mountains and *you're* scared." She tucks her legs beneath her on the sofa and rests her chin on one hand. In the firelight and candlelight, her eyes glisten cat-green.

I smile at her but can't deny what she's said. Sneaking a glance at the clock, I see it's past nine and we need to be up before five. I consider ditching the rest of the process. But remembering how I might have avoided feeling so alone on Jackson if I'd had this very talk, I press on. "I'll start us off on goals. My first is to bag my seventeenth peak."

Ginny cheers.

"Larry didn't tell me you'd done so many," says Clara. "That's impressive!"

"Oh, Cheryl's amazing," says Ginny. "You should have seen her when we did the Hancocks."

I wince. Probably both Clara and Lee are faster and stronger than I. I also worry Ginny's allusions to our hikes together make the other two feel excluded. I hurry on. "Another goal is to enjoy myself. I want to connect with everyone and to get to know you two better." I nod at Lee and Clara. The easy part is over. "I've learned part of my pleasure in hiking, my passion really, comes from getting in touch with nature." I drink some water. "Which means that for part of the time, I'd like to hike alone." I can feel my shoulders inch up towards my ears. "I hope that doesn't sound anti-social," I add lamely.

Seconds tick by. Then Clara says, "You know, I'm glad you said that. I like to hike alone part of the time, too, and I never thought to ask for it. That will be one of my goals also."

Whew.

Ginny pipes up. "I'm fine with that unless it's at a hard place. I don't like to be alone where it's steep or rough, or if we have to cross a big stream."

I make a note then turn to Lee, who hasn't weighed in.

"I find that people hike at different speeds, so we get separated sometimes anyway," she says. "And I like spending time alone."

I relax a bit despite what I'm about to say. "My last goal, not my least, is to be a good leader. Part of being a good leader—I think anyway—is asking for help when I need it. Not so easy for me." I'm better at it since cancer, but not if I'm the leader. "I want each of us to speak up. If you're hungry or tired or scared, sick of talking or need us to distract you, say so." I'm talking to myself as well. "Every problem in a group is a group problem. And groups solve problems better than individuals. I hope you'll trust me on this one." I mean every word so much I feel naked.

No one comments. Clara looks open, Ginny proud, Lee considering. I've had enough of the spotlight. "Clara, I've written down your goal of hiking alone for a while. Anything else?"

Clara pulls her hair back and twists it into a loose ponytail. "I don't like it when people whine about the kind of day it is. Or the mud or bugs."

"But Cheryl's saying something else." Ginny leans forward. "She means speaking up about what's inside us. Which is very different from complaining about external things we can't control."

Lee doesn't say anything and I can't read her face. Clara says, "I guess I'll have to see it in action."

My three companions, one by one, state their goals. I'll have occasion to remember them when we're on the trail.

∽

In the full dark of 6:00 a.m. in mid-October, we bounce down a potholed dirt road toward Whiteface.

A quarter of an hour later, Clara clicks on the wipers. "It's snowing." Sure enough, fat white flakes launch themselves at the windows. Nobody says a word. I'm thinking about the ledges and I doubt I'm the only one. We find the parking area and Clara turns off the ignition. We sit staring out at the sleet and snow—they seem to be alternating—as the windows fog over.

I tap Ginny's shoulder. "Could you run us through the PHL for our backup mountain next door, Mt. Passaconaway, just in case we need to hike something without ledges?"

Ginny turns around and looks sheepish. Though she agreed to put together our Personal Hiking Log for Passaconaway, she confesses, "I procrastinated until last night and fell asleep before I could do it."

I try not to gape. No time to deal with my irritation now. We can use the map, of course. But I'm a words woman, a writer. I want descriptions and milestones and sign posts for the mountains I face. I reach down by my feet and pull out the bible, hand it to Ginny, and ask her to read aloud the description of Dicey's Mill Trail up Passaconaway. As she reads, I pick out milestones and trail turnings and calculate distances between them at what feels like warp speed. Clara and Lee silently wait. Dicey's Mill Trail is nothing to sniff at: 9.4 miles round trip with fifty feet more elevation gain than Whiteface. I'm pink-cheeked from adrenaline by the time I produce a hand-written, bare bones PHL to guide us. I zip the back-up PHL into a hiking vest pocket, saying with forced cheer, "It's like bringing an umbrella. Now we won't need it at all." Just in case, I ask if everyone brought her trail map.

Ginny and Clara nod. "I don't have one," Lee says.

Is leading hikes always like this? I provided everyone my tried-and-tested list of what to bring and made a special point about having the map. I planned a backup mountain. Where have I gone wrong? I tell Lee, "You'll just have to stick close to one of us."

That settled, we start tightening bootlaces and grabbing things from packs. Clara says she noticed an outdoor toilet. She and Ginny open the front doors to head off for a pit stop, when Lee clears her throat. "I'm a little anxious about this weather," she says. Pauses. "Because I didn't bring my jacket."

Clara slams her door. Before I can gather my wits, the former campaign director who's just driven over an hour in the dark on a crater-pocked road turns to Lee. "You've got to be kidding me! You don't have a rain jacket?"

I envy how easily Clara puts it right out there.

Ginny shuts her door. Nobody's going anywhere.

There's more. Lee owns up that she did not bring any foul weather gear at all. No rain or wind pants, no gloves, no hat. All things on my packing list. All things I showed everyone last night, layer by layer. And what about all that expertise from the Himalayas?

The silence grows active as we each work through what lack of a protective, waterproof layer in snowy, sleety weather means.

Lee cannot do the hike.

And we cannot leave her in the car for eight hours.

She could take the car and go somewhere, I suppose. And come back for us, when? Nobody brought a cell phone; they rarely work in the mountains. After weeks of logistical preparation and months of training and anticipation, we have to give up our climb.

Ginny turns her blue eyes and open California look toward Clara and me. "This is partly my fault. I saw Lee debating whether or not to bring her jacket and I should have said something." Ginny later will reveal she didn't want to seem bossy—controlling—to someone she'd just met. Maybe the Himalayan credentials intimidated us all.

Lee speaks up, her voice tense. "I could use the first aid blanket Cheryl lent me. As a cape." She's probably been thinking about this since it began to snow. "I really don't want to ruin this for everybody. I'm sorry. I just get so hot when I hike."

So does everybody else, I want to snap. Only hours later do I piece together that Lee has always hiked in Nepal during her vacation in *August*, sweating through semi-tropical weather. While I pictured her in crampons and snowsuit wielding an ice axe, she was picking off leeches that slid from the vegetation as she passed. This is her first hike in the Whites, her first hike outside the Himalayas, and her first hike with me instead of a professional trekking guide. Who probably checked over all her gear or brought it for her.

She has just taught me an important hike leader lesson: Never Assume.

"Okay," I say, tapping my thigh as I think. "Brainstorm, everybody. What have we got besides emergency blankets?" I rummage around the cargo area behind the back seat. "Plastic grocery bags. We can tie those together. Anybody have a big garbage bag you brought as a pack cover?"

"No," says Ginny, "but I did bring two pairs of rain pants and an extra fleece because I wasn't sure which ones I'd need. Lee can borrow a set."

Ginny to the rescue! She's the tallest, so the clothing will fit if Lee rolls up the pant legs. "That's great, " Lee says. "Thanks. I'm sure that will be plenty with the Mylar blanket on top."

"You can use my extra pair of socks as gloves," Clara offers.

"And it looks like the snow is letting up," Ginny adds.

"Houston," I cry, "we have a mission!"

We get out of the car, outfit Lee, and take turns at the comfort station. A furtive sun peeks in and out from behind scurrying clouds. I take the improved weather as a good omen.

We march along Ferncroft Road looking for Squirrel Bridge and the start of the Blueberry Ledge Trail. The sky clouds over again, but with our event going forward and nothing wet and sloppy falling on us, the mood of the group improves. I feel my energy rise in a blend of excitement, anticipation, and fear—the specific tang of a climbing adventure.

As we stride through woods, Ginny and Lee behind us, I learn that Clara has left political organizing to look for work in the field of conservation, a direction that complements her obvious love of mountains. I mention a few folks I think might be able to provide some leads. As we continue talking, I notice frost-stiffened grass by the side of the road and trees wearing icy coats. Nothing drips from branches or leaves overhead, so the temperature hasn't warmed in the last half hour. Even with a dilettante sun, I expected some melting.

We arrive at Squirrel Bridge and, for the second time that morning, the bottom drops out of my stomach. The stream over which our wooden bridge arches is caked with ice. Even at this low elevation the wooden bridge is rimed with the stuff that can kill you on ledges higher up.

Our feet slip as we cross the flat surface. Somebody whoops as she slides, but the hollow sound of my boot steps echo inside my chest where I want joy to be. Once across the bridge we come, in both senses, to a fork in the road. To the left the Blueberry Ledge Trail leads up to Whiteface, our goal. Straight ahead lies the gravel road that begins Dicey's Mill Trail toward backup Passaconaway. Which do we take?

We pause in the crossroads. The need for a decision sends me back to the fire-lit living room last night when we stated our goals. I replay Clara's mellow yet commanding voice saying she wants to complete the hike safely, get a lot of exercise, and enjoy spectacular views—the views from Whiteface. Except in this weather, the safety factor suggests relatively viewless Passaconaway. Getting exercise will happen either way. She also said, "I want to get away from the city and experience wilderness. I want that serenity you get from hiking in the Whites." Me, too, I'd said at the time. Won't either mountain offer us that serenity? Not if we're afraid of sliding off ledges.

Ginny's first goal was to get to the top. "But I also want to have enough energy left to get back down and not hate it. Usually the descent is exhausting and painful and I hope to do better than that." With the snow and ice, I'm not sure we'll get to the top of Whiteface. If we do, the trail conditions will require more, not less, energy on the way down.

Ginny also wanted time alone. "I really enjoy the spiritual side of the hikes Cheryl and I've done. And I want to see lots of fall color. I want to appreciate autumn, the season of transition." Everybody agreed. Which argues for Whiteface and the panoramic views.

Lee hoped to get to the place where "my brain stops and my body takes over. It's so satisfying to find a rhythm and follow the flow." She also wanted to hike alone. "When I hike alone I can just *be*. Be in my body and in nature." Though we all want to, I don't think anyone should hike alone if the Blueberry Ledge Trail is snowy, icy, or wet.

I squint, trying to remember Lee's other goals. Oh, yes. I see her leaning forward a little and setting down her mug to say, "I feel like I've been living this split life where my athletic endeavors are in Nepal and then I come home to Boston and work. I want to see if I can do what I love in my own backyard, to find out if I can enjoy the Whites."

Would she enjoy Whiteface or Passaconaway more? How the hell do I know?

As for me, if we make it to the top I can exchange the blue pin on my wall map for a red number 17 with either mountain. I'll also get to know Lee and Clara better whichever one we choose. But my last goal is the killer: to be a good leader.

During the few seconds it takes me to consider everyone's goals, two men and a woman have shown up, all long, lean, and weathered. Our little group walks over to their little group. I ask them where they're headed.

The woman responds. "We're thinking we'll do the loop. Up Whiteface and across to Passaconaway, then down Dicey's Mill."

Following a hunch I ask, "You've done it before?"

"Twice."

"You're not worried about the ledges being too slippery?" Ginny asks.

The woman shrugs. One man pokes at the ground with a hiking pole but the other man says, "Hey, if it happens, we'll turn back. We'll still have spent a nice morning in the woods." They march off on Blueberry Ledge Trail.

We look up at the sky, but it's hard to read. Oyster-colored clouds with a hint of blue that could mean the sun will poke through eventually. Or not. I pose the question directly: "Whiteface or Passaconaway, folks?"

We follow the threesome down Blueberry Ledge Trail, but slowly, because we're debating. Everyone agrees it's risky to head up Whiteface, though it might clear up. Or it could, in the predictably unpredictable manner of the Whites, warm up so much we face wet, dripping rocks. Each of us voices her longing to see the famous views. Perhaps each secretly longs to test herself, as I do, on the ledges. We fall silent.

We pass an open green field with a picturesque set of white farm buildings. Watching over them stands a cluster of maple trees dressed like tall sentries in bright uniforms of burnished orange. Farther away a mountain presents a hazy blue-gray shoulder. We pause to admire the view. Ginny takes a picture. "I did warn you I like to take a lot of pictures."

So far everyone admits that the ledges might be too dangerous and no one feels certain about forging onward. On the other hand, no one speaks up for choosing our backup. I'm uneasy about continuing up Whiteface but prefer to come to a consensus, so I ask them to vote. One by one, each woman says she could go either way and that the decision is mine.

The unanimity—the formality—of their stance surprises me. I feel flattered. Honored. Burdened. Part of me wonders if they're deferring to me because no one else wants the responsibility while the voice of my father the executive barks, *Oh for crissakes, lead!*

Clara asks me a pivotal question. "How would you feel if we continue on to Whiteface but we get to the ledges and have to turn back?"

I look at her and something clicks. "I guess I'd be . . . if we had a backup that was a sure thing but we tried Whiteface instead and missed doing a whole mountain today . . . I'd be pissed."

Clara takes a step back. I'm surprised again. Doesn't she, who is also pursuing The 48, or Ginny whose goal is to get to the top, feel the same way? Maybe I should have said *disappointed* instead of *pissed*.

"Well, that decides it for me," Clara says. "I don't want you to be angry. Let's do Passaconaway." Ginny and Lee quickly agree with Clara.

Hang on. "I don't mean I'd be pissed at *you*." I say. "I mean I'd be pissed at . . . the result. The lost opportunity." Looking back, I doubt that was the whole truth. I'd have been furious with myself for not speaking up when I should have and some of that would likely have spilled over onto them.

No matter, they're of one mind now. "On to Passacon-away then," I say and we do an about face, back to Dicey's Mill Trail. Soon we're enjoying an old logging road blan-keted with colorful fallen leaves, through which we scuff our boots like kids. Now that we know what we're doing and we don't have to worry about the ledges, we're carefree and chatting away. Birches glow like immense marigolds lighting up our path.

When we pass another farmstead, we stop to admire a long line of scarlet sugar maples rippling in the wind like a wall of fire. Behind them a foothill with the same bright hues is crowned with a wreath of gauzy white mist. Forget the ledges, our view is stunning. "Now *this* is autumn," Ginny says, satisfaction deepening her voice. While the rest of us agree, I mentally tick off one of her goals.

As we begin to climb, it snows again, but we are so warmed by exertion (Clara's goal) that Ginny and I hike in tank tops. We never get too far apart but we do have silent times to reach for the spiritual experience each of us craves. Lee manages with the borrowed gear, though she can't pause for long. She tells us when she's cold and we move on. No one feels stuck being last. I discover I do not slow anyone down except Lee. She is faster than me but, for the first time ever, it doesn't bother me.

Passaconaway
4,043 ft — 10/15/2003

27. THE TICKET

The week before Thanksgiving, Larry flies to Florida on one of his frequent trips to tend to his father, now ninety-one and suffering from Parkinson's. On these visits, he and his father reminisce about his mother, talk about Casey, and watch the news. Larry pays the bills and confers with Jack's doctors and caregivers.

Wednesday evening I sit on the red sofa in the den and fold laundry, waiting for *The West Wing* on television. In her bedroom, Casey scrambles to finish her homework so she can join me. When the phone rings, I assume it's Larry.

"Sorry I missed you on your birthday, kid," says my brother.

He still calls me *kid* when I'm over fifty. It's one of the things about Bill that I love. For sure, I am a kid to no one else. "Hey, thanks for trying. Twice," I say, wincing. I meant to call him back, but life got so hectic these days.

"Well, I'm calling with—" the line bleeps to announce I've got another call coming in so all I hear next is, "news."

I ignore the other call, smiling in anticipation of his news, only to hear him blurt, "Cindy died. They just called Mardy from Dracutt Home. I'm on the road for work and I'm not driving back to Houston tonight. No reason to. It's dark and . . . "

I don't absorb anything else he says. Cindy's dead? My sister is no longer alive?

". . . let you know what we decide after Mardy and I go over to the funeral home. I don't think there's any reason to have a funeral or viewing. It's your decision but I don't see why you'd want to come down here."

Words come out of my mouth. "People have different feelings about these things." My sister is dead?

"Sure they do. I'm just saying I don't see why you would."

"I can't believe she died. It doesn't seem . . ."

"Well, if you decide to come, you'd better make up your mind quick. They can only hold the body for thirty-six hours. We're going to have her cremated because that's what Mother wanted . . ." I tune out again, then hear, "The Cindy you knew died two years ago."

He talks about embalming her body if I insist on coming. I'm speechless. He sounds almost angry. It will be months before I remember both how angry I was after our father's death, and that anger is one of the stages of grieving. It will be eight years, after Bill dies and I am the only one left of our lottery family, before I fully appreciate some other things: how much I'd relied upon Bill and Mardy, as the oldest and physically nearest, to bear the burden of my mother and my sister; how he stood between me and the most frightening aspects of aging; and how much I wanted my big brother simply to be there, a permanent fixture in the firmament of my life.

I have to get off the phone. I can't listen anymore. I mumble I'll call him tomorrow, and hang up. I stand up, laundry falling from my lap to the floor, and go sit in the chair at Larry's desk, longing for him. I pick up the phone and call Florida. When he answers, I barely get out the news before I start to cry. I'm holding the phone in one hand, my other hand covering my face, when Casey walks in.

"Oh, Mom," she says softly and bends down to hug me. "What?"

"Cindy," I tell her between sobs. "Died."

She leans her head against my arm. I manage to tell Larry I'll call him tomorrow after carpool, that I just have to cry now. He doesn't want to let me go; he hates that he's not here, but he acquiesces.

"Do you want me to find someone else to do carpool in the morning?" Casey asks.

I nod and she heads off with the phone. I drop my head onto the desk and weep. Distantly, I hear the phone ring. Casey comes back. "It's Bill. Do you want to talk?"

I take the phone. Amidst tears, I tell him I can't talk right now.

"Well, you have to," he says, sounding like our father. He tells me he just spoke with Mardy, who said he was wrong. They had more time to decide about embalming so I didn't have to let them know tomorrow if I was flying down. She said to tell me I should not feel rushed. Surprising me, he adds brusquely, "We love you."

That brings on more tears. I say I love him, too, and hang up.

Casey takes the phone from my hand. "I know this is really sad, but I don't want to feel anything right now. I just want to zone out and watch *West Wing* for a while. Is that okay?"

"Of course, honey." At fourteen, her year-long worry that I would die from cancer is still fresh and she's been through the death of my mother, Jackie, Kate, three of Larry's beloved aunts, an uncle, and two cousins. She worries about Jack, the grandpa she adores. I know grief about Cindy will consume her later, but for now, she is calm. She says she'll take any calls that come in.

I feel guilty letting my child shield me, but for the space of a few hours, I need to be alone to mourn not the silent crone who had come to need a wheelchair or, before that, the aged woman who confused Casey with Bill's grown daughter and forgot my name, but the sister of my youth. Memories wash over me from when I was four, five, six, seven and she was truly three years older and bigger. I close my eyes and see a parade of matching cowgirl outfits with hats and holsters; fluffy organza Easter dresses and baskets of chocolate bunnies and eggs; matching pairs of slippery Chinese pajamas, hers pink and mine green. By special dispensation, Cindy was allowed to make her First Communion with my class so we both wore flouncy white dresses and flowered headbands with veils.

We played so much make-believe together in those years. I was Roy Rogers, climbing up the corner mailbox that I pretended was his horse while Cindy, who didn't like climbing, played Dale Evans on the ground and rode a stick. I was Zorro and she Sargent Garcia. She wore a feather like Tonto and I a scarf for my mask as the Lone Ranger.

In my mind, I hear her Elvis and Mitch Miller records, watch her conduct the band and sing along with every song. We stand in the driveway of our house in Skokie, Illinois, Cindy wearing the veil from her communion dress as she acts the part of the bride in the play I wrote for us to perform. We splash together again in the waves of Lake Michigan, metal beach tags pinned to our suits, our lips blue with cold.

Once she became a teenager, she always chose a boyfriend, some boy at her school or a friend of Bill's or, later on, one of my friends or boyfriends. I remember how difficult it was to go out on dates and leave her behind. Again I hear her preach alone in her room, loud and vehemently, like Billy Graham whose fervor appealed to her. I see her at Larry's and my rehearsal dinner holding up her wine glass to toast "our dead father up in heaven."

My sister, the partner of my childhood, is gone, and I feel like someone's cut off one of my limbs. Throughout the years, at different ages and capacities until she couldn't anymore, Cindy had played with me, willing to dance and sing whenever I asked.

But Bill's also right—for years she hasn't been the Cindy I want to remember. I don't have to sacrifice being with my family in Cambridge when I need them the most. It's hard to do, but I agree there's no need for a funeral, and I don't go to Texas.

⌒

The year bleeds into a new one. In the first weeks of 2004, Larry comes with me into the little changing closet, as he's done for the last three years since my diagnosis. I wear the cotton gown open in the front. He sits on the bench in the tiny room until I come back from the mammogram machine cradling my crushed breast. Then I sit on his lap while we wait to see if cancer has recurred.

The technician knocks. Larry and I cling to each other. "Nothing has changed," she says, smiling. "You're free to go home." Free. The word echoes in my head. I remember my friend in cancer support group who, after ten years of battling breast cancer, tried a new drug that took her into remission. She said it was like being handed a ticket that read, *You can leave now. You're free to live.* Her face glowed with determination to do exactly that. She left support group and started a foundation to research breast cancer.

Three years later when the cancer returned, she died.

For however long it lasts, even without my sister or mother or father or Kate, every clean mammogram is my ticket to live.

28. TO THE TOP

I take my ticket to live and bag peak after peak, finishing my twenty-fourth mountain mid-summer, halfway through The 48. In the fourth year after chemo, I still get acupuncture every third week to support my immune system because when I don't, I catch everything catchable. In my workouts, I spend almost as much time stretching as strengthening, and each week I attend yoga classes. The aging body that survived cancer requires these things, and I've learned to listen to her.

During a training session in which I huff up an inclined treadmill, Cathy, by now a close friend as well as coach, asks what it feels like to be at the midpoint of my quest. She's good at posing questions and pausing to mark the moment.

Before I answer her, I think back six years to Tripyramid when Kate, Sarah, and I discovered 4000-Footers. How little I knew then! I had no idea Kate wouldn't be with me past the first five peaks, that cancer would cause a two-year hiatus in my quest, or how much I would come to love and respect these flinty White mountains. I tell Cathy I understand now, that what calls me to hike isn't simply proving I'm strong or fast or that I can succeed. For one thing, each climb reunites me with Matanna, my lost breast, my lost self. For another, hiking deepens my friendships. And these sustained doses of the natural world have become a profound, necessary source of nourishment.

"I've grown confident," I add. It's immensely satisfying to review my progression, both physical and mental; to note that the passion for hiking keeps me fit and offers concrete challenges that tap into skills from both my business and writing careers. Climbing feeds my work as a writer by providing not only material, but also a process that helps me meet writing goals along with my hiking goals. Being in the mountains fills my creative and spiritual well, that fecund internal soup from which writing emerges.

"It's kind of amazing," Cathy says, "when you think about it. Your quest has continued despite cancer, chemo, Tamoxifen, side effects. Kate's death. Cindy's. Your broken wrist. Your knee. Years of physical therapy." She pauses. "I'm really proud of you."

As she looks up at me from her chair, her eyes fill. Mine do, too. "In spite of all that," I murmur from the treadmill, "maybe because of it, I can't wait for my next mountain."

Cathy nods.

"I think the next twenty-four mountains will go faster. Take fewer years." The moment I say this aloud, a wave of sadness passes through me like a ghost. While there are fabulous mountains all over the country—all over the world—that I'd love to hike, I hear myself confess, "I don't really want my quest to end. No other mountains could ever mean as much to me as the Whites."

❦

By fall of 2004, I've climbed Mounts Liberty, Flume, Jefferson, Adams, Madison, Field, Willy, Cannon, Galehead, South Twin, North Twin, and Garfield—twelve 4000 Footers, the most ever in one year. I'm thrilled and proud. But despite my care regimen, I pay a price. A benign but painful nodule appears on the instep of my right foot. I also have trouble raising my arm, which triggers flashbacks from shoulder surgery seven years before. Though I'm luckier this time and it's not a bone problem, both injuries require PT. Instead of an attorney, I should have married a physical therapist.

Then late one snowy, bitter, February night going out to walk Juniper, I lose my footing and crash down the front steps on my right hip. "You didn't break anything," the nurse tells me after an X-ray, "but you dropped a couple of pints of blood in there." The reservoir of my energy runs dry, leaving me with a dragging exhaustion so reminiscent of cancer that I visit my oncologist. She says it's not unusual, even four years out, to find oneself with periods of utter depletion. "You need to do less," she advises.

After my best hiking season ever, I'm forced to cut down to just one mountain for 2005. It's hard not to feel discouraged. I promise myself that my one lone mountain will be momentous. I select Washington, the biggest of them all. With Cathy's encouragement and support, I make the event even more meaningful by persuading a sports magazine to buy an article about the climb itself, explicitly marrying my writing career with my passion for hiking. I sell the event as a mother-daughter climb. I will lead three other women in their fifties up one of the four deadliest mountains in the country, a statistic that lands Washington in a group with much bigger massifs: Denali, Rainier, and Hood. Plus, we'll be bringing along three teenaged daughters, one of them my own.

By the end of April, I've spent hours reviewing my hiking process and necessary gear with the mothers. I've picked trails, worked out logistics, and booked two huts for our group—Joe Dodge Lodge at the base of the mountain and Lakes of the Clouds hut near the summit where we'll overnight before descending. I promise my hikers that the morning after summiting Washington, if weather and our bodies permit, we'll climb Monroe next door before we descend. They're excited to add another peak. For me, hiking Monroe means I can revisit the spot where Sarah and I scattered Kate's ashes, something I never expected to do but now adds emotional significance to the trip.

My injuries mean I can't do my full training regime, but I'm confident I can intensify my workouts in the crucial six weeks before our grand endeavor.

Fate, however, has other ideas. In yoga class, I tear the medial meniscus in my right knee again. The knee balloons up and throbs enough to prevent sleep. The doctor also informs me the cartilage beneath the kneecap has worn away, both from overuse (hiking) and from structural misalignment (scoliosis). She says all I can do now is try to reduce the inflammation, and hope.

Distraught, I tell Cathy, "I have to do this climb! Six people depend on me. I've already booked the huts. I've contracted my first article." We create a program of aggressive icing, ibuprofen, and rest. For two weeks, Larry covers both our carpool shifts to Casey's distant high school to spare my right knee. I stop doing Porters, yoga, strength building, cardiovascular workouts, and walks. Instead, I focus on mental training, the mind being the engine of the body. Over and over, I picture myself and my group on the climb, summiting to a chorus of cheers.

Five weeks later, when the swelling and pain have subsided, I'm sent to PT. The therapist announces, "The tissue around the knee's in trauma. Worse, your quadriceps aren't strong enough, especially the inner quads."

"How's that possible?" I've hiked twenty-nine 4000-Footers for crying out loud. I look down at my legs. They look strong enough.

"Too much work is being done by the knee itself. You

need to build up those inner quads. We might resolve the acute problem in two-to-three weeks, but it will take six months, maybe a year, of exercises to fix the mechanics."

"That can't be right," I say. "I have a major hike coming up!" She makes a rueful face.

That night, I dream I'm standing in the middle of a boxing ring, alone. It looks like I have no opponent but then the fighting begins. In cartoon fashion, I throw my right knee down to the mat. My knee retaliates, jerking into my chest hard enough to knock me over backwards, flat on my ass. My dream-self thinks, *This is absurd. The knee is the adolescent of the body. You know you can't control a teenager.*

~

At 6,288 feet, Washington is the highest mountain in the Northeast and well over a hundred people have died climbing it. Winter is the most perilous time, which we will avoid. There's a hair-raising auto road to its top, but like other hikers, we'll haul ourselves up the hard way. The trails are numerous, steep, and often confusing, but the severe and unpredictable microclimate does the real damage. Hikers can begin climbing in sweltering mid-summer and within a few miles find themselves battling rain, hail, or snow driven by hurricane-force winds. You need to come prepared.

Preparing is something I know how to do. I make sure my hikers carry everything that might be called upon to save a life, possibly theirs, on the mountain.

Thankfully, my hiking buddy is coming. Ginny will bring Mandy, at eighteen a striking young woman with long ash blonde hair who is already taller than her mother. She's a strong hiker from summers at camp and an avid skier in winter. She was two years ahead of Casey in grade school so I know her only slightly, enough to know she's intellectually inclined and quiet, at least when I'm around.

251

Intrigued by big bad Washington, Casey agrees to participate despite the fact that, at fifteen, she prefers to spend as little time as possible in my presence. Knowing her friend Ansu will come helps.

Ansu is Lee's adopted daughter. Lee and I have climbed other 4000-Footers since she hiked up Passaconaway without her jacket. A friend of Ansu's family in Nepal, Lee brought Ansu to the States when she was ten to be educated here. Because Ansu dropped back a few grades to learn English, she's in Casey's sophomore class though she, like Mandy, is eighteen. Ansu is Casey's height, nearly 5'4", and sturdy with lovely caramel colored skin, short blue-black hair, and dark eyes. Perhaps because she comes from another culture, Ansu is a congenial teenager who actually enjoys conversing with Larry and me. She climbs with Lee in the Himalayas in summer, runs cross-country at school with Casey, has tons of energy, and a wonderful, ready laugh. Having traveled with her once, I also know she can, like my own teenager, be moody. Especially with Lee, who is coming, too.

Our last participant, Rachel, is someone Ginny met and connected me to because Rachel was the only person either of us knew who had actually done all the 4000-Footers. She finished a decade ago. I've spoken with her on the phone but have never actually met the woman I esteem. Since she's already summited Washington, she says as we near the top she'll take a cutoff to the hut and meet us there. Rachel's adult daughter can't make it, so she joins us as a solo mom. To my mind this leaves her, the eldest by three years, free to mother us all. I welcome her experience on our expedition, especially in my current physical condition. It helps to know I can count on her as backup leader should we need one.

In mid-June at the start of the famous Tuckerman Ravine Trail, the temperature barely reaches 50°F and the fog is so thick we can't see the tops of the trees, much less the mountain itself. It has required endless chivvying to get everyone ready and at 8:15 a.m., we start much later than I wished. A big yellow sign warns: *Try this trail* only *if you are in top physical condition, well clothed and carrying extra clothing and food. Many have died above tree line from exposure. Turn back at the first sign of bad weather.* We mothers grow quiet reading this. The teens whisk right past it. Our forecasted weather is, at best, iffy. No storms are predicted but there's a 35 percent chance of rain—not that either prediction can be trusted on Washington—and mere rain, treacherous on the rocky parts of the trail, could end our trip altogether.

I'm tense. During last night's pre-hike session at the base lodge, I warned everyone my injured knee could force me to turn back at any point. Facing the most formidable mountain I've ever encountered, my hip is painful, my foot aches, and I haven't trained *at all* during the last seven weeks.

Lee is also on the injured list. She broke a bone in her foot and just got out of her cast three weeks ago. She assures me she's fine, that she's already been running on it but, strong as she is, it's hard not to be concerned.

The Tuckerman Ravine Trail is the classic route up Washington and despite my nerves, I get tingly just setting foot on it. If all goes well today we'll scale 4250 vertical feet, about three and a half times the Empire State Building. We'll gain all that altitude in a scant 4.2 miles, making this my most strenuous hike.

"I hope the fog disappears," Rachel says as our group takes off, one of the few things she's said since we met at the lodge yesterday. "The views will take your breath away." Rachel's long gray hair suits her well-worn backpack and hiking clothes, making her look something like a woman who'd have gone "back to the land" in the '70s. I'm having a hard time getting a fix on her personality since she's so reserved. Probably she's one of those strong, silent types.

"I'm counting on the scenery to be the payoff," Ginny responds.

"I'm cold," says Ansu, bouncing up and down on her toes. She gives me her beautiful smile, white teeth contrasting with the navy ski cap she's already pulled down to her eyebrows. "Can we go faster?"

Within five minutes the group divides like a reproducing cell as the three teenagers shoot ahead. "Wait!" Ginny calls after them. "Our fearless leader should lead us."

The three girls stop and turn around, Ansu looking startled, Casey exasperated, and Mandy polite.

"We have to stay together!" Ginny hisses to me. "It's too dangerous!"

How well I know that desire for control, especially under stress, but I shake my head at my hiking buddy. I yell up to the girls, "Stop at every junction till we catch up. We have to stay close after Hermit Lake, so enjoy this part." I wave them on.

When Ginny's mouth tightens to a thin line I explain, "They can't get lost here and they'll go nuts if we rein them in the whole way. I promise we'll all be together when it counts."

She says no more. Until that moment, I haven't quite understood how bringing our daughters along adds a hair shirt of worry. Listing our fears last night, no mother mentioned concern for her daughter's safety, including me. How absurd that was.

～

The first couple of miles through woods are surprisingly pleasant. The trail winds upward and we constantly gain altitude, but the grade feels kinder than I anticipated. So far, aided by large doses of ibuprofen and a massive, hinged black brace, my knee is holding up. If I can make it to Hermit Lake, halfway to the top, I may be able to continue on. I'm not sure I could bear having to quit. Besides, I'd worry constantly about all of them, especially my progeny. And what kind of crap article would quitting make?

We stick close to a book-time pace because of the weather. If it's going to rain or worse, here worse tends to happen in the afternoon. The sooner we get to the top, the safer. We spy a red trillium still in bloom and admire the plunging waterfall of Crystal Cascade, but I don't let us linger. I find myself in a great mood despite Ginny's and my clash of wills, Rachel's unbroken silence, and the oppressive grayness.

The unrelenting ascent has everyone but Rachel stripping to shorts and shirts despite the fog and dripping greenery. After 2.4 miles and nearly as many hours, Ginny, Rachel, and I arrive at Hermit Lake, meeting up with the teens and Lee, who hiked with them for the last half-hour. We settle on the porch of Hermit Lake Shelter for a brief lunch. Fortunately, it's spitting, not raining, allowing us to enjoy all the verdant foliage surrounding picturesque Hermit Lake on the floor of Tuckerman Ravine. Tucks, as it's known, is a glacial cirque on the southeastern flank of Washington, a uterus-shaped granite bowl scoured out by a mile-high train of ice roughly 12,000 years ago. From where we nosh on trail mix and sandwiches, we can only see the foot of the Headwall, a sheer half circle of rock thrusting up and up into clouds and fog. The Abenaki people named this mountain Agiocochook—*Home of the Great Spirit*—and the majesty of Tuckerman Ravine makes clear why.

Even in the middle of June, behind the cloak of fog gleams the brightness of snow. Here the annual snow pack averages about fifty-five feet, and because of the snow and ice remaining today, the second half of our trail—which would have been easier to climb—has been closed. We detour to Lion Head Trail instead. Parts of Lion Head, too many parts we'll discover, are a great deal steeper and rougher.

"I'm happy to sweep," Rachel volunteers and I give our most experienced member a grateful smile. Nobody else wants to go last.

Soon the trail becomes slabs. Boulders. Rocks. In other words, we are no longer on anything resembling a trail. We climb through an explosion of rock. How long will my knee cope? Cairns and blazes painted on stones suggest a way through—up—the monstrous southeastern cone of Washington. It's unusual to be only 4500 feet high and yet above tree line. At a similar latitude in Wyoming, for example, tree line occurs at 10,000 feet. Both places have screamingly harsh winters, but Washington's average annual temperature is 27°F and it hasn't ever recorded a temperature above 70°F, suggesting the trees can't compensate for the winters by growing enough in other seasons. Whatever the reason, there isn't a tree in sight.

As we climb, the temperature drops. We've zipped on pant legs, added fleeces, and—everyone but my daughter—hats and gloves. The steepness and miserable footing soon exacerbate our differences in pace. Ansu and Casey forge ahead, Mandy and Lee either with or slightly behind them. I'd like to be with them, too, but Ginny wants me with her or better still, right behind her. Rachel creeps along behind us, ever more slowly. I constantly call ahead to our rabbits to wait so I can keep Rachel in sight. I don't understand her sluggishness. Though I hate to burden my knee with a single unnecessary step, I turn down the trail to discover what's up.

"It's always hard for me to breathe around 5000 feet," the woman I think of as my back up leader informs me. "I just have to slow down to catch my breath."

She didn't think this was worth mentioning last night

when we all listed our fears? No wonder she volunteered to go last.

"You go on ahead, I'm fine by myself," she says, sitting down on a rock.

She must know that's pure horse pucky. We're having a hard time in this fog not straying from the route marked among the rocks. She's slow, she's older, and she's obviously suffering. I can't leave her alone. Nor can I make her go faster. I'll just have to let her hike her pace and keep track of her.

Apologizing to my knee, I climb back up to Ginny, who's now accompanied by Lee. When I explain the situation with Rachel, their eyes widen. "Good grief," Ginny comments. "She should have said something when you invited her."

Lee nods. "I'll hike up and tell the girls."

I scrutinize her face. "How's your foot? You need some Vitamin I?"

She smiles, a thoroughly welcome sight. "Don't worry," she says kindly. "Apart from being cold, I'm fine." And off she goes.

My knee is working, but the pain is insistent. I uncap the bottle of herbal tincture I call Miracle Oil given me by Lili Cai, my acupuncturist, remove my knee brace, and rub oil around the joint. "Sorry, buddy," I say as Ginny turns her head. I quite like the pungent smell.

As we trudge upward, I exclaim over the sizes and shapes of the rocks and how fortunate I feel that I'm able to do this hike at all. Since her one outburst on the Hancocks, Ginny has never gone negative on a trail, but Washington and worry about Mandy must be getting to her. She complains about the weather. The endless rock hopping. The utter lack of views. How the group should stick closer together. How Rachel should have warned us so we could have opted not to bring her. How if this is the famous Washington, you can stick it.

At first I respond with empathy—everything she says is true—but when that doesn't seem to help, I tune her out. I have joy welling up inside. The corners of my mouth keep turning up even as my head swivels like an owl to keep track of Rachel behind, Lee and the girls ahead. Gratitude and glee that it's not completely raining fill me. The surface of the stones hasn't gone slippery. Nothing has iced up. Lichen adds hues of lime and mustard. I have plenty of energy left and am surprisingly strong, just as my affirmation proclaims. Inside the brace, my knee bends and straightens, straightens and bends. It's true the brace has rubbed off a bunch of skin, but the burning sore seems a small price to pay for a knee that levers me up boulders.

We catch up to Lee and the teens lounging on a set of large stones. Everyone takes advantage of waiting for Rachel to snack. When it starts to rain, we dive into our packs for rain jackets. We're all in various stages of sticking our arms and heads into protective clothing when I notice Casey hasn't moved. "Honey," I say, "put on your rain gear."

"I'm fine." She doesn't even look at me, just continues munching an apple.

"You may be fine now but it only takes a few minutes to get chilled and your shirt will be wet. The temperature will drop as we climb. Remember hypothermia?" I'm not exaggerating.

"I'm too hot, okay!" she snaps. "Just leave me alone."

I stare at her, thinking. Maybe she has a headache. She's been plagued with migraines since puberty. I remind myself she's not stupid. Nor can I make her wear a jacket. I'll have to trust that she's taking care of herself, not merely rebelling. Trusting her on Washington requires a galaxy of effort.

After Rachel arrives, we allow her time to refuel then once again pick our way up rocks. Both Lee and Ginny quietly contrive to let me know how unwise it is for Casey to go bare-armed in the rain and, while I'm glad they're protective of my daughter, I am clearly the worst mother on the mountain.

It gets colder. Rachel goes slower. We can't afford to go slower. We need to reach the top before dusk so we don't have to depend on headlamps to make our way through the web of trails crossing the upper cone of Washington, the stuff of nightmare.

Lee climbs down to Ginny and me to say she's having a hard time holding the girls back. "They're just so cold," she says, her own lips looking faintly indigo. "Having to stop and wait makes them colder."

"I'll go hike with them awhile," I say, "can you two hang together?" I know Ginny doesn't want to be left alone. "Make sure you keep an eye on Rachel." Rachel worries me. I also want to throttle her. I'm pretty sure I'm not the only one. If ever I thought I controlled anything on a hike, or in life, I'm certainly being schooled today.

As I get closer to the girls in the fog, I note Casey is wearing her jacket. The rest of us all wear warm hats too, but I'm grateful for small mercies. We hike along until they edge ahead. "Just keep us in sight, please, or you'll lose us. Jog in place if you have to." I pull my polypro hat lower on aching ears.

When Ginny and Lee draw near, Lee springs forward as if she's been frustrated by Ginny's pace. I'd like to hike faster too, but won't abandon my buddy. We heave ourselves up knee-high boulders casting around for signs we're still on the trail. I search inside myself for that wellspring of joy, but the best I can manage is a kind of peaceful numbness where my legs and arms do what they know how to do. The temperature drops some more. The wind picks up. We climb.

Around 2:00 p.m., in the sixth hour of a climb the bible says should take a bit over four, I find that despite the knee brace, the Miracle Oil, and a truckload of ibuprofen, I have to press my lips together to keep from groaning. Hiking ahead of Ginny to check on our four rabbits, I find them sitting on a ledge the wind slices through, freezing the tips of my fingers and nose. I suggest we back trail to some giant boulders that can block the wind. Lee and Mandy follow me down, but when I look back I see Casey and Ansu haven't budged. Instead, they're taking out snacks. I shout to them to come down, not just because we need to reconnoiter, not just because I'm worried they'll chill themselves to the point of danger, but because they are seriously pissing me off.

They ignore me. Their lack of response detonates Lee. "This is not the place for teenaged rebellion!" she screams. "Get down here. Now!"

I'm impressed.

Ansu obeys Lee. Casey follows Ansu, still insisting they are okay by themselves. I lose patience and fine her a night of talking on the phone with her boyfriend. We are all furious, slamming food containers on the rocks, jamming things into packs, guzzling water while our eyes spark.

~

At last we arrive at the trail Rachel can take to Lakes of the Clouds Hut. The fog remains so I hand her a walkie-talkie.

"I don't need it," says the woman who doesn't breathe well in altitude.

"For my sake."

Rachel agrees to radio me when she arrives at the hut. Now that the moment we've all been eager for has arrived, I'm loath to let her head into the fog by herself. What if she hits her head or gets lost? We haven't seen anyone else on the trail. I remind myself she's walking into a flattish, well-travelled area, and even if slow, she's got more experience on this mountain and doing 4000-Footers than any of us.

We hike on considerably faster. Ten minutes later I test

the walkie-talkie to see how Rachel is doing, but she doesn't answer. Swell.

We now find ourselves waiting for Ginny. Her mouth draws down from concentration and exhaustion. I suggest, "One of you rabbits lead, but the rest of you sweep. Ginny and I'll get in the middle of your energy sandwich."

"But I hate going last," Ansu says.

Ginny turns. "Well, so do I!" she snaps. "I feel all this pressure to keep up. I've already fallen once and I don't want to fall again!"

Silence. None of us knew she'd fallen. We stand there as if concussed.

"I'll lead," Ginny proclaims and with a wave of her hiking pole, storms off. After a look at me, Casey follows her. I watch them go. Lee volunteers herself and Ansu for sweep, leaving Mandy as my companion. I pick up my feet and force them up the next rock. It gets harder each time I stop to start up again. I slog upward, too tired even to curse. Behind me, Lee and Ansu wait to give us a sizeable head start. Looking up, I notice Casey's not crowding or chivvying Ginny, she's accompanying her. I hear the sound of Casey's voice and see her point, suggesting footholds. It dawns on me that my rebellious daughter is helping my hiking buddy. Glory be.

With every lunge upward, I lean more heavily on my poles, trying to ignore the pain in my knee, trying not to think or feel. I just keep heaving myself up and over, up and over. Mandy climbs at a faster pace. Time fades away.

Lee and Ansu appear on rocks beside me with sweaty faces, panting. "We raced each other," Lee explains. I nod. They stay with me a few minutes until I tell them they don't have to. Ansu bounds off to catch Casey and Ginny. Lee confesses she's gotten a headache. I grunt sympathetically. I try to raise Rachel on the walkie-talkie. Still no response.

Head down, I don't even notice Lee has left until I come

upon Ginny. "The crest's just ahead," she says. "The others went on, but I wanted to summit with you, buddy."

That's my Ginny. We haul ourselves up a few more steps and then, as if I've slammed into an invisible barrier, I stop. Perhaps because my buddy is here to lean on, I suddenly can't endure another step. "I've hit the wall."

Ginny doesn't curse or try to push me, though she must be cold and eager to finish. She suggests I sit on a rock and eat something, and when I don't move, gets out her trail mix and puts the open bag in my hand. I take a little trail mix and chew, my throat so dry I can hardly swallow. I'd drink water if I weren't afraid of throwing up. Constant pain and lack of training have taken their toll.

"You can do this, buddy," Ginny encourages. "It's not far."

She packs up her trail mix and I follow her, placing my feet in her footsteps, unable to figure out even that much for myself. Drafting behind my buddy, I finally climb over the last rock to the apex of Washington.

And discover . . . a parking lot. I'd forgotten about the auto road. There are also several buildings, including an observatory planted here to record the impossible weather. Ginny guides me into a cafeteria. Cafeteria? I'm in a daze. But I smell soup, hot soup.

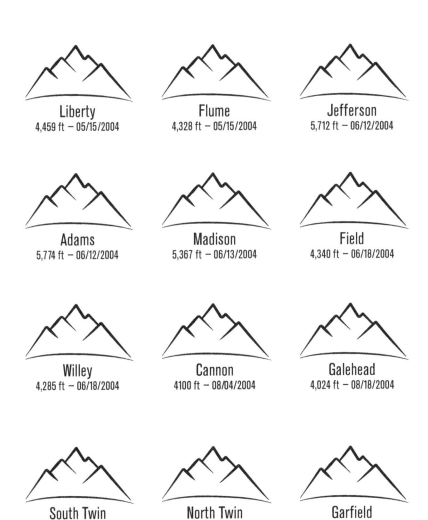

Liberty
4,459 ft – 05/15/2004

Flume
4,328 ft – 05/15/2004

Jefferson
5,712 ft – 06/12/2004

Adams
5,774 ft – 06/12/2004

Madison
5,367 ft – 06/13/2004

Field
4,340 ft – 06/18/2004

Willey
4,285 ft – 06/18/2004

Cannon
4100 ft – 08/04/2004

Galehead
4,024 ft – 08/18/2004

South Twin
4,902 ft – 08/19/2004

North Twin
4,761 ft – 08/19/2004

Garfield
4500 ft – 08/20/2004

29. DOWN

It's 4:30 p.m. And even colder. We've spent an hour on Washington's summit.

"Okay, women," I say, "time to get moving. Dinner at Lakes Hut is at 6:00. At least the last 1.5 miles are downhill. Here's the thing." I clear my throat and Speak Up. "I won't be going with you."

"What?" Ginny says. Though I warned them all, they look stunned.

"I barely made it up. My knee's so swollen it won't bend. No way could I get to Lakes or hike down tomorrow."

"But where will you sleep?" Casey asks, looking around.

"A shuttle can take me back to Joe Dodge Lodge, honey. I'll wait for you there tomorrow.

"I'm so sorry," I add, but I'm too drained to feel anything except how little choice I have. I hobble outside with them to find the trail, a path of stones dropping into pea-soup obscurity. I hug Casey, relieved she doesn't seem to mind my departure. She, Mandy, and Ansu start off, rock-hopping down the mountain, followed by Ginny and Lee. I watch until they disappear into fog. Only then do I feel pangs of guilt, regret, and the loss of not visiting Kate atop Monroe.

❧

A week later, moms and daughters gather at a cheerful Thai restaurant to celebrate having climbed Washington. Rachel can't make it. As we pass around platters of steaming food, we commiserate over the lousy aspects of the hike, debrief our hopes and fears. "I'm never hiking that high with Rachel again!" someone vows, and the rest agree.

Once we've cleared the air, we spend our time savoring the good moments of the climb and our accomplishment. No one, including myself, questions my counting my one-way hike as having bagged Washington. I've repressed the rule of the Four Thousand Footer Club that one must get both up and down a mountain by foot, leaving me quite sure I earned the red pin—number thirty—that I gleefully stuck on my wall map. I'm proud of my almost fifty-five-year-old, post-cancer body; proud of my daughter and the other mothers and daughters; proud that I made the dreadful decision to bail on the descent so that no rescue party had to risk themselves saving me. I feel this way until age sixty-three, when I climb Washington again with three other women, this time in September, hiking down in sleet and hail, and shoved off balance by 50-60 mph winds.

The mother-daughter climb sends me back to PT. Reluctantly, I give up forever the mainstay of my strength and cardio training—Porters—and turn instead to the elliptical machine at Healthworks. I need to reserve what's left of my knee for actual mountains.

In the spring of 2006, now that Casey's a second-semester junior, the beast known as the college search process commandeers our spare time, leaving me to plan a mere two treks for the coming summer. Besides, my knee still isn't strong. This is all true, and all that I'm aware of at the time.

In May, Ginny and I climb Mt. Carrigain in an unlikely, swampy 90°F that feels more like the rain forest of Costa Rica than a spring day in New Hampshire. The vista from the fire tower on top rewards us as Ginny and I wrap an arm around each other, hiking buddies and, by now, best friends.

The week after Carrigain, despite all the mountains in my legs, I have a hard time getting up and down stairs and am scarcely able to walk. Regardless, my internal clock ticks. Seventeen mountains remain to complete my quest. I organize a foursome for my second trek of the year. Clara, a good friend now after several hikes together since Passaconaway, her new husband Evan, Larry, and I will climb Mt. Moriah in August. When this plan first emerged the prior winter, Moriah excited me. The trail offered a long ridge walk full of views, and I've saved this mountain to do with Larry in hopes that it will remind him of the western trails he loves.

Mid-summer, as soon as she's recovered from having her wisdom teeth extracted, Casey comes down with a severe case of mono, and though she's miserably sick—and after two weeks of wisdom teeth care, I'm sick of playing nurse—I'm glad it happens now instead of at college so I can take care of her. After several weeks, she recovers enough to finish her internship with state representative and political legend, Alice Wolf. Though Larry and I would prefer Casey to rest before senior year begins, I notice how gleeful she sounds each day when she tells me she's going to work at the State House. I hide a grin that's two parts pride and one part relief since by the time she walks out the door, she's interrupted my writing three times to yell for help finding her favorite heels, her subway pass, and her lunch bag—as if only a person who's given birth can locate missing objects.

Much of the time she treats me as if I'm occasionally interesting but not at all relevant, an artifact from her former life. Unless something really bothers her, in which case, she tends to want to talk at approximately midnight. I adore my daughter. I'd take a bullet for my daughter. And I'd like to be the good mother who offers wisdom whenever asked. But all I really want to do when she's hurt by life is to go after somebody with a blowtorch. And then go back to sleep.

When I see Cathy the week before Moriah, I'm too ashamed to tell her I wish I hadn't involved another couple because Larry would be delighted to cancel the event and, for the first time, so would I. But I can't fool Cathy. "Something wrong?"

"Mothering a teen should receive hazardous duty pay," I grumble. "Then there's climate change and the war in Iraq." I tell Cathy that after Moriah, I want to take Juniper to Waterville Valley for a few days and do nothing but walk in the woods, not talk to anybody or read a newspaper, just lie on the sofa with Junie watching old movies.

Cathy smiles, but looks at me keenly. "What else?" Only then do I ask if she's ever completely uninterested and unwilling before an event. "Sure," she says. "Happens to athletes all the time. It's a way of conserving energy."

⌒

At the long wooden breakfast table in Joe Dodge Lodge the morning we hike Moriah, Clara looks happy, Evan playful, and my husband wary. You have to love a man who hikes, for your sake, mountains he doesn't like anymore. At least I've brought along Clara, one of his favorite people. Marriage clearly agrees with her and Evan. They smile all the time and their faces look softer. Evan is Larry's height, six feet, and my age, nearly fifty-six, with gray hair, wire-rimmed glasses, and a delightful British accent. He's a gentle man who likes birds and the game of bridge and plays the bassoon. In fact, bridge is how he and Clara met, and they both are becoming bridge masters, maybe even life masters, something I admire without really understanding. Evan's also a good sport. His inaugural 4000-Footer venture was a two-day hike in the Presidentials with Clara and me and a couple of Clara's friends and, though it nearly destroyed his knees, he's back for more. He and I are the only two using hiking poles, and I'm the only one with a large black knee brace. Perhaps age tells. Larry's our junior by four years and Clara by ten. Clara is as outgoing, warm, and frank as Evan is reticent, cool, and precise. They make an engaging pair.

The mid-August day is warm and drizzly. Mercifully, given the rocks and ledges coming our way, the rain stops when we start hiking. The humidity remains formidable, and the sky blazes steel gray with enough glare to make us squint. And there are bugs, lots of bugs.

Moriah, 4,049 feet tall, ranks forty-first in height of the 4000-Footers. It is the first mountain I've attempted in the Carter-Moriah Range, a wild, knotty backbone boasting eight mountains over 4000 feet that, as the bible points out, would receive far more attention and respect were it not for its prodigious neighbors, the Presidentials. Moriah's the last big New Hampshire peak on the Appalachian Trail.

We decide to spot two cars and hike a 9.5-mile loop to enjoy a variety of scenery. We will ascend by Stony Brook Trail for 5.1 miles with 3122 feet of elevation gain, more gain than summiting North Peak on Tripyramid with a mile less in which to do it. The ridge trail, however, promises breathtaking views of the Presidentials to our west and, if the weather clears, a glimmer of the Atlantic Ocean over fifty miles to the east.

Except for one perversely steep bit early on, the trail winds pleasantly through the woods, crosses a stream, and passes a small cascade and pool. But the humidity and heat become their own burden and, at any given moment, I swear I'm supporting a pound or two of mosquitos. Clara ties a bandana around her forehead to keep the sweat and bug spray from stinging her eyes.

Evan and I hike together as Clara and Larry chat behind

us. We spy a hummingbird. Rather, Evan the birder does. I notice something slender whizz by and he identifies it, thrilled to have caught his first glimpse of a hummingbird in the wild. Then, predictably, the path steepens and we do nothing but search for breath. Once we reach the ridge, we all gratefully leave behind the bugs and oppressive heat of the last 3.6 miles. The sky turns a delicate powder blue. The sun appears. We stop for lunch, and I mug for Larry's photos. At this point in my life, I dye my short, spiky hair red like my mother's, which adds a certain zest to the pictures. But the most telling image shows me with one boot waist-high on a steeply slanted ledge as I strain forward: Woman Stretched Thin Over High Rock.

The hike is much harder for me than I expected, even now on the ridge where the outlooks are excellent. I had hoped that, after Carrigain with Ginny two months ago, Moriah would be less daunting, my legs less heavy. My feet have launched an all-out attack on my nerve endings, so I try to weigh less, succeeding about as much as you'd expect. We're only in the second quarter for crying out loud, with 1.4 miles left just to reach the summit, and already I want this hike over. The others converse about politics, work, movies. People they know. Whatever. I'm not really listening. Something's off for me. It can't be possible, but it's as if I'm bored.

I try to focus on wildflowers. For the first time outside a book, I spot mountain cranberry. The tiny alpine plant has brought forth its red berries from nothing but a fissure of dirt between two ledges of gray rock. Shouldn't that inspire me? I crawl up a crevice in the face of a twenty-foot-high boulder, my hiking poles clipped to the back of my vest to free both hands. This should excite me, no?

After what seems like forever, we arrive at the summit of my thirty-second 4000-Footer. The views are majestic. I know this because Clara and Evan and Larry say so.

Everyone else drinks them in like precious dew. The vista is nice I guess, but I can't slip into the sense of expansiveness, of *soul*, that sustains me. I don't even feel like doing the peak dance, but Clara insists.

She, Larry, and Evan have a fine time descending the Carter-Moriah trail which is littered with constant, steep, slanted ledges I would infinitely rather have come up than be going down. I'm in a continual crouch trying to maintain control and not slide off the mountain, my quads and knees bunched and shaking, trying to manage vertigo. In my head, I'm yelling at myself for agreeing to a loop trail when I *knew* we should have simply returned the way we came. Unfortunately, I haven't cared to lead much on this hike. During the pre-hike talk last night, I felt like I was going through the motions, and all day on the trail I've done nothing leaderly. Let them take care of themselves.

When the ledges finally end, I tell the others I'm going ahead alone for a while. I'm desperate to get in touch with the mountain. With myself.

But I can't go fast enough to escape the sound of their voices. How can they be so blasted cheerful? I want to blame them, but the truth is no matter how hard I try, I can't plug into nature enough to feel the magic. All I'm aware of is each individual stab of pain and, worse, the overriding sense that I'm sick to death of hiking. I can't remember why I put myself through such misery.

Nor does Moriah conjure up many happy associations. The Wailing Wall in Jerusalem is located on Mt. Moriah. God commanded Abraham to slit the throat of his son Isaac on Mt. Moriah. As a child, I heard a mournful cowboy song *They Call the Wind Moriah* that cut into my heart. As I force myself to march downward, the plaintive tune takes over my brain.

Moriah also rhymes with "pariah," another aspect of

how I feel right now. By force of habit, I look around for something to distract me. Nothing. Wait. There's something, but what is it? I bend down for a closer look. The plants, if they are plants, are only an inch or two high. Two pale hospital-green leaves stick rigidly out from each stem. The heads of the flowers are appalling. They are round and pasty with sections outlined in bloody red veins, their centers staring up at me with a flat, dead, green eye. The head is fringed with brown blobs. The whole thing looks sick. I straighten up and walk on quickly. If cancer ever grows in the wild, I have just come face-to-face with it.

I stomp along, dismayed. Disgusted by the rocks, the heat, the bugs. When I tire of that, I berate myself for being weak. After so many mountains, how can it still be so hard? Larry works out less and look at him. Maybe I'm not cut out for 4000-Footers anymore. Maybe they are simply beyond me. Maybe I've gotten too old, too injured. Why should I erode what's left of my knee on these obnoxious Whites?

After we finish Moriah, though I'm nearly 70 percent of the way through my mountain quest, I want to quit. My body hurts and my knee won't bend, but pain isn't the reason. Pain ends eventually. The truth is worse than pain: I'm just not interested anymore. Sixteen mountains remain and not one of them gets my juices flowing.

After eight years and thirty-two mountains, I have lost my passion.

Washington
6,288 ft – 06/17/2005

Carrigain
4,700 ft – 05/31/2006

Moriah
4,049 ft – 08/19/2006

30. GONE

I tell Cathy, "I didn't love Moriah like the others did and . . . the worse part is, it feels permanent." I'm not working out, I'm slumped in Cathy's chair. "It's like my heart is dead to the Whites. To nature." Tears prickle. "I'm a woman without a country."

"Oh," Cathy says quietly. She lets the dust from that bomb settle before she starts telling me things in an encouraging voice. Whatever she says, I'm not listening. I'm poking around deep inside myself. Is it Kate? Can I not finish without her? Have I made Kate into some paragon she couldn't have been in real life and now no one can stand in her place? That can't be true—there's Ginny, after all. I'd go see Ginny right now, but she's on vacation. Maybe I only truly enjoy hiking with one buddy, one who relates to nature the way I do. Did.

Did?

What if it's simply time? What if, after eight years, I no longer lust for the Whites? What if my hiking process, the remaining peaks, and the Four Thousand Footer Club no longer matter to me? Maybe thirty-two mountains have given me enough challenges and successes. Maybe I don't need them anymore. Maybe I'd be happier climbing out west or someplace new and exciting, like Patagonia. Who says I have to do all the 4000-Footers? I can set my own rules, define my own success.

Part of me silently screams, *But Matanna is there! Don't abandon her.* A different part responds that I'm still tied to this quest only because I've had cancer and an amputation. Will I never be free of that legacy?

～

At home, I call my hiking buddy, interrupting her time with her family. When she hears what's going on she says, "I wish I were there so we could go hike together right now." She understands my sadness and confusion, my fear about giving up on a goal I've been working toward for so long. "This is life-changing," she declares.

I consider the possibility that I'm just scared, afraid of failing the remaining climbs. Like many peak baggers, I've saved some of the hardest mountains for last. Some require gear I don't have, like a tent or a backpacking stove, for camping overnight. Others demand a whole other level of endurance, like Owl's Head that is eighteen miles round trip. Maybe I just can't cut it anymore. Whatever the reasons, I no longer love to hike.

Who the hell am I?

31. ULTIMATUM

I mourn for ten days, miserable and uncertain.

Then I'm on the Starr King Trail, attempting my thirty-third 4000-Footer. Alone. I don't even bring Juniper. If I can't rediscover my ardor for the White Mountains today—by myself—I'm giving up my quest.

Both Larry, despite being in the middle of a real estate deal, and Casey, despite her summer job with the Humane Society, volunteered to come with me to Waterville Valley. Not to intrude, they understood I needed to climb alone, but to save my knee and hip from driving, help unpack the car, and wait for me in our apartment so that, whatever the outcome of the hike, I wouldn't face it alone. I was grateful, but declined their offers. I needed to face this alone.

⌒

It rains as I drive northeast to the trailhead, lightening to a wet mist by the time I set boots to ground. New boots I've broken in by walking around Fresh Pond. With luck, the new boots will lessen the pain in my feet during the last miles of the day. This far north, in late August, the trees have already been touched here and there with a scarlet finger, a brush of gold. The damp, 60°F weather raises goose bumps on my skin.

The bible said Mt. Waumbek is so isolated and has such a variety of vegetation from prior logging ventures that one was bound to see wildlife. The thought of bears and moose tempers the freedom I feel not having to lead or worry about anyone else. Already I've accomplished one thing: I carry all I need. By paring down food and water, I've managed to cram everything into my hip pack and vest pockets. It makes me feel lighter, as if my needs are slight, though the stakes for this trek are so high.

Cataloguing my hopes and fears the night before—without Cathy because I didn't know when I saw her last week that I was going on this journey—I surprise myself. I don't actually fear injury or wild animals, bad weather or my body's weaknesses. What I fear is the power of my mind. To drag myself down. To keep me from enduring 7.2 miles on my own. To quit when no one else is around to see.

When I head into the woods to relieve myself before hitting the trail, I nearly step on a colony of tiny, delicate, pinkish-lavender plants. Reaching down, I tip up the hooded blooms shaped like miniature iris but on inch-long stems. Heal-all, a plant named for its tenacity and its medicinal powers. Also known as self-heal.

❧

After two hours, I'm panting up the steep sections and getting a bit twitchy.

I've already invited the spirits of my mother, my father, my sister, and Kate along with me. My mother loved plants and supported my successes. My father bore pain stoically and must have been familiar with swampy conditions like this in the Pacific during WWII. Cindy was always ready to join me at play. Kate because she was Kate. I've spoken, too, with Matanna, evoked her presence in the woods on this lonely mountain—I need every part of me here today.

But the sense of my lost ones' companionship has worn off, and I catch myself startling at forest sounds. By now my knee hurts and my back aches and I'm weary and these sensations are taking over my brain. No one else appears to be on the mountain, so to buck myself up, I sing. Out of my mouth comes the country-twanging plaint Linda Ronstadt popularized in the 1960s, "When Will I Be Loved?" The lyrics complain of being cheated and mistreated, put down and pushed around, and being generally luckless at love. I croon them for a long time. Had I felt like that about Moriah? I guess I did.

Waumbek stands 4,006 feet high, a moderate climb. I haven't done it before because it lies so far north it always seemed arduous to get to. It has been.

Waumbek, meaning "white rock," tops the other peaks in the Pliny Range. The range forms a half-circle in a geological formation known as a ring dike, according to Smith and Dickerman in *The 4000-Footers of the White Mountains, A Guide and History*. That half-circle is what remains from a huge upwelling of fiery magma through a semi-circular crack in the earth, magma that piled high and cooled quickly into the dense rock of the Pliny Range.

It's hard to picture Waumbek as molten lava when it's so solid beneath my boots, but it does feel wild and primitive. The trail, muddy and wet from earlier rain, breaks down frequently into running rivulets. Moisture drips from the vegetation. The rocks and roots are slippery, requiring my concentration. No rain falls, but it must be near the dew point because, though it's cool, my face streams sweat. Ten feet above my head, a ghostly mist hangs in the trees in a sweltering blanket of silver. In the intense humidity, my glasses fog over and I have to swipe them clear with a bandana. Bugs launch themselves at me.

I haven't seen so much as a single boot track in the mud. It's been days, at least, since anyone climbed up here and the spiders have been busy. Every step I take breaks open one of their artistic traps. Layers of damp, sticky cobweb cling to my hair, my face, my glasses, my neck, my hands, my arms. The first few times I couldn't help shivering at the atavistic feel of the stuff, but I've long since given up trying to brush it off. When the angle of light permits me to see the webs, I thrust a hiking pole through first. My poles, too, have gone gray with webbing.

Spiders. I don't see the creators of the webs, though obviously they are here in abundance. Grandmother Spider, Native Americans say, was the giver of writing, the weaver of stories. I apologize aloud for the works of art, the lifelines for trapping food and incubating eggs that my journey destroys. I ask the spiders to understand that I, too, am weaving my life and that this day, this path, looms large in my story.

Periodically something sizeable crashes through the forest nearby. I never see an animal, but the hindbrain urges me to hurry, go faster. I catch myself loping along the trail and then the forebrain admonishes, *Be careful. Don't get injured. No one will find you for a very long time.* I was right to fear my own mind.

The trail and woods are lush with plants. Spotted Jew-elweed nearly reaches my waist, the flowers reminding me of orchids, small orange ones whose pouting lower lip is dusted with rosy red freckles. They brighten the misty day considerably.

It's definitely berry season. I pass orange and scarlet hobblebush berries, red bunchberries, and the bright agate berries of blue-bead lilies. Then I notice something like a berry but so large and red and loaded with seeds, I figure some hiker has thrown away a half-eaten cherry tomato. Dis-gusted, I kick it into the brush. But twenty paces later, I see another one, then small groupings of these things that are obviously the fruits of some plant. A mile later, I locate one last stem that has leaves on it. Three leaves, to be exact, of a very familiar shape. I smile when I grasp that trillium, my first wildflower friend, accompanies me today. She has lost her flower and her leaves are going, but though worn down to essentials, she remains herself.

~

I arrive sooner than expected at Mt. Starr King, the peak before Waumbek. Despite what my bible claimed, even in the cleared out space at the top there are no views for anyone less than twelve feet tall. It must be time to buy myself a new edition.

I should stop and rest. Eat, though I'm not hungry. I take out one of the granola bars I brought because they are nourishing and weigh little, then put it back. I hate granola bars. Sitting down on a rocky outcropping, I rip open a small bag of potato chips. To balance my diet, I choke down a handful of trail mix.

Whap-whap-whap. I bolt upright, then force myself to turn slowly to face whatever predator wants my food or me. What creeps out of the forest instead, on teeny bird legs, is a bunch of gray jays. They surround and eyeball me only to whirr off again when I sit down. A few moments later, the Bear-Coming-To-Eat-You noise happens again, but I tell my stupid heart to relax, it's only the jays. Again they hop out to give me the once-over. Any movement sends them flapping off, but they always come back, hoping for handouts.

It would be nice to share a laugh at my fear with hiking companions. If I were with other people, I wouldn't have been so afraid in the first place. But I have to be alone to turn today into the sorbet that cleanses my palate for the richness of hiking with others, of hiking at all.

I march toward Waumbek's summit. At eye level, a fallen log is propped up beside the trail by its root ball. The log is carpeted with thick spongy beds of emerald moss, little spiky lime mosses that look like they would hurt to touch but instead are as soft as feathers, star-shaped mosses arrayed in rows like an army of miniscule pines, and lichens fading from orange to yellow to bone. And there, at the end of the lichen trail are my favorites, British Soldiers that stick up on tiny stalks with teensy scarlet pillows on their tips.

After arriving at the top of my thirty-third peak, I glance around the wooded summit, then turn to retrace my steps back down. Catching sight of my own boot prints coming toward me in the mud, I feel like Robinson Crusoe. For a moment it's as if no other human has ever been here and the thought is exhilarating. My affirmation for the third quarter rings strikingly true: *I love hiking alone.*

I look myself over and grin. My arms and legs are spattered with mud. My glasses are so dirty I keep brushing away bugs that aren't there. I put my hand up to the sticky webbing in my hair and discover that, because of cobwebs and bug spray, my hair stands on end in clumps clotted with bits of bark. My clothes are drenched with sweat and damp mud. Squashed insects freckle my arms and neck. My face is webby and, I can tell from the smooth dryness beneath my exploring fingertips, splotched with dirt. I smell fecund, like earth and rain and stone. Like the woods. Like the mountain.

Waumbek
4,006 ft — 08/29/2006

32. ENDGAME

Larry and Casey promise to hike with me at least twice a year until I finish The 48. I can't ask Ginny or Sarah to carry the tent, two sleeping bags, stove, utensils, and the food we'd need for some of the 4000-Footers that remain. I buy a tent big enough for three people and a small dog. Having nearly lost it, I refuse to let anything shake my determination to finish my quest. During the summer of 2007, Larry, friends, and I bag five peaks: Mounts Whiteface, Zealand, West Bond, North Kinsman, and South Kinsman.

In September, four women and I embark on the most ambitious two days of hiking I've ever planned. The first day Ginny, Sarah, Rosemary, and I will climb the five peaks of the Wildcats, across the road from Washington.

Ginny and Sarah, dauntless hikers and intimate friends, I know I can count on. This will be Rosemary's and my first big hike together. We only met a year ago at Fresh Pond. I noticed her, a fit-looking woman my age but a couple of inches taller, with glasses and blond hair, strolling along with a Bichon Frise, one of Juniper's tribe. I walked over to pet the dog, Samson, and suggested we walk together sometime, a play date for Junie as well as for me. It turned out Rosemary,

a political activist like us, knew Larry from the 2006 gubernatorial campaign. A big-hearted psychotherapist, she was filled
with energy, passionate about the environment, and, through
her kids at the Cambridge high school or her husband or
her church, seemed to know everyone in Cambridge. Before
long, we were good friends taking care of each other's dogs.
To prepare for this hike, we'd trained on Wachusett a couple
of times, just the four of us: Rosemary, Samson, Juniper, and
me. Rosemary proved sure-footed and strong-legged. Samson
had become my grand-dog's best friend.

But the Wildcats aren't for little dogs. We face 3150 feet
of elevation gain and 5.1 miles of trail reputed to be markedly
steep and rough. Though all five summits top 4000 feet,
only two of them count for the 4000-Footer list because not
enough elevation change separates the others. Once across
the peaks, we'll descend into Carter Notch to spend the night
at Carter Notch Hut. There we'll pick up another hiker,
Valerie, a college classmate of mine though she and Sarah
scarcely know one another.

Valerie and I've been friends for decades, but we've
never hiked together. Our friendship began at a pre-reunion
party in Washington, DC, where we both lived, just before
our tenth reunion and continued after we both relocated to
Massachusetts. We also share an interest in politics. She's
even run for selectman in her town. A scientist, she loves
the outdoors. She and her partner also have a second home
in New Hampshire where they kayak and hike, and they've
trekked all over, including Alaska and Nepal. A quiet woman,
Valerie is both gentle and confident. Though not tall, she has
a sturdy build and exuberantly volunteered to carry all my
extra gear needed for the hut. I didn't take her up on the offer,
but, like Clara's offer for Passaconaway, it impressed me.

After a night in the hut, the five of us will scale Carter
Dome, Middle Carter, and South Carter, giving me ten

4000-Footers for my year's total. If all goes as planned, in these two days we'll climb 14.5 miles and gain over 6000 feet of elevation—the depth of the Grand Canyon.

At the end of our Wildcats and Carters expedition, only five mountains will remain to fulfill my quest. Circling Fresh Pond with the dogs a few days before our trip, Rosemary asks me how it feels to have thirty-eight mountains under my belt. I sing her a few exuberant lines from "Guys and Dolls," one of Casey's childhood favorites, implying that I'm so happy if I were a bell I'd be ringing my fool head off.

I've also studied the five mountains that remain after this trip, their heights, trails, and difficulties. I've plotted a course through them for next year. Though I'm eager to meet each one, I want to finish The 48 in 2008, just before I turn fifty-eight. I'm curious to see what comes around the corner, what new challenge I'll take on after this marathon of mountains. I'm ready now for my quest to end.

Larry has made it clear how happy he'll be when I'm done and we can hike somewhere else. Somewhere with trails kinder to feet and knees and with more constant views, somewhere like the West. Or New Zealand. Despite the stunning early fall days we are currently enjoying, he can't go running because he still suffers from plantar fasciitis in his foot—a consequence of hiking two 4000-Footers carrying all our camping gear a month ago. I think the fact of the injury bothers him more than the actual pain because it resulted from careening two miles down the wrong trail, a mistake for which, though all four of us on the hike had our Personal Hiking Logs and maps, we both blame me.

On that venture we had ended up descending the Zea-cliff Trail, an untamed and not-well-maintained knee and ankle buster that was exhilarating, wild, and occasionally scary. Because of overgrown brush, it was hard to judge one's footing and with all the weight he was carrying, the arch of Larry's foot paid the price for every misstep. The mistaken trail also ruined our plans for bagging four peaks, managing only two instead. Sarah and Nolan, her husband, exclaimed over the rugged beauty of the trail, completely unfazed by the change in plans that resulted. But Larry smoldered, and I smarted from my error.

My hiking buddy, too, was quitting the Whites as she followed her husband and his new job across the continent to California. The Wildcats/Carters venture was the last climb together we could be sure of. We hated to lose each other and the easy intimacy we'd developed as hiking partners and best friends who lived in neighboring towns. We worried about maintaining our relationship with a whole country between us. We cried together, we hugged, we hoped. The Wildcats and Carters could well be our 4000-Footer swan song, and I wanted it to be an endeavor to go out on.

∾

Ginny, Sarah, Rosemary, and I take a much-needed break to sigh over the views of Washington and the Presidential Range that loom just to our west, then push on. The name of our trail, "Wildcat Ridge," is an exercise in false advertising. One does not clamber up Wildcat E and then saunter across a pleasant ridge to Wildcats D, C, B, and A. No indeed. The trail unfurls with all the crests and valleys of a roller coaster that we haul ourselves up and down step by weary step. In addition to the five peaks, we encounter so many nobs, sags, hogbacks, and unspecified bumps that it's often hard to tell which are the actual summits.

By the time I stand at the top of the frighteningly steep pitch leading down from the last peak to Carter Notch Hut, dinner, and our meet-up with Valerie, it's late afternoon and chilly. The early autumn light has faded to sepia and my bare legs are covered with gooseflesh. Waiting for my three friends, I peer over the edge of the peak down a rocky incline so vertical it's like a set of 90° stairs. I see two men about ten feet down the trail and watch them for a few moments before stepping back to let them get up before our group blocks their way.

The men yell up their thanks and continue ascending. "Oh my God," one of them grunts, "this trail hates human knees. And I have fifty-five-year-old knees!"

"Know what you mean," I respond. "My knees are fifty-seven."

He raises his silver haired head, now about even with my aforementioned knees where I stand above him, and gives me a quick once-over. "You sure don't look fifty-seven."

I don't know what to say.

All through dinner at the hut Sarah, Rosemary, and Ginny tease me and threaten to tell Larry about my new beau.

At breakfast in the hut dining area filled with wooden picnic tables and benches, I send nervous glances out the windows at the cold curtain of rain and catch my friends doing the same. Like other hikers in the hut, we consume heaps of hot oatmeal and scrambled eggs the hut crew, mostly college kids working here before returning to school, bring to each table. We drink cup after cup of tea or coffee that steams in the damp air.

After most people clear out, we squeeze close together on the benches to review our situation. I go over our options. "We can continue on to Carter Dome, South Carter, and Middle Carter—9.4 miles and 4600 feet of elevation gain—as planned." We all heard the hut crew present the weather forecast. The temperature outside is currently 35°F. Icy rain is expected to continue for a couple of hours down here in Carter Notch, but no one can predict what will happen a few thousand feet higher up where it will be colder. Thunderstorms are expected in the afternoon. Then again, things could improve suddenly in the way that weather in the Whites sometimes does.

I look at their intent faces. No one says anything. They're waiting to hear the next option. "Or we could jettison our plans and hike out to the car via Nineteen-Mile Brook Trail, the one Valerie took to meet us here. It's 3.8 miles with a 1900 foot elevation loss, a so-called 'family' trail," I say. "Valerie, you want to tell us what it's like?"

"It's a piece of cake," she grins. "Like a walk around your Fresh Pond. Except it'll be slightly downhill."

"There will be rocks and roots, of course, the way there always are," I add. "And today, they'll be wet and slippery."

A silence ensues. Valerie breaks it first. "You can all go on if you want, but no way am I climbing mountains in this weather. Just not worth the risk." Her eyes seek mine. "I'm out."

I don't let her decision linger in the air to infect the others. "Okay, but I want to go on. To summit even just Carter Dome, to try anyway." I figure if we bag the Dome, I can come back and do the remaining Carters by myself. But to climb all three some other time means organizing another two-day hut hike with others to help carry the extra weight required. "If we find it's too slick or the weather worsens," I say, "we can turn around and come down at any point."

"True," Sarah says. "But coming down if it's slippery will be worse than going up."

No arguing that.

"And what about the potential thunderstorms?" Ginny says. "I for sure don't want to be up there all exposed if there's lightning."

That's sensible, too.

Rosemary ventures, "We could test it out, go up a little way. Maybe we could do the whole thing."

"I asked the hut guy his opinion," Sarah says. "He said if it were him, he wouldn't go to the Dome today. He's afraid that not only would it be wet, it could be one giant icicle." The image of ice-rimed rocks kills anyone else's remaining interest in forging ahead. I'm outvoted.

Back in our unheated cabin with the six bunks, everyone rushes around packing her stuff and running to the bathroom, preparing to hike out to the car. Our breath fogs in the cold.

As I brush my teeth in the women's bathroom, memories of the thwarted trip to climb all the Bonds and Zealand sting me. Today makes two trips within a month of each other where I've only partially achieved my goals. Just as I near the finish line, it moves further away. I tear up.

I wipe my eyes, grab toothpaste and towel. I've got something to say. Back in our room, only Rosemary is missing. Once she arrives we all stand in the narrow cabin in which we slept, or tried to sleep. It feels oddly colder in here than outside, and it's dim, the only light leaking down from a couple of small, high windows obscured by rain. My friends are all suited up to go. Their packs wait on bunks or on the floor. Their boots are laced.

I stand in front of my bunk and face them. "You know I always say to Speak Up so you don't have to carry whatever's on your mind by yourself. Well, I have to speak up now." As of one accord, they all sit down on the nearest bunk, except for Valerie who leans comfortably against a wall. I appreciate that, the sitting and the leaning, the settling in, offering their attention even though they're ready to go. I love my hiking friends.

I sit too, perched on the edge of my bunk. "I'm close to completing The 48, and I'm really, really ready to finish. Right now I'm so disappointed it actually hurts." I press a hand against my chest. "I don't blame you," I clarify. "It just kills me to look out," I fling my hand toward a window, "and know that Carter Dome is right there, within my grasp. I'm this close—and I'm going to pass it by." My hand shuts into a loose, empty fist.

I swipe the back of my fist across my cheeks. Rosemary digs in her pockets and reaches out to hand me a tissue. She says, "This must be really hard for you. Especially since you gave up time with Casey before her gap year abroad to do this hike."

Tears roll down my face. "I don't know why it matters so much to me. It shouldn't. I get that. But it does. I just want to end the season with forty-three peaks, so I have only five to do next year. I could be sure I'd finish then." Except about Kate, I've never cried on a hike before.

Ginny leans forward. "I'll fly back to do the Carters with you next summer. I promise."

Sarah makes the agreement sound psychiatrists make, humming in the back of her throat. "Me, too." Rosemary and Valerie add their offers as well.

I look into each of their faces. They're concerned, uncomfortable, compassionate, and right here with me in this awkward, intense moment and I know I have to tell all my truth. "I'm afraid," I murmur. "I know it's not . . . I mean, I'm okay. I know I'm okay." It's hard to push the words out. My voice drops to a whisper. "But what if I get sick again? What if I die and I'm not here next year to finish?"

There's a pause. Then Ginny gets up and comes over to sit next to me on the bunk. "Oh, buddy," she says, and holds me close.

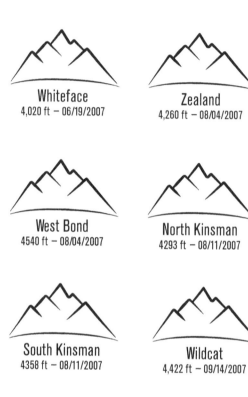

Whiteface
4,020 ft – 06/19/2007

Zealand
4,260 ft – 08/04/2007

West Bond
4540 ft – 08/04/2007

North Kinsman
4293 ft – 08/11/2007

South Kinsman
4358 ft – 08/11/2007

Wildcat
4,422 ft – 09/14/2007

Wildcat D
4,050 ft – 09/14/2007

33. ISOLATION IN
GOOD COMPANY

It's a moist, warmish morning around 65°F on Monday, September 29, 2008. Though we don't know it yet, today the flailing stock market will crash, the worst drop since 1929. Freddie Mac and Fannie Mae and AIG have already been bailed out. Banks, securities firms, and other insurance companies look about to topple. People are beginning to lose jobs. Economies the world over are shaken and so are those of us hiking today. Everyone we know is trying to figure out, as are we, the personal impact and how bad things will be for how long. But today, we five have set aside our worries to immerse ourselves in the natural world that seems, by comparison, settled and stable and safe. Over the summer, with various combinations of Ginny, Sarah, her husband Nolan, Rosemary, and Larry (sometimes with Juniper), I've summited Carter Dome, Carter South, Middle Carter, Owl's Head, and Cabot.

My forty-eighth and final mountain, Mt. Isolation, awaits. It is almost ten years to the day since I began my many-peaked quest.

Having parked a second car down the road where we expect to end up, Larry, Sarah, Nolan, Clara, and I are on the Glen Boulder Trail. Accompanying us is Sophia, Sarah and

Nolan's dog, a long-legged, shaggy-haired black beauty—
Juniper's pal and hiking companion, though this climb is not
for my wee grand-dog. This is the same trail that everyone on
the mother-daughter hike cursed coming down from Washington, only we're going up it.

In the early morning dark, with our headlamps lit, we
resemble a string of cyclops making our ungainly way up a
trail littered with rocks, fallen leaves, and roots, forbiddingly
slippery from a week of pounding rain. In places, the path
resembles a brook. I remind myself to be cautious, to avoid
injury with 13.3 miles ahead of us, but inside I sing with
excitement. Today I am invincible.

Yesterday I had concerns. The elevation gain today is
hefty—3800 feet—and, of course, once we gain it, we've got
to lose it again coming down, all in the same day. No overnight at Lakes of the Clouds or any other hut. I worried that
Larry's plantar fasciitis could recur, that my knee would act
up, that the wet conditions would make the footing dangerous. We have to negotiate our way across the Rocky Branch
River numerous times as we descend the Rocky Branch Trail.
The bible said one of the crossings could be "extremely difficult," two words I was not happy to read, especially after
last week's storms.

For the river crossings Larry carries our water shoes,
in hopes the river doesn't rise too high or flow too fast for
us to wade across. I make a mental note to remind everyone
to unbuckle their packs before crossing. People who slip can
drown when the weight of their packs pins them under. Yet
here in the damp chilly dark, I virtually thrum with delight.
Passion buoys me, and gratitude. I am healthy and strong.
Though I know I control appallingly little, in life or on a hike,
I'm confident. No way can I fall. No way can I fail. Not today.

We'd scheduled the hike for Saturday but had to switch
plans when thunderstorms raged. Poignantly, that unforeseen

shift means I will finish this last mountain on the ninth anniversary of Kate's and my last hike together, Lincoln and Lafayette.

I'm exuberantly fit and ready. A month ago, after dropping Casey off at Colorado College for her first-year orientation, Larry and I hiked for three amazing days in the Rockies. On our second day someone on the trail told me about The Fourteeners, mountains 14,000 feet and higher. "There are fifty-seven of them," she said.

"There are?" I asked, my voice avid.

Larry pressed my shoulder. "Don't even think about it."

We did, however, climb a Fourteener—Mt. Sherman—one with less technical difficulty than most 4000-Footers in the Whites but more extraordinary views. When we found ourselves looking down on clouds and circling hawks on a steep, narrow, sandy trail, he kept me going despite my altitude-exhaustion and vertigo. He knew how triumphant I would feel after summiting, and he was right.

Back home again, I finished off mountains number forty-six and forty-seven, Bond and Bondcliff, with Sarah, Nolan, and Gwen, a political friend who happens to also be a rock climber. We hiked the two Bonds in a glorious 11.2-mile adventure that so filled me with mountain energy, I nearly burst my skin.

All of which meant now is the moment for Isolation. Bless them forever, my comrades reorganized their lives to make today's revised date possible. Sarah rescheduled patients. Nolan, an architect who helped us renovate our house, moved meetings. They're here despite the fact they'll have to leave at 3:00 a.m. tomorrow to get back to Boston for Sarah's commitments. I can't imagine finishing The 48 without Sarah, but I'm glad Nolan is here too. He's a strong hiker, one who enjoys whatever a mountain throws his way. He never complains, never minds carrying extra gear. In fact, on a climb this summer, he carried Juniper when she wore out. He has the kind of quiet, firm patience that makes him marvelous with animals. He jokes a lot and can make me laugh even when things are tense. We've been friends for the thirty years he and Sarah have been married.

Clara took off two precious vacation days to join us. Larry cancelled work plans and did the same. They know I can't do mountain number forty-eight without them, nor do I want to. Larry, the man who doesn't like 4000-Footers, has nonetheless scaled seventeen of them at my side. Sarah has accompanied me for sixteen, Nolan for seven, Clara for six. Lately she's taken a furlough from The 48, but she insisted she had to be with me when I finished my quest, and she's trained all summer to prepare.

Having hiked this trail and unable to bear doing it again, Ginny, who now lives in California, is missing. Ditto my daughter, who is immersed in the new world of college far away in Colorado.

∼

Up we clamber, gaining altitude. Despite chattering, happy as a monkey, I notice that Larry my mountain goat climbs more slowly than usual. In fact, he's stumbling.

"Are you okay?" I ask.

"I'm not sure. It's like I have no depth perception. I can't tell where the rocks are."

We bunch together so the light from my headlamp in front of Larry and Nolan's behind him, can add to the glow from his own. We slow down to be sure he can negotiate the stony, rough footing. Slowing down is my suggestion, but it's hard for me to do. I'm ready to tap dance my way up. I tell myself *I'm just warming up*, my usual first-quarter affirmation, but soon switch that to something more giddy, more accurate—*My feet are as light as feathers.*

Once the sun rises, we switch off our lamps. We've warmed considerably from climbing and the temperature has increased, too, though mist dampens our clothing and hair. The trail steepens and stays steep. We launch ourselves up and over numerous large rocks, often scrambling with hands and knees on this trail that looks like a rocky chute, just one big ravine over from the famous Tuckerman. At some of the hardest spots, Nolan and Larry—back to his sure-footed self now that it's daylight—offer Clara a helping hand.

Soon we're above tree level. Mist permitting, we get marvelous views of the Wildcat and Carter ranges across the way. As promised, Ginny and Sarah joined me in June to climb the Carters, so I nod to them like old friends, and we enjoy the sweeping view southward into the endless green thicket of the Dry River Wilderness.

Up ahead on our trail perches the eponymous Glen Boulder. Sixteen feet high by twelve feet wide and sticking up on end, Glen Boulder is so massive you can pick it out from Route 16 far below. Though they are not, the many tons of stone appear precariously balanced. Passing beneath Glen Boulder I pat its rough skin, but quicken my pace.

We're wearing rain jackets with our hoods up. My hair, plastered to my cheeks and scalp, drips from the mist. Beyond Glen Boulder, we enter an enchanted lane of slender white-trunked paper birch trees, elegant and eerie in the gray mist. I wonder what Kate would have said about this sight. I imagine her pausing, pulling her camera from her waist belt, shaking her head at the mystery and beauty of it. Adding up the years, I'm startled to realize she'd be sixty-four now. Would she be finishing the 4000-Footers today too? I like to think so. I suddenly miss her so powerfully my jaws ache. I touch a passing tree trunk. I wish I could talk with Kate now about Casey and my empty nest.

Thinking of my daughter, my eyes sting. The only way

I could let her begin her walk away from us into a life all her own, was by driving from her campus straight into the Rocky Mountains. I wish I could see her face and pull her close, the body that used to live inside me and now can pick me up.

When the birch lane ends, we hike along ledges, then follow a sweet green path through a forest of tiny firs that, due to the ferocious weather, only grow waist-high. The two shortest among us, Sarah and I, laugh and stride like giants. The wizened firs give way to huge fields of grasses, gently rounded like the curve of the horizon, that have turned a fiery burnt sienna for fall. Below us a dense wall of wooly cloud blocks our view, but above that glows an azure sky. Our path of stones cuts through this unexpected meadow atop Washington's southernmost flank. The way is marked by two-foot high cairns of gray rock marbled with shining quartz. The cairns stand to one side of the stony trail, a row of uneven pillars marching across the great upward swell of red-brown grasses on into the future. To the east the clouds, fabulous layers of lavender and white, continue to rise but ahead of us the sun shines. As we hike on, the blue sky grows more saturated with color, burning rich ultramarine.

How Ginny would have loved this view! I wish I could turn to her now. Were she here, I'd probably spill the tears of joy and relief that threaten to overwhelm me. At the same time, I'm glad she doesn't have to endure this hike that's longer and as arduous as our Washington trek, retracing some of the same ground. When we talked by phone yesterday, she said she'd be thinking of us today, sending me energy for this last climb, and I feel as if she's put an arm around me, pulling me onward.

When we arrive at the wooden signpost pointing to Davis Path—our trail to Isolation—I'm stunned. "Already?"

Behind me Clara says, "Well, I should hope so. We've been hiking four hours!"

"We have?" I feel frisky as a lamb. My heart beats a staccato message—*2.8 miles left, nearly done, the end of the quest.* I take a few slow breaths, trying not to think ahead. I don't want to miss anything by leap-frogging the moment.

The trail pitches downward now, descending over a thousand feet. Afterward, we hump upwards then drop down again for four hundred fifty feet, having to shed altitude from the 5,175-foot-height we reached on Glen Boulder Trail, down to the 4,300 feet of Isolation. It may not be so tall as other mountains, but getting to it is a challenge—Isolation is aptly named.

When we reach the short spur that leads up to the 360° panorama of the summit, Clara suggests everyone hike ahead of me and tells me to wait at the bottom until they give the signal. A plan appears to be afoot.

Clara calls down when it's time and I race up, grinning like a madwoman the whole way. Too late, I think about pictures and wonder about the state of my mist-dripping, wind-blown hair. I look up to see Larry holding the camcorder. He carried a camcorder all the way up here? I adore that man. When eventually I view the film, I observe myself click my way up the mountain with my poles, looking like a very large, very eager, stick-legged insect.

As I approach Larry, I'm greeted with a sound I've never heard before in the Whites. Kazoos! Clara secreted them up in her pack. She, Sarah, and Nolan blast out a kazoo rendition of "For She's a Jolly Good Fellow" while Larry films. As Nolan parades around the broad rocky summit, I fall in behind him. With my two friends behind me, we march several turns around the summit, collapsing into laughter. I bend down and kiss the round metal geological survey marker embedded in stone that confirms the summit of my final peak. I hug Clara fiercely, then Sarah, then Nolan who whirls me around in a circle, then Sophia, who licks my face. I run over to Larry and push away the camcorder. We smooch dramatically while he dips me over backwards, one leg up in the air.

We all (except Sophia) do our traditional peak dance. Even Larry, who generally avoids making a fool of himself. The five of us kick up our boots, wiggle, and flap, making pseudo-cool faces and looking as ridiculously joyful as possible. We sing and dance until we are laughing too hard to continue. My sister would have loved this part of a hike.

Larry pulls another surprise out of his pack. He's drawn me a picture of all forty-eight mountains. Beside them stands a small hiker proclaiming in a cartoon bubble, "I got me 48!" I crush it to my chest and kiss him again.

We loll around the expansive summit eating lunch until I say I have a surprise of my own. I light a tea candle, which promptly blows out in the wind. After two more tries, I give up. "I couldn't ever have done the past ten years without you," I tell them, my voice cracking. I hand each one a tiny figurine carved from bamboo. For Sarah, our Pisces who finds new ways of framing situations on a trail, there are two tiny fishes. Larry gets a ram because he's so nimble in the mountains and, I can't help but add, so stubborn. To Clara, I present a horse to represent the horses of her childhood but also her strong, frank, openness. Nolan gets a frog because he never slips when crossing streams, even carrying Juniper or someone else's pack.

I've also brought the list of dates I climbed each 4000-Footer and who came with me, and I'm just about to begin intoning this solemn list and what it means to me, when I notice the others packing up. What about my speech?

"We've spent two hours up here," Clara says. "We've gotten behind Cheryl time."

We no longer hike concerned about book time. Now we follow what Clara christened "Cheryl time"—my estimate of how long it will really take us to finish. It's a pleasure not to compare ourselves to someone else's standard but to simply create, and accept, our own. We do so many more things on a hike besides following the trail. For this reason, I've estimated today's venture will take fourteen hours.

For me, the seven hours it took us to reach the summit rippled past. Today I have no concept of time. There is only each jeweled moment. I wish Casey were here to see me like this, the mother she believes wakes up each morning in order to plan.

Before we strike off onto the east branch of Isolation Trail—we have 7.3 miles to climb down—Sarah gazes around the summit for a last time and sighs. "It's so comfortable, I could live here."

I have a hard time tearing myself away as well. This is my final good-bye to Matanna. No longer do I feel I am missing a part of my self. I am my new normal now. I leave Matanna here, at rest and at home in my beloved Whites, knowing I can visit whenever I choose, but also knowing I have other mountains in my future.

Despite all I've experienced to the contrary, I expect the downhill hike to be a cakewalk now that the real drama—reaching my forty-eighth summit—is done. We hike onward, me last. Sophia comes back to check up on me, good shepherd that she is. When she leans into my thigh, I stop to pet her. "Junie bagged seven peaks with me," I brag. At the sound of her friend's name, Sophia's ears twitch.

Our trail soon turns into a stream. A flowing stream. We descend by stepping from the back of one rock to the back of another, just as one would crossing a stream, except that this stream goes vertically down the side of a mountain for 2.6 tricky, muddy miles. A person can't help but slide off the stones and roots into the water and mud. We all were concerned about river crossings, but we never thought we'd be hiking down inches of running water *all the time*. It's as if the Whites can't let me go without a final kick in the pants to remind me who's in charge.

The first time we cross the Rocky Branch River I make it, with some help from Nolan, all the way to the last stepping stone when my left boot slides off and submerges itself completely in the river. Shit! I take off my boot and upend it to watch water pour out. My sock is soaked. Digging out the spares I always carry, I gratefully put one on. Twenty steps later, the dry sock is drenched from the inside. Which is why one tries not to slide off the side of a rock into a river. As we continue down, I slip, and slide, and fall. We cross the river three more times, each crossing more time-consuming as we take off boots and socks to wade through the rushing river that comes up to my thighs. I thank Larry again for bringing the water shoes.

We hike on, tired and footsore. I plod along on autopilot while looking out for our turn-off onto Rocky Branch Trail, a milestone that really should appear any moment, a thought I've had for the last fifteen minutes. Apparently I'm not the only one who's had this thought. Larry marches from the end of our group where he's been hiking sweep, up to me in the lead. "We missed it," he says. "We've missed the junction."

I stop. "No, we haven't." The others gather around us.

"We have," Larry insists.

"There's no way I passed it! I've been watching for it since the last crossing. And even if I somehow managed to miss it, how could all four of you have walked past it, too?" I look around at Sarah, Nolan and Clara. "What do you think?"

"I didn't see another trail," Clara ventures.

"Me either," Sarah says.

Nolan shakes his head.

"We've got to go back." Larry is adamant.

"Are you kidding me?" Going back means adding distance to a hike that's more than thirteen miles already. Going back means going uphill through the miserable riverbed of a trail we've just come down when we've been hiking for over ten hours, when he's wrong. I know he's wrong.

Neither my husband nor I say it aloud, but beneath our argument surges a river of our own—the memory of my mistake on Zealand, the one that took us two miles in the wrong direction and gave Larry plantar fasciitis. I ask my friends their opinion, but they defer to us, or rather, to the winner of our argument. Sarah's face creases with worry. Nolan has a hard time standing still. Clara slumps onto a downed tree. They wait.

I shake out my map. "Look," I say to Larry. "Here's our first water crossing." With my finger on the line of the trail, I walk him through each place we crossed the river. "Four times, not five times. Five times would mean we've missed it, but we haven't. See? We've got to keep going. Only another quarter of a mile, half a mile at most, we'll hit it. I *know* we will."

This is absolute role reversal. Larry has the better sense of direction and he's the Map King. I get why he thinks we've passed it. With all the water it's taken us nearly three hours to descend less than three miles. But I have not mistaken the trail as I did on Zealand.

I stand my ground.

Larry concedes, but I doubt he's convinced. We all slog on. After five minutes, Nolan volunteers to hike ahead to scout. I suspect he's itching to shed pent-up anxiety, and danged if I don't want someone to find Rocky Branch East as soon as possible myself. Meantime we pick our way through rivulets, rocks, puddles, and roots.

The seconds tick by. Then the minutes. No chatter. We wait. Hope. If we have to turn back, it will be dark as we search for a trail problematic enough to have eluded us the first time in far better light. We will have added another mile to our trek but far worse, it will break the faith my friends have placed in me. After forty-seven mountains, on my final 4000-Footer, I will have failed as a leader.

Then Nolan hollers. Before I can ask anyone else what he said, I see him jogging around a bend toward us, waving us on. "Just around the corner!" Our heads lift. My fanny pack feels lighter. Our pace surges.

A week after the hike, Clara will tell me, "Cheryl, I have never loved you more than when you stood up to Larry about finding that trail. Larry was panicking and the rest of us were panicking but you didn't. You never backed down. It's hard to stand up to your honey. You were so strong."

Gradually the light fades, and we dig out our headlamps once more. Switching them on makes the dark really dark. Not one of my companions complains about how the hike is dragging on, how no restaurant will be open by the time we get down, how muddy and chilly they probably feel, how rife with potential injury our descent is. They are amazing.

When at last we reach the car, it's 8:45 p.m., an hour past Cheryl time, but it doesn't matter. "Thank you all for such an astounding, incredible adventure!" I say.

"We got to hike three hours in the pitch dark!" Clara says, enchanted.

At the lodge we don't take time to shower, but change into dry, mud-free clothes and meet back in the living room of the Lodge to celebrate. Sitting on a sofa and a couple of chairs, everyone dumps whatever food they have left from the hike onto a coffee table. It's a meager haul, but I'm too ecstatic to eat anyway.

We open bottles of wine and toast repeatedly. To each other, to me, to Isolation. We celebrate the conclusion of the dream that kept me coming to the Whites for ten years, to reveal and teach and test myself in the demanding school of nature. Here, I've been fortunate enough to create and deepen friendships. Here, I've been able to face my fears, endure my losses, recover from cancer, and let go, drawing sustenance from a home that fed my soul and healed me. With linked hearts, we salute the waters and wilds of forty-eight unforgettable, life-threatening, life-affirming mountains.

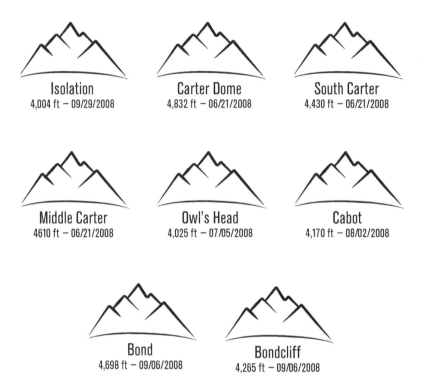

Isolation
4,004 ft – 09/29/2008

Carter Dome
4,832 ft – 06/21/2008

South Carter
4,430 ft – 06/21/2008

Middle Carter
4610 ft – 06/21/2008

Owl's Head
4,025 ft – 07/05/2008

Cabot
4,170 ft – 08/02/2008

Bond
4,698 ft – 09/06/2008

Bondcliff
4,265 ft – 09/06/2008

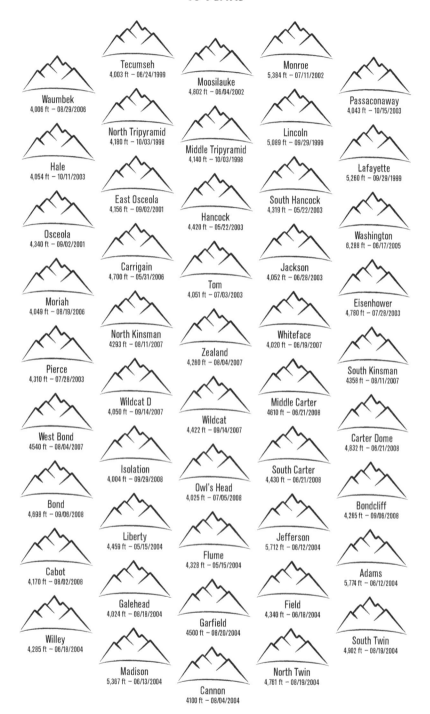

Waumbek
4,006 ft – 08/29/2006

Hale
4,054 ft – 10/11/2003

Osceola
4,340 ft – 09/02/2001

Moriah
4,049 ft – 08/19/2006

Pierce
4,310 ft – 07/28/2003

West Bond
4540 ft – 08/04/2007

Bond
4,698 ft – 09/06/2008

Cabot
4,170 ft – 08/02/2008

Willey
4,285 ft – 06/18/2004

Tecumseh
4,003 ft – 06/24/1999

North Tripyramid
4,180 ft – 10/03/1998

East Osceola
4,156 ft – 09/02/2001

Carrigain
4,700 ft – 05/31/2006

North Kinsman
4293 ft – 08/11/2007

Wildcat D
4,050 ft – 09/14/2007

Isolation
4,004 ft – 09/29/2008

Liberty
4,459 ft – 05/15/2004

Galehead
4,024 ft – 08/18/2004

Madison
5,367 ft – 06/13/2004

Moosilauke
4,802 ft – 06/04/2002

Middle Tripyramid
4,140 ft – 10/03/1998

Hancock
4,420 ft – 05/22/2003

Tom
4,051 ft – 07/03/2003

Zealand
4,260 ft – 08/04/2007

Wildcat
4,422 ft – 09/14/2007

Owl's Head
4,025 ft – 07/05/2008

Flume
4,328 ft – 05/15/2004

Garfield
4500 ft – 08/20/2004

Cannon
4100 ft – 08/04/2004

Monroe
5,384 ft – 07/11/2002

Lincoln
5,089 ft – 09/29/1999

South Hancock
4,319 ft – 05/22/2003

Jackson
4,052 ft – 06/28/2003

Whiteface
4,020 ft – 06/19/2007

Middle Carter
4610 ft – 06/21/2008

South Carter
4,430 ft – 06/21/2008

Jefferson
5,712 ft – 06/12/2004

Field
4,340 ft – 06/18/2004

North Twin
4,761 ft – 08/19/2004

Passaconaway
4,043 ft – 10/15/2003

Lafayette
5,260 ft – 09/29/1999

Washington
6,288 ft – 06/17/2005

Eisenhower
4,780 ft – 07/28/2003

South Kinsman
4358 ft – 08/11/2007

Carter Dome
4,832 ft – 06/21/2008

Bondcliff
4,265 ft – 09/06/2008

Adams
5,774 ft – 06/12/2004

South Twin
4,902 ft – 08/19/2004

EPILOGUE

2015

Sarah went on to complete her forty-eight 4000-Footers, then planned for and led Nolan to finish his.

Ginny climbed Half Dome (8,800 feet high) in Yosemite, a truly vertical and arduous fourteen-mile hike.

Clara fulfilled her dream of hiking daunting Mt. Katahdin (5,269 feet) in Maine, an eleven-mile venture.

Her first year in college, Casey climbed Pike's Peak (14,115 feet) in Colorado, at night, to watch the sun rise from the summit.

Cheryl co-led hikes for the Appalachian Mountain Club.

Larry and Cheryl celebrated Cheryl's sixtieth birthday by hiking two Great Walks in New Zealand, the Abel Tasman and the Kepler.

QUESTIONS FOR DISCUSSION AND REFLECTION

1. Cheryl's quest begins with a long-term goal: summiting the forty-eight 4000-Footers in the White Mountains to find success and join the Four Thousand Footer Club. How does the meaning of this goal change over the course of the story?

2. How does the death of Kate, best friend and hiking companion, shape Cheryl's journey?

3. In what ways are your own friendships similar to or different from those portrayed here?

4. *48 PEAKS* is an interlocking narrative of action and reflection. In what ways does each component contribute to Cheryl's life and to the memoir?

5. What physical challenges does Cheryl face and how do these both thwart and strengthen her?

6. How would you describe the characterization of hope in the book? How does hope play a role in your own life?

7. The author recalls childhood events. How does she include and reflect on these memories, and what do they add to the unfolding story?

8. What do you think of Cheryl's hiking process? Can you envision uses for the process other than hiking?

9. What role does nature play in the narrative? In the title of the memoir?

10. Cheryl's First Rule for Hiking is "Speak Up." What are the risks and benefits of such a rule?

11. On each hike, even the solo ones, Cheryl has companionship. How does she maintain her relationships with those who are present and those who are not? How do these relationships sustain her and enhance her experiences?

12. Cheryl ponders the nature of leadership and authority within groups. How would you describe her leadership style? What are examples of how she exercises leadership?

13. In what ways does Cheryl change over the course of her quest and how do these changes manifest themselves?

14. Considering your own life, which of Cheryl' experiences resonate with you? What insights does *48 PEAKS* provide for your personal journey?

ACKNOWLEDGMENTS

Many people have contributed to the life of this book. I'm grateful to those who helpfully read drafts and re-drafts of chapters in numerous writers' groups over the years; you made me a better writer. Meg Senuta did the invaluable service of commenting on the entire book—twice.

Early on, Dr. Allan Hunter, professor and author, encouraged me to believe I had a story and could tell it, offering many hours of acute insight.

I'm forever grateful to the Vermont Studio Center for a month-long residency grant that offered the time and space to review my first draft and plan my next.

Editor Jami Bernard's fine eye and ear helped clarify and tighten 48 Peaks in its final stage. Ellen Goss Goldsberry's early edit improved the course of subsequent drafts. Special thanks to Brooke Warner, Cait Levin, and the wonderful team at She Writes Press who brought *48 PEAKS* into the world, and to Crystal Patriarche, Savannah Harrelson, and the terrific folks at SparkPoint Studio who made its presence known. I'm indebted to the helpful community of great writers they've created, in particular to Barbara Ridley and, especially, to Belle Brett, publication buddy par excellence.

I would not have met my hiking goals or finished this book without the weekly support and wisdom of my friend and trainer, Dr. Cathy Utzschneider, founder of *M.O.V.E!* and author of a book by the same title as well as of *Mastering Running*.

My hiking comrades know without a doubt there would have been no quest without them. They provided companionship, wisdom, humor, and affection as well as carried my gear. Using their book names, I thank, from the bottom of my heart: Sarah, who summited seventeen peaks with me, Ginny (fourteen), Nolan (eight), Clara (seven), Kate (four), Rosemary (four), Lee (four), Evan (three), Cecile (three), Dakota (three), Gwen (two), Alexandra (one), Ansu (one), and Mandy (one).

My two hiking buddies provided the partnership that kept me going. I would never have begun my quest without Kate beside me. I'd never have finished without Ginny, who so willingly took up the baton and infused our endeavors with her bright spirit. Nor without Sarah—able, close comrade on so many treks.

I am indebted to the Appalachian Mountain Club staff and volunteers who set, maintain, and preserve the trails as well as protect the mountains and forests I love; to the hut and lodge staff; and to the volunteers who manage the Four Thousand Footer Club.

Last but never least, my family hung in with me for the ten years it took to climb The 48 and deal with the physical consequences. They accompanied me many times: Larry on eighteen peaks, Casey on nine, and Juniper on seven. They encouraged me sweetly and, as the years rolled by, adamantly to finish this book. They kept me alive on the cancer trail and continue to fill my heart.

If nothing else, I hope my story encourages readers to spend more time in nature and to protect our amazing planet and the vast web of life of which we form but one part.

ABOUT THE AUTHOR

C heryl Suchors began writing at age six, when she wrote a play starring her sister and herself. She continued to write poetry until she took a detour through the business world for twenty years. She holds degrees from Harvard Business School and Smith College. Her fiction, poetry, and essays have appeared in *City Book Review, Limestone, The Distillery, RE:AL*, and *HerSports*, as well as in the anthology *My Other Ex: Women's True Stories of Losing and Leaving Friends*. In her business career she coauthored the book *Own Your Own Cable System*. She lives in Cambridge, Massachusetts with her husband and a plethora of plants. She continues to hike every chance she gets, most recently in Poland and Canada.

Author photo © Andrea Joliat

Juniper takes a break atop South Kinsman.

SELECTED TITLES FROM SHE WRITES PRESS

She Writes Press is an independent publishing company founded to serve women writers everywhere. Visit us at www.shewritespress.com.

Naked Mountain: A Memoir by Marcia Mabee. $16.95, 978-1-63152-097-6. A compelling memoir of one woman's journey of natural world discovery, tragedy, and the enduring bonds of marriage, set against the backdrop of a stunning mountaintop in rural Virginia.

Gap Year Girl by Marianne Bohr. $16.95, 978-1-63152-820-0. Thirty-plus years after first backpacking through Europe, Marianne Bohr and her husband leave their lives behind and take off on a yearlong quest for adventure.

Body 2.0: Finding My Edge Through Loss and Mastectomy by Krista Hammerbacher Haapala. An authentic, inspiring guide to reframing adversity that provides a new perspective on preventative mastectomy, told through the lens of the author's personal experience.

Blue Apple Switchback: A Memoir by Carrie Highley. $16.95, 978-1-63152-037-2. At age forty, Carrie Highley finally decided to take on the biggest switchback of her life: upon her bicycle, and with the help of her mentor's wisdom, she shed everything she was taught to believe as a young lady growing up in the South—and made a choice to be true to herself and everyone else around her.

A Leg to Stand On: An Amputee's Walk into Motherhood by Colleen Haggerty. $16.95, 978-1-63152-923-8. Haggerty's candid story of how she overcame the pain of losing a leg at seventeen—and of terminating two pregnancies as a young woman—and went on to become a mother, despite her fears.

Postcards from the Sky: Adventures of an Aviatrix by Erin Seidemann. $16.95, 978-1-63152-826-2. Erin Seidemann's tales of her struggles, adventures, and relationships as a woman making her way in a world very much dominated by men: aviation.